From Cape To Cape
THE HISTORY OF
LYLE SHIPPING COMPANY

Frontispiece

Three masted iron ship *Cape Sable I*, completed by Thomas Wingate & Co. of Glasgow in 1874.
This fine vessel was typical of the trading vessels of the period. The Lyle house flag flies from
the main mast.

From Cape To Cape

THE HISTORY OF LYLE SHIPPING COMPANY

John Orbell
Head of the Business Records Advisery Service,
Business Archives Council

WITH
Edwin Green
Archivist, Midland Bank Limited

AND
Michael Moss
Archivist, University of Glasgow

PAUL HARRIS PUBLISHING, EDINBURGH

First published 1978 by
PAUL HARRIS PUBLISHING
25 London Street, Edinburgh

ISBN 0 904505 26 X

British Library Cataloguing in Publication Data
Orbell, John
    From cape to cape.
    1. Lyle Shipping Company – History
    I. Title   II. Green, Edwin   III. Moss, Michael
    387.5'06'541428   HE945.L/

ISBN 0–904505–26–X

Printed and bound in Great Britain by
Morrison & Gibb Ltd, London and Edinburgh

Contents

List of Illustrations

List of Tables

Acknowledgments

I am extremely grateful to the Directors of Lyle Shipping Co. for their help and encouragement in writing this history of their firm. In particular I wish to thank Mr. William Nicholson, formerly Chairman, Mr. Herbert Walkinshaw, the present Chairman and Managing Director, and Mr. Tom Shearer, Mr. Marshall Gibson, Mr. Iain Noble and Mr. Tim Noble, Directors, for their invaluable assistance. I owe many thanks to Dr. Percival Agnew, past Chairman of the Company, who has taken an enthusiastic interest throughout the project. I am most grateful to Lieutenant Colonel Michael Lyle, Honorary President of Lyle Shipping Co., to Mrs. Lyle; and to Air Marshal Sir Anthony and Lady Selway for their help, interest and warm hospitality.

Several present and retired members of the staff of Lyle Shipping Co. have been of great help. In particular I wish to thank Mrs. Isabel Barnes, Mr. J. Begg, Miss Agnes Bell, Mr. D. T. Border, Captain R. D. Love, Captain D. M. Taylor and Mr. R. Wallace, the Company's chief cashier until the 1960s. Mr. A. A. McAlister of H. Hogarth & Sons Ltd has greatly assisted in the provision of photographs. Mr Hugh Clark has helped with the composition of the schedule of masters on pages 187 to 190.

Widows of former Lyle masters and chief engineers have also given great help. In particular, I wish to thank Mrs. Gladys Cagney, Mrs. A. M. Duguid, Mrs. K. M. Fairgrieve, Mrs. L. C. McGlashan, Mrs. K. A. King and Mrs. Jane Wright.

Many of the business associates of Lyle Shipping Co. have displayed much interest and, when possible, have given assistance. In particular I wish to thank the Adelaide Steamship Company, Adelaide; Mr. A. J. B. Agnew, Penney Castello & Co.; Mr. A. Binks, Tilney & Co.; Mr. R. E. M. Davidson, Anderson, Fyfe, Stewart and Young; Mr. Jan Eriksen, Haugesund, Norway; Mr. F. Harting, Ruys and Co., Amsterdam; Mr. E. D. Holland, Managing Director, John T. Rennie and Sons, Cape Town; Mr. Heinz Lind, Hamburg; Mr. L. H. Lording, London Manager, British Phosphate Commissioners; Mr. J. S. Parson, Hodder Whitwell Ltd, Avonmouth; Mr. M. L. Richardson, Senior Vice President, Anglo-Canadian Shipping (Westship) Ltd; Mr. M. J. Schneider, Vice President, Tite Ship Agencies Inc., New Orleans; Mr. George Thomson, Branch Manager, Bank of Scotland, George Square, Glasgow; Mr. F. Twiss,

John Kilgour & Co. Ltd; Mr. A. C. Tyler, General Manager Marine, Montreal Shipping Company Ltd; Mr. John Watt, Assistant Secretary, Bank of Scotland Head Office, Edinburgh; Mr. D. White, Laurence Prust & Co.; and Mr. T. A. Wiggins, United Baltic Corporation, Kiel.

I am most grateful to the following for the help they have given; Mr. John Bates and Mr. Jack Sime and the excellent staff of the Scottish Record Office; Mr. D. A. C. Bennie of H. M. Customs and Excise, Greenock; Sir Henry Birkmyre; Sir Frederic Bolton, Chairman of Bolton Steam Shipping Co. Ltd; Dennise Box and Ruth Cobley; Mrs. Eve Brown; Mr. Michael Crowdy, Chairman and other members of the World Ship Society; Mr. L. N. Cogie, Norwalk, U.S.A.; Mr. Robin Craig, University College, University of London; Mr. John Firn of the Department of Social Economic and Research, University of Glasgow; Commander J. R. Finlay; Mrs. Rita Hemphill; Dr. Katrina Honeyman; Mr. Tony Hugill; Mr. John Hume of the University of Strathclyde; Mr. David Kerr who has provided much information concerning his ancestor, John Kerr; Mr. Michael Knowling; Mr. William Lind who has greatly helped with the provision of photographs; Sir William Lithgow who has made available photographs and who kindly allowed me access to the Lithgow Business Papers deposited in the Scottish Record Office; Mr. John Lyle, President of Tate and Lyle Ltd; Mr. G. A. Mackay of the Centre for Sparsely Populated Areas, University of Aberdeen; Mrs. Manchester of Baillie's Library, Glasgow; the staff of the Mitchell Library, Glasgow; Mr. Osbon of the National Maritime Museum; Mr. Reginald Pigott for his excellent work in drawing graphs and diagrams; Mr. T. C. Pollock, the Factor of the Ardgowan Estates; Mr. Stephen Rabson, Group Librarian, P. & O.; Mr. N. Richards, Anderson Hughes & Co.; Mr. R. W. D. Ross; Captain Jim Scobbie who kindly made available notes on his seafaring ancestors who served in the sailing ships owned by the Lyle family; Mrs. Ruth Sirton; Mr. Frank Smith of the General Council of British Shipping; Mr. J. E. Somner, Technical Adviser, Tate and Lyle International for his comments on my script; Mr. S. P. Valentine. Head of Economics and Public Relations Department, the Stock Exchange; the staff of the Strathclyde Regional Archive; and Mr. Arnott Wilson, Trainee Archivist, The University of Glasgow.

In particular four people have given invaluable help. Mrs. Mary Cree, personal assistant to the Managing Director of Lyle Shipping Company, has typed scripts which at times have been almost obliterated with corrections and has performed too many of my chores. For her help, interest, enthusiasm and cheerfulness I am most grateful. Alec Ritchie worked as my research assistant for two months. His hard work and great interest coupled with his dry humour have been very greatly appreciated. Edwin Green and Michael Moss have advised on source material and have edited my scripts with meticulous care. Their enormous help and support have been invaluable and their unbounded enthusiasm has been greatly infectious. I am deeply grateful to them. I must also thank their charming wives, Hilary and Lynne, for their kindness and warm hospitality on very many occasions.

Most of the photographs in this volume have been drawn from the Company's archives. Those apart, some illustrations have been reproduced from collections in the hands of private individuals or public institutions. The author would like to thank the following for permission to reproduce illustrations:

D'Antonio Guido, Venice, Figure 9.1.
The Imperial War Museum, Figure 7.5.
Mrs. A. King, Figures 6.3, 6.10 and 6.12b.
Keeper of the Records of Scotland, Upper Clyde Shipbuilders Collection, Figures 9.2 (a), (b) and (c).
David Kerr, Esq., Figures 2.3, 2.4 and 2.5.
William Lind, Esq., Figures 3.5, 3.6 (a) and (b), 3.7, 4.2.
Sir William Lithgow, Figures 5.1, 5.2, 5.3, 6.2, 6.4.
Mrs. L. C. McGlashan, Figure 6.12a.
Marine Photography, New South Wales, Figure 9.5 (b).
National Maritime Museum, Figures 3.2, 3.4, 3.7 (a), 5.5, 6.6, 7.1, 7.2, 7.8.
Port of Bristol Authority, Figures 7.11 (a) and (b), 9.5 (a) and 9.6.
Air Marshal Sir Anthony Selway, Figure 6.13.
Tom Shearer, Esq., Figure 6.11.
Skyfotos Ltd, Figures 1.3, 7.10, 8.3, 9.3, 9.4, Appendix 3.2, Appendix 3.6.

I. Prologue

When the product of any particular branch of industry exceeds what the demand of the country requires, the surplus must be sent abroad, and exchanged for something for which there is a demand at home. Without such exportation, a part of the productive labour of the country must cease, and the value of its annual produce diminish . . . It is only by means of such exportation that this surplus can acquire a value sufficient to compensate the labour and expense of producing it. The neighbourhood of the sea coast, and the banks of all navigable rivers, are advantageous situations for industry, only because they facilitate the exportation and exchange of such surplus produce for something else which is more in demand there.

(Adam Smith, An Inquiry into the Nature and Causes of the Wealth of Nations, 1776, edited by R. H. Campbell and A. S. Skinner, Clarendon Press, Oxford, 1976, p. 372.)

This history was originally intended to mark the 150th anniversary of the Lyle family's first recorded shipping venture and to trace the origins and growth of the present Lyle Shipping Company Limited. However, during the researches it was discovered that the purchase of a part ownership of the *Helen MacGregor* in 1827 was preceded by several earlier shipowning ventures by members of the Lyle family.

The Lyle family had been general merchants in Greenock since the early eighteenth century and their investment in shipping and coopering at the turn of the century was a natural extension of their commercial activities, paralleled by similar diversification amongst other merchant families in the town. After surviving the depressed decades of the 1830s and 1840s, Abram Lyle III (1820–1891), then the head of the family, in partnership with John Kerr junior built up one of the most successful shipping concerns in Scotland with probably one of the largest fleets in the United Kingdom. As an integral part of his business interests, Abram Lyle III extended the family's cooperage and invested in the sugar industry. After Kerr's death in 1872, he became a shipowner in his own right and continued to expand his Glebe sugar refinery until, by 1879, it was the largest in Greenock.

Adverse trading conditions in the 1880s forced Abram Lyle III and his sons to consider how best to react to changed circumstances. Characteristically the Lyles seized their opportunity and decided to construct a modern low cost

Figure 1.2
Cape Sable II, completed by Lithgows Ltd in 1936, steaming fully laden up the English Channel sometime after the Second World War. She was ordered by the Newport Line and bought by Lyle Shipping Co., after being several years on the stocks.

Figure 1.1 (*pages 2, 3*)
The newly built four masted steel barque *Cape Clear II* constructed by Robert Duncan & Co. of Port Glasgow, adjusting compasses on her trials in the Firth of Clyde in 1892.

refinery. Thwarted in their ambition to build their new factory in Greenock, they moved to London. In the twentieth century their sugar business became one of the largest in Britain, merging with Henry Tate & Sons of Liverpool in 1920 and by a policy of progressive takeovers achieving a dominant position in the British sugar trade in 1976. During the 1880s and 1890s the establishment and subsequent nurture of the new refinery diverted the family's capital and management away from shipowning. However, the Lyles' association with ships and shipping was preserved, perhaps from sentiment, by A. P. Lyle (later Sir Alexander Lyle Bt., 1849–1933), who had remained in Scotland after the move to London. A limited liability company, The Lyle Shipping Co., was formed in 1890 to take charge of the family's shipping interests. The venture was not a success; the fleet was equipped with sailing ships which, although they could be traded profitably, were fast being made obsolete by improved and more economic steamships. In 1900 the Company was wound up.

Undeterred, A. P. Lyle tried again and a new limited company, Lyle Shipping Co. Ltd, was established in 1903. The new concern had strong management recruited from outside the family, and was backed by John Birkmyre, the wealthiest lower Clyde merchant of the time. With a fleet of new steamers and judicious control the concern asserted itself and expanded against the prevailing trends in the industry. Like many of its competitors the Company emerged from the First World War with a strong balance sheet, healthy reserves and a greatly increased experience of complex ship management. Fortuitously, the Directors did not commit themselves to investment in new tonnage after the Armistice, largely because building berths were fully booked by their larger competitors. In 1920 on the return to peacetime trading the concern was reconstructed by liquidating the old Company and transferring the unencumbered assets and reserves to a new one.

This new Company immediately faced the challenge of the inter-war slump. Careful management, strengthened by a special relationship with Sir James and Henry Lithgow, enabled the Company to withstand the economic blizzard of the 1920s and 1930s. As a result the Company and its subsidiaries not only survived and made profits, but emerged in the late 1930s with a modern fleet which was well placed to take advantage of the upturn in trade. During the Second World War profitability was tightly controlled by the government and the Company suffered in consequence. With the coming of peace the Directors, encouraged by the buoyancy of the freight market and by the Lithgows, pursued a vigorous investment policy which brought rewards.

In 1953, as a consequence of the post-war Labour Government's fiscal policy on the taxation of private wealth, the Company went public. During the 1950s the Board was lulled into a sense of false security by the prolonged boom and the 'never had it so good' atmosphere of the time; punitive company taxation raised by successive Conservative governments denied the Company adequate resources for re-investment. Such ships as were added to the fleet were ordered and designed in the light of current requirements rather than future needs. Nevertheless healthy profits were recorded until 1958/59 when there was sudden downturn in the economy. Until 1963 the Company experienced a grave financial crisis, comparable with the worst years of the 1930s.

Recovery began in 1963 when forward looking policies on ship replacement, financial gearing and marketing were adopted. A fleet of modern handy-sized bulkcarriers designed to enter the maximum number of ports in developing countries was built up. The management's resolve was strengthened by the financial incentives provided by the Labour Government. An expansion in the size of fleet required the Company to break into new trades. This was achieved by well judged salesmanship and a determination to give the customer every satisfaction. Time charters were arranged to bring the Company a steady income and thus financial security. In 1968 Scottish Ship Management Ltd was established by Lyle Shipping Co. and H. Hogarth and Sons Ltd to manage jointly the two companies' fleets. This development gave both concerns greater flexibility of operation and reduced costs, with the added advantage of presenting an image of substance and reliability to potential customers.

The increased strength of Lyle Shipping Co. in the late 1960s enabled the Directors to embark on a programme of diversification to relieve the Company's dependence on the shipping cycle. In the 1970s the Company invested with success in the developing North Sea oil industry. Seaforth Maritime Ltd was formed in 1972 on the initiative of Lyle Shipping Co. to operate a fleet of eight supply vessels to service drilling rigs. From 1973 it established with success a series of subsidiary companies to service the offshore oil industry. The experience gained from this venture led Lyle Shipping Co. to form Lyle Offshore Group Ltd in 1975. This Company owns two of the most sophisticated diving support ships at work in the North Sea and through its operating subsidiaries has a substantial share in the embryonic offshore oil maintenance industry. Lyle Shipping Co. also now owns stakes in North Sea oil and gas discoveries, and has insurance broking and precision engineering subsidiaries.

In the history of shipping, and in the evolution of British business as a whole, Lyle Shipping Co. offers a case study in the development and relative importance of financial control and management expertise. In the highly competitive world of shipping, these aspects of the Company's performance have always been essential to its survival. The Lyle family in its early ventures in shipping did not make any distinctions between the functions of ownership and management of

Figure 1.3 (*opposite*)
The bulkcarrier *Cape Horn IV*, built by Haugesund Mekaniske Verksted, Haugesund, Norway in 1971, on trials. She is one of the Company's new fleet of handy-sized bulkcarriers, capable of entering most ports, especially those in less developed countries.

their ships. The Lyles acted both as owners and as operators, using the minimum of external finance or specialist help. This pattern was characteristic of British tramp ship operation in the nineteenth century, when specialist ship management was slow to emerge either in privately owned fleets or single ship companies. With the control and direction of the business concentrated in the hands of the Lyle family, the outlook of the business was dominated by the need to support the family's other interests in cooperage and sugar-refining. In practice, these were short-term goals and it is doubtful whether the Lyles held to any long-term strategy for their shipping interests.

In the twentieth century, since the formation of the Lyle Shipping Co. in 1903, the business has been transformed by the recruitment of professional ship managers and the increasing use of external finance. This readiness to seek managerial and financial expertise has been essential to the modern development of the Company, allowing the Company to strengthen its methods of financial control and to develop a long-term strategy. In more recent years, during a period of radical change in the shipping industry, the Company has chosen diversification within the Scottish economy as a corner-stone of its business strategy. On a broad base of experience and expertise this diversification reflects the complete transformation of tramp shipping business and the sure recovery of Scottish trade and industry since the 1960s.

2. 1791-1872
Sugar and Ships

In 1829, Daniel Weir wrote of Greenock that its 'progressive improvement from a small fishing village to its present state has been but little more than the work of a century'.[1] In 1680 Greenock was just 'a row of houses'.[2] The original harbour was built in the first decade of the eighteenth century, and by the 1720s Daniel Defoe was able to comment on the town: 'it is . . . well built, and has many rich trading families in it. It is the chief town in the West of Scotland for the herring fishing, and the merchants of Glasgow, who are concerned in the fishery, employ the Greenock vessels for the catching and curing the fish, and for several parts of their other trades, as well as carrying them afterwards abroad to market'.[3] As the tobacco trade between America and Glasgow developed during the eighteenth century, Greenock prospered. Large ships could not travel up the Clyde to Glasgow until the engineers John Rennie and Thomas Telford undertook the widening and deepening of the river between 1807 and 1826. Before that time, Glasgow merchants used Greenock and Port Glasgow, conveniently placed at the river mouth, as their principal ports of entry. The quays on the riverside at Greenock were constructed in 1788.[4]

In the mid eighteenth century John Lyle had moved to Greenock from Argyll and had rapidly established himself as a merchant. His sons, Abram I and Gideon, entered the weaving and coopering trades respectively. In 1791 Gideon, by then an established cooper, together with his partner, Abram I's eldest son Robert, purchased the family's first vessel, the *Christies*, a thirty ton sloop. The other partners in this venture were James Morrison and Archibald McLean, Greenock mariners, and the sloop was almost certainly one of the many 'fishing buses' [boats] for which Greenock was well known.[5] Gideon Lyle's motive in acquiring a share in the ship was doubtless to provide a tied outlet for the products of the cooperage, since at the time a large number of barrels were used for storing salted and cured fish. In 1799 Gideon Lyle in partnership with his fellow cooper, Dugald MacPhaedran, and Donald Mactavish, a mariner, bought the fifteen ton sloop *Lucy*. The following year Robert Lyle in association with William Newsham, a Greenock plumber, and William Campbell, a mariner, purchased the thirty-one ton sloop *Cluster of Pearls*, and Gideon Lyle with Robert Turner, a smith, and Malcolm Morrison, a mariner, the forty-six ton sloop *Friendship*. All these vessels were designed to

Figure 2.1

An engraving of the port of Greenock in 1829, with the harbour filled by merchantmen and the recently developed steamships in evidence. On the right two sailing ships can be seen on the stocks. The smoking chimneys belong to a group of sugar refineries.

participate in the West Coast fishing trade.[6]

Meanwhile Greenock had become more prosperous. The port had survived the decline of the Glasgow tobacco trade following the American War of Independence and, despite the Napoleonic Wars, Greenock's trade grew. The East India Harbour and its associated dry dock, designed by John Rennie, were completed in 1805.[7] During the next decade cotton textiles proved to be the most valuable Scottish export. Although there was only one cotton mill in Greenock, most of the goods manufactured by the large West of Scotland textile industry were exported through the port. Greenock's other major export was coal, which was shipped in vast amounts. Besides cotton textiles and coal, exports included refined sugar, linen, hardware and cutlery.[8] In 1815, 359 vessels totalling 60,497 tons cleared the port with such goods for America, the West Indies and Europe. Amongst the principal imports were timber and whale oil from Canada and Newfoundland, and sugar molasses and rum from the West Indies. During 1815, 322 vessels of 56,228 tons unloaded at Greenock 3,170 hundredweights of cocoa; 309,871 hundredweights of sugar; 22,219 hundredweights of molasses; 236 hundredweights of pimento; 59,754 gallons of brandy; 780,945 gallons of rum; 160,174 gallons of wine; 67,369 pounds of tobacco; and 4,665,725 pounds of cotton.[9] The expansion of imports of sugar and raw cotton in the early decades of the nineteenth century, replacing the tobacco trade, was responsible for a rise in gross receipts at Greenock's custom house from £15,231 in 1728 to £455,597 in 1823. This was a larger revenue than that of any other Scottish seaport.[10] The composition of Port Glasgow's trade was similar to that of its larger neighbour, but only a third of the size.[11]

From the turn of the century Greenock's industries were mostly concerned with maintaining the shipping fleets. Shipbuilding was well established. By the 1820s Scott's (founded in 1711) had the 'most complete' yard in Scotland. In 1826 Robert Steel and Co. launched the *United Kingdom*, then 'the largest and most splendid steam vessel built in this country'.[12] Other industries servicing the shipping industry included rope making (notably the Gourock Ropework Co. at Port Glasgow, established in 1771), the weaving of sail canvas, brass founding and the manufacture of steam engines. The principal industry processing imported produce was sugar refining, which in 1829 'had been carried on with great success' and employed 'an immense tonnage in carrying both raw and refined sugar'.[13] Closely connected with this industry were the coopers of Greenock 'who carry on a most extensive trade in both the foreign and home market'.[14] (Figure 2.1)

Robert and Gideon Lyle gave up their shipowning interests in the first years of the century[15] and concentrated on making barrels for Greenock's developing sugar industry. No figures are available for imports of raw sugar into Greenock for this period but the local sugar refining industry was expanding rapidly. By 1812 five refineries were at work and in the following twenty years a further six were built and existing ones enlarged.[16] The growth of the business created considerable opportunities for established coopers such as Robert and Gideon Lyle. During the late 1810s Robert and Gideon took Robert's brothers, Abram II and Edward into partnership.

With the increase in prosperity of Greenock's sugar trade the Lyles expanded their cooperage business and resumed their shipping interests. In about 1820, to effect these developments, Abram Lyle II entered into partnership with William McDonald, an established cooper, who had taken over the weaving shop of Abram Lyle I in 1815 and converted it into a cooperage.[17] By 1821 the

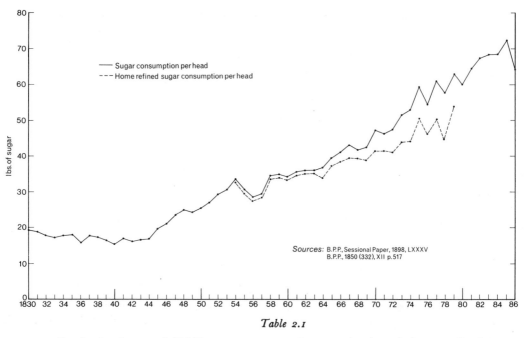

Table 2.1

Graph showing total British sugar consumption per head and home refined sugar consumption per head, 1830–1886.

partnership was raising £340 by mortgaging its premises.[18] A further £550 was obtained from a local blacksmith in 1827,[19] again secured by mortgage, and was used to finance the purchase of Robert and James Bannatyne's cooperage in the same year.[20] Two years later two further loans of £420 and £320 were obtained from a local doctor and writer (lawyer) respectively.[21]

In addition these loans were probably used to fund the purchase of shares in ships employed in the West Coast and Atlantic trades. In 1816 Gideon Lyle bought a shareholding of 21/64ths in the 104 ton brigantine *Commerce*, which since 1809 had belonged to John Kerr I, a Greenock merchant, and his mariner son, John II. During 1825, in partnership with John Kerr II, Gideon Lyle acquired the *Maria*, a twenty-seven ton vessel built in 1791. In the same year Abram Lyle II purchased a shareholding of 8/64ths in the *Belmont*, a vessel of 294 tons that was fitting out at Aromueto, St. Johns, New Brunswick. Two years later in 1827 in partnership with William McDonald and Duncan Gibb, a Liverpool trader, he purchased the *Helen MacGregor*, a 210 ton barquentine newly built at Miramachie, New Brunswick.[22] In December Lyle advertized the despatch of the *Helen MacGregor* from Greenock to Trinidad and invited enquiries about freight or passage arrangements.[23] (Figure 2.2.) It is probable that Lyle became a partner in the *Helen MacGregor* to bring sugar or molasses

NOTICE TO SHIPPERS.
FOR TRINIDAD,

THE coppered and copper-fastened fine *new* Brig of 210 tons, HELEN M'GREGOR, ROBERT SHEDDEN, Master, is taking on board goods, and will be dispatched for the above mentioned island on the 10th instant.

This vessel being built of the very best materials, and having her cabin newly fitted up, affords excellent accommodation for passengers, and is also a most eligible conveyance for dry goods.

For freight or passage apply to Messrs. Abram Lyle & Co., Greenock; or to
WIGHTON, GRAY & CO.
Glasgow, 6th Dec., 1827.

Figure 2.2
An advertisement in the *Glasgow Herald* of 3 December 1827, declaring that the brig *Helen McGregor* will take passengers and cargo to Trinidad. This announcement marks the Lyle family's first known interest in a shipping venture.

to Greenock in his own casks and sought to reduce his losses on the outward journey by advertizing for freight.

Other ventures soon followed. In August 1828 the *Albion* arrived from Trinidad with twenty puns of molasses assigned to Abram Lyle II. In December the *Rebecca* docked from Quebec with a cargo of barrel staves and the following day the *Elizabeth* arrived from Demerara with fifty puncheons of molasses.[24] Abram Lyle II does not seem to have held shares in these vessels, but in 1828 in partnership with John Kerr II and his brother Robert Kerr, he acquired the *Foundling*. This vessel of 205 tons had been captured from the French by HMS *Honourable* in 1814 and partially rebuilt by Robert Steele & Co. of Greenock in 1823.[25] In December 1828 she was despatched by Lyle to Demerara with a cargo of bricks, coal, wooden hoops, lime, pin packs, wheel barrows, potatoes and 100 empty puns. In the same month the *Helen MacGregor* returned to Greenock with 496 casks of molasses and one barrel of rum assigned to Lyle. In December 1828 and February 1829 he sent three cargoes of molasses coastwise to Liverpool.[26]

During the 1820s the pattern of Greenock's trade changed. Coastal shipping, particularly up the West Coast of Scotland, declined and the total tonnage of foreign-going vessels increased. The original harbour was rebuilt in 1824 at a cost of £20,000 to make it 'as commodious as any in the kingdom'.[27] In 1828 the number and tonnage of vessels entering from foreign ports and clearing Greenock was 220 equalling 57,101 tons. In addition, 250 ships amounting to 32,750 tons were recorded sailing from Greenock to Ireland. In 1799 the number of ships leaving Greenock for both Ireland and foreign ports had been 363 totalling 37,476 tons. By 1828 there were 249 vessels totalling 31,929 tons registered at Greenock, compared with 200 ships of 30,771 tons registered at Aberdeen, Scotland's second largest port.[28]

Greenock's trade was small by comparison with the larger English ports. In 1821 there were 822 ships of 178,047 tons registered at Newcastle-on-Tyne and 557 ships of 81,808 tons at Stockton-on-Tees, the two principal North East coal ports.[29] As early as 1808 there had been 993 ships of 162,343 tons registered at Liverpool and in 1828 1,311,000 tons of shipping entered that port, of which 520,158 tons or 40 per cent had come from foreign destinations.[30] In the 1810s Liverpool's trade in the commodities imported into Greenock was between five and ten times as great. During the 1820s and 1830s Liverpool, with its ever more prosperous hinterland in the industrial North and Midlands, was able to expand its import and export trade to the detriment of its West Coast competitors, particularly Bristol and Greenock.[31] In 1830 even Bristol, which was in decline, could boast a registered fleet of 316 (or 318) ships totalling 49,535 tons.[32]

By 1829 the Greenock coopers were well-known and engaged in both a national and international trade. In that year there were several firms at work in the town: John Buchanan and Co., Messrs. Baine, Robert Glass, William Chisholm, Robert Jamieson and Messrs. Abram Lyle & Co., as well as several smaller enterprises. They were independent of the coopers who made barrels for the herring-curing trade[33] and they were also separate from the cooperages who supplied barrels to the wine merchants. The independent coopers of Greenock supplied the sugar refineries with barrels (wooden-hooped for solid substances) for holding sugars and especially molasses. Between 1825 and 1827 over 10,000 empty casks (mostly made in Greenock) were exported from Scotland;[34] this total was over and above the barrels shipped filled with sugar or flour, or with coal or other goods to reduce transport costs.

Gideon and Robert Lyle appear to have retired from business some time in the late 1820s and left the cooperage under the management of Abram Lyle II. A. P. Lyle writing in 1922 believed that at one time Abram Lyle's merchanting business was worth between £20,000 and £30,000, 'no mean fortune in those days of moderate things'.[35] But the thirties were not as prosperous for him as the twenties. The *Helen MacGregor* and the *Belmont* were sold in 1829 to be followed by the *Foundling* in 1832.[36] In that year MacDonald left the partnership.[37] This marked the end of the Lyle family's first venture into shipping. More mortgage agreements were made by Abram Lyle, one with the Renfrewshire Banking Co. for £1,000 in 1833[38] and another for £300 with a local merchant in 1837.[39] Banks rarely gave medium or long-term credit in the early nineteenth century, and the Renfrew Bank loan was almost certainly a temporary expedient.

More positive evidence of Lyle's financial plight is provided by his difficulties in paying feu duty. The duty totalled about £5 per annum yet in 1838 Lyle was no less than £18:5:1d in arrears and had made no payment since 1835. In 1837 the superior's factor wrote to him that 'I have now to intimate that if these arrears as well as the feu duty of the present term be not settled . . . the most peremptory measures will be adopted against you'.[40] In 1840 he wrote again stating 'I have waited somewhat patiently in the expectation that you would have settled the arrears owing . . . and I have only to mention that unless the amount is paid . . . I will be obliged to proceed with impounding the ground'.[41] Similar letters were sent in the 1840s, a decade of trade depression.

In the 1830s and 1840s Lyle was in continuing financial difficulties and when he died in 1849 he is reputed to have left 'seven thousand pounds less than nothing'.[42] His will shows him to have been a man of modest means. His daughter inherited the whole of his estate amounting to the insurance valuation of £150 on his household goods which had been destroyed by fire shortly after his death, rent due from property in which he had an interest but did not own, and his one third share in the stock and profits of Abram Lyle and Sons, valued at just £100.[43] It is probable that the remaining share in the business was divided equally between his surviving sons, Abram III and Robert. His obituary in the *Greenock Advertiser* ran to no more than two lines.[44] His downfall was probably the result of heavy losses incurred in merchanting. In a period of slow sea voyages and poor market intelligence fortunes were made and lost overnight. For Abram Lyle II, the risks were heightened by a lack of experience and aggravated by intemperance.

Of his two sons Abram III was the most able and it was he who laid the foundations of his family's fortune. He had been educated at Murray's School, 'an establishment of merit and the best which Greenock then possessed' and had later worked in the office of a local lawyer. However his 'desire to make money was unquestionably there' and soon he gave up law in favour of a career as a merchant and a mariner. He had 'a passion for work' and was 'intolerant of all sport and amusement'.[45] These were qualities which would be needed to rebuild his family's business. His success was to depend on his friendship with John Kerr III, the son of his father's partner in the *Foundling*.

After the sale of the *Foundling* in 1832, John and Robert Kerr had continued to own ships. During 1829 they had purchased a shareholding of 22/64ths in the 176 ton brig *Helen* for trade with the West Indies and in 1830 they had become half shareholders in the *Williamina*.[46] In 1832 Robert Kerr and James McBride entered into partnership and established themselves as shipowners. In the 1840s the firm of Kerr and McBride would become one of the leading shipowners in Greenock.[47] John Kerr II remained in business on his own account; in 1835 in partnership with James Boyd, a Glasgow merchant, he bought the *Esquimaux* built in Canada in 1832; in 1838 he acquired a majority stake in the brig *Margaret*; and in 1840 a half share in the barque *Margaret Poynter*. Kerr seems to have traded these vessels up the West Coast of Scotland in partnership with Boyd, John Poynter, a Glasgow chemist, and Archibald McNeil, a cattle dealer in Inveraray. John Kerr II died in 1845 and he left all his shares in the vessels which he owned independently of his brother Robert to his son John III, then aged twenty-one. In that year John Kerr III became sole proprietor of the *Esquimaux* and two years later, in 1847, he purchased outright the barques *Amanda* (from Kerr and McBride), *Isabella Cooper* and *Consort*. Abram Lyle III was appointed master of the *Consort*, but his career as a sea captain was brief; the *Consort* was wrecked in the Western Ocean on 29 March 1847.[48] At about this time Kerr and Lyle with more success speculated in a shipment of silver watches and red herrings to the West Indies.[49]

It is not known if Abram Lyle III obtained another command, but on his father's death in 1849 he took over the management of the cooperage; with the business worth only £300 in 1849 this was to be an uphill task. Capital was needed for expansion. Retained profits, which were a major source of capital finance in the nineteenth century, were depleted or non-existent. Family loans were a second source of finance, but Abram III's immediate family was impoverished and it is unlikely that he married into much money. Mary Park, who married Abram III in 1846, was the daughter of a Greenock tanner and a smalltime shipowner and the sister of a local draper.[50]

In order to rebuild their father's business Abram III and Robert had little choice other than to pull in their belts and live frugally. Progress was accordingly slow and in 1850 their position had not improved. The factor of the Ardgowan Estate wrote to Abram in a sharper tone than he had written to his father: 'I have sent repeated notices to pay the arrears of feu duty owing upon your several properties but to these no attention whatsoever has been given. I have now to intimate that if a settlement . . . be not made within four days from this date I will have recourse to judicial proceedings'.[51] Abram was living on a knife's edge.

One reason for the subsequent recovery of Abram's fortunes was the gradual reduction in sugar duties in the 1840s. In 1844 the duty on colonial muscovado (unrefined sugar) was £1.26 (£1:5s 2d) per hundredweight, on foreign muscovado £3.29 (£3:6s 2d) and on refined sugar £8.82 (£8:16s 5d) and these duties had been pushed upwards during the previous century. From the late 1820s, there was a good deal of public agitation for the repeal of duties on corn and other foodstuffs, leading to the formation of the Anti-Corn Law League in 1833. The activities of the League epitomized the growing belief in the commercial and social advantages of free trade. Tariff reductions were gradually extended from corn to other similar commodities. By 1853 duties on colonial raw sugar had been reduced to between 50p (10s) and 58p (11s 8d) per hundredweight and to between 60p (12s) and 65p (13s) on imports from elsewhere. In the following year colonial preference was removed, making imports from non-colonial countries (including raw sugar from the East Indies) more competitive. Duty on raw sugar import was finally abolished in 1874.[52]

The impact of the reduction of duties on sugar consumption was remarkable. After 1844 consumption per head of population which had remained almost unchanged since before 1820 increased rapidly. With occasional reverses, for example in the mid-1850s and late 1880s, this was sustained and even quickened up until the end of the century (Table 2.1). The volume of imports is not documented but at a time when little refined sugar was imported, consumption was a realistic measure of the volume of trade. For Lyle this buoyancy of the sugar trade was of the utmost importance. His livelihood as a cooper was largely dependent on the prosperity of the refining industry. Between 1850 and 1870 the number of refineries in Greenock grew from eleven to fifteen and most of the established refineries were rebuilt and extended.[53]

During this period Abram Lyle III became more closely associated with John Kerr III. Between them John Kerr and Abram Lyle were to build the largest fleet at Greenock and engage in many merchanting ventures, eventually becoming two of the wealthiest and most successful businessmen on the Clyde. 'It is worthy of note', commented the author of *Family Notes* in 1922, 'that no formal contract ever passed between these partners. Such note-book jottings were all and yet they never had a dispute over results or reckonings. It was a strange and striking thing this close friendship. . . .'[54] They complemented each other with great effect: 'Mr. Kerr's boldness, audacity rather, would take the form of swift intuitive action, while [Abram Lyle's] touch of caution (with its share of boldness too) must have been at times a beneficial restraining influence in the combination'. Lyle and Kerr never operated as a single firm, and both businesses retained their distinct trading identities. Like Abram Lyle, Kerr may have been active in the cooperage trade. A John Kerr, cooper, was listed in the *Greenock Trade Directory* of 1845; the address of the business at 9 Nicholson Lane, was the former premises of Abram Lyle II.[55] The entry had been deleted two

Figure 2.3

John Kerr (1823–1872), with Abram Lyle as his partner, established the Diamond 'K' fleet which had become one of the largest merchant fleets in Britain by 1870. With other associates, the two laid the foundations of the Lyle sugar refining empire.

years later. (Figure 2.3)

After his purchases in 1847 John Kerr expanded his fleet continuously until his death in 1872. The *Isabella Cooper* was mortgaged in 1848 to Archibald Robertson and James Mackenzie, shipbrokers in Glasgow, probably to provide funds for the purchase in 1850 of the twenty-year-old *Lady Cornwall*. In 1850 John Kerr in joint partnership with Robertson and Mackenzie acquired the newly built *William Campbell* (340 tons), *Margaret Smith I* (258 tons) and (possibly on his own account) the new *Elizabeth Campbell* (316 tons) and the ten-year-old *Retrieve*.[56] One of his early ships, the *Jamaica*, was fifty years old and a second, when acquired in 1853, was twenty-three years old. Altogether Kerr operated some eleven second hand vessels in his first five years in business which made possible the cheap and rapid expansion of the fleet. By 1851 Kerr owned six vessels of a total of 1,693 tons. Some of these craft were owned for only a short time. The *Mountaineer* was purchased in 1851 and sold in 1854. Similarly the *Lady Cornwall* gave five years service and the *Bucephalus* was disposed of after four years. Partly because of their age, many of these early vessels were lost, the *Esquimaux* in 1850 on a voyage from Havana to the Clyde, the *Retrieve* in 1851, the *Amanda* in 1852 and the old *Jamaica* was burnt out in 1855. (See fleet list on page 192.)

During these early years the Kerr fleet was only of average size. In 1849 few Greenock shipowners operated more than two or three vessels. Twenty-eight of the seventy-three firms owned just one ship and eighteen of the others no more than three. Nevertheless, when compared with the largest firms Kerr's business was middling. At the time Thomas Hamlin and Co. was the largest Greenock shipowner with eleven ships weighing 5,939 tons, followed by Robert Cuthbert with 5,056 tons and C. MacMillan and Co. with 3,110 tons.[57]

During the 1850s, John Kerr ordered more new ships, mostly from the shipyard of Archibald McMillan & Son of Dumbarton. The *Isabella Kerr I* (442 tons) was delivered in 1852 followed by the *Agnes Taylor* (399 tons), *Demerara I* (523 tons), *Archibald McMillan* (498 tons), *John Ferguson* (499 tons), *Trinidad I* (485 tons) and *Barbadian* (569 tons), all built between 1852 and 1856.

By the mid-1850s the foundations of the great fleet of the 1870s were already laid. The growth of the Kerr fleet was perhaps the most remarkable feature of Greenock's shipping industry before the coming of the Peninsular and Orient Steam Navigation Co. to the port in the 1870s. In 1849 the total registered tonnage at Greenock had amounted to 68,358 tons of which Kerr owned a mere 161 tons. By 1857 total tonnage had grown by just 5,331 tons to 73,689, yet despite this sluggish growth, the 'Diamond K' fleet, as Kerr's ships came to be known after the conspicuous house flag they flew, had expanded to 8,676 tons.[58] Most of the small and second hand vessels purchased while the fleet was being established had been disposed of. Their place had been taken by larger purpose-built craft constructed by Archibald MacMillan & Son of Dumbarton. The

Figure 2.4
The three masted barque *Agnes Taylor*

Figure 2.5
The three masted barque *John Ferguson*.

new ships remained with the fleet for many years unless lost. By 1859 the average displacement of Kerr's ships had grown from 185 tons to 425 tons in eight years, equalling the mean displacement of Greenock registered ships. At the end of the 1850s Kerr was the largest of Greenock's eighty-six shipowners. His main rivals, J. and W. Stewart, Thomas Hamilton and Co., Macarthur and Binnie, and D. M. Larty and Co., owned 3,936, 3,730, 3,763 and 3,770 tons respectively. Only ten firms owned more than 2,000 tons of shipping.[59]

John Kerr's success in expanding his fleet depended on the financial support of Robertson and Mackenzie (later James Mackenzie on his own), who no doubt also arranged cargoes, and the business acumen of Abram Lyle III. Between 1851 and 1858 Robertson and Mackenzie, or Mackenzie, took a 50 per cent stake with Kerr in nine vessels. Two other craft purchased in 1853–4, the *Isabella* and *Marchioness of Ailsa*, were jointly owned by Kerr and other partners. After 1855 Kerr owned all the vessels in his fleet outright or in partnership with his sons and traded them in conjunction with Abram Lyle.[60] After their ill-fated experience with the *Consort* in 1847, Kerr and Lyle seem to have become regular partners in merchant ventures. In 1855 they purchased jointly the *Pursuit* at London for £1,070 and immediately despatched her to Trinidad. In the same year Lyle loaned Kerr £5,850, half the cost of a vessel under construction at Greenock to enable him to take delivery and made a similar loan to allow him to purchase the *Varna* lying at Liverpool.[61]

During the 1860s Kerr and Lyle profited from the growth in trade and Kerr purchased more new ships. In 1864 the first 1,000 tonner joined the fleet as flagship and was named *Isabella Kerr II* (after John Kerr's wife). With her hull constructed of wood and iron, she was the first composite ship to be owned by Kerr. Measuring 1,415 tons, she was twice as big as any of the 'Diamond K' ships in service. She was still the largest ship registered at Greenock in 1870. Later in 1864 the *Queen of the Lakes*, another 1,000 tonner, was acquired and a second composite ship, the *Ceylon*, was purchased two years later. (Figures 2.4 and 5)

In the late 1860s a further seven vessels of 1,200 tons each were added to the fleet, perhaps the most significant investment decision to have been made by the partners by that time. Two more craft of the same class were constructed in 1871 to replace the *Malabar* and *Sinde* which had both been lost soon after completion. A much larger sailing ship, the *Culzean*, of 1,572 tons was also completed in this year. All of these vessels were built of iron which had been used since the mid-1830s for constructing the hulls of steamships, but had only become economic for use in sailing ships in recent years.[62] As the shipbuilding trade was depressed, Kerr was able to place contracts with Robertsons of Greenock, J. & G. Thomson, who had recently established the Clydebank yard, and R. Duncan and Co. of Port Glasgow, all of whom normally constructed iron hulls for steamers. The link with Duncan's anticipated Lyle's close relationship with Russell's and Lithgow's in later years. Although Kerr had chosen to build iron ships, there were still doubts amongst many sailing ship owners about the competitiveness of iron sailing ships on longer routes where speed was essential. Iron hulls were more prone to fouling than the copper bottoms of the traditional wooden boats, which reduced their speed. In 1870 six of the seven ships overdue from China were made of iron. By 1872 the 'Diamond K' fleet of twenty-four ships at 21,693 tons in total was valued at £198,631.[63]

The expansion of the 'Diamond K' fleet in the 1860s was at the expense of the smaller Greenock owners. The number of shipowners in the port, which had risen from thirty-three to sixty-eight between 1849 and 1857 fell to fifty-four in 1870. However, between 1857 and 1870 the tonnage registered at Greenock increased by 55 per cent to 114,236 tons. Over the same period the displacement of the 'Diamond K' fleet rose by 261 per cent to equal 20 per cent of Greenock's registered shipping. In 1870 the 'Diamond K' fleet was more than twice as big as its closest rival, R. Shankland & Co. Comprising twenty-seven vessels and with 22,623 tons it exceeded that company's fleet by almost 14,140 tons. The next largest fleets were those of J. and W. Stewart with 7,359 tons, Henry Ferguson and Co. with 7,234 tons and G. Adams with a tonnage of 6,122 tons. Only seventeen firms owned more than 2,000 tons. Kerr and Lyle not only operated the largest fleet at Greenock, but the best equipped. The average displacement at the port was 617 tons and only twenty-six ships (seven of them traded by Kerr and Lyle) measured more than 1,199 tons.[64]

Throughout their partnership as merchants and shippers, Kerr and Lyle were committed to the West Indian trade and their vessels sailed almost exclusively to that area. (Table 2.2.) In 1849 no cargo was sent to any other destination while in 1856 twenty-one of the firm's twenty-three cargoes went to the West Indies. A few ships began to venture elsewhere; the *Varna* was wrecked in Tasmania in 1857. By the 1860s the range of destinations had extended, partly reflecting the expansion in Far Eastern and Australian trade after the curtailing of the East India Company's monopoly in 1833. One Kerr and Lyle ship sailed for New Zealand in 1863, another to Hong Kong and five more to Montreal. Two years later a 'Diamond K' ship sailed to Singapore and two others to Bahia and at that time the *Madras I* was wrecked in the China Sea, to be followed by the *Ceylon* lost on a voyage to Bombay in 1868. However as late as 1869 the destination of the vast majority of 'Diamond K' ships remained the Caribbean.

Imported cargoes were received exclusively from the West Indies. In the years for which data is available only one cargo came from elsewhere, Mauritius. Hence ships which originally sailed to destinations such as Montreal, Mauritius and the East must then have sailed, possibly in ballast, to the West Indies to return home with a cargo of sugar. Descriptions of the cargoes carried and their sea routes on the second leg of the journey are not recorded.

Table 2.2

Destinations and Origins of Cargoes sent from and received at Greenock in Kerr and Lyle Ships

Year	Number of cargoes to West Indies	Number of cargoes from West Indies	Number of cargoes to elsewhere	Number of cargoes from elsewhere
1849	6	2	—	—
1853	17	15	1–Mauritius	—
1856	21	21	1–Calcutta 1–Mauritius	1–Mauritius
1859	15	24	1–Bombay	—
1863	18	13	1–New Zealand 1–Hong Kong 5–Montreal 5–Mauritius	—
1865	15	20	1–Montreal 1–Singapore 2–Bahia 2–Mauritius	—
1869	21	24	3–Bombay 1–Calcutta 1–Mauritius	

Source: Clyde Bill of Entry

Table 2.3

The Extent of Kerr and Lyle's Interests in Cargoes Shipped to Greenock in their Ships

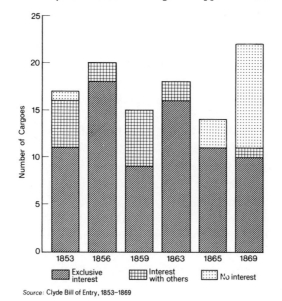

Source: Clyde Bill of Entry, 1853–1869

Sugar was the chief commodity imported into Greenock by Kerr and Lyle, making them the principal suppliers to the Greenock sugar refining industry. Occasionally, very small quantities of cotton, rum or coconuts were shipped, but every cargo was almost entirely made up of sugar or molasses. The large discrepancy between the number of cargoes received at and sent from Greenock by Kerr and Lyle indicates that some cargoes were shipped into other United Kingdom ports. Between September 1866 and May 1867 nine 'Diamond K' ships arrived to load goods at Greenock, mostly with no cargoes, all having sailed from either London or Liverpool, the principal sugar importing ports.[65] This disparity makes it impossible to estimate the volume of trade handled by the fleet.

A wide range of goods was exported from Greenock. Coal was mostly sent to Montreal; cast iron, railway sleepers, stores and coal went to India. Coal was also the most important commodity shipped to the Caribbean, but a great variety of other commodities were also exported. The cargo of the *Demerara I* which sailed to Havana in 1855 was typical. She carried 30,860 yards of colour cotton, 5,850 yards of plain cotton, 56 square yards of plain linen, hardware, hosiery, slabs, stationery, barley, cheese, oats, 70 barrels of ale, 66½ hundredweights of wrought iron and 305 tons of coal.[66]

Kerr and Lyle had a financial interest in nearly all the cargoes their fleet brought to Greenock. In some cases they owned the entire cargo. The partners also despatched cargoes in vessels they did not own, including the *Ann of Sunderland* in 1849. (Table 2.3.) After the termination of Kerr's partnership with Robertson and Mackenzie, Kerr and Lyle seem to have been able to finance most of their ventures from their own resources. Only in 1857–58 did Kerr have to raise loans on any of his ships; the *Berbice I* and *Margaret Smith II* were mortgaged to the Bank of Scotland for £14,000. The mortgages were discharged in 1860.[67] In combining merchanting with shipowning Kerr and Lyle were not exceptional. The Greenock trades directories never made a distinction between the two groups while at Liverpool half the leading cotton importers had shipping interests in the 1850s.[68]

For the crews of the 'Diamond K' fleet, like those of other merchant ships of the period, life afloat was unpleasant. Loss of life at sea was heavy. In the sixteen years before 1865 some 20,000 British ships were lost and on one night alone 195 went to the bottom.[69] Between 1845 and 1872, twenty-nine of the seventy-five ships operated by Kerr and Lyle were lost, wrecked, abandoned or burnt out. Poor maintenance, over loading and bad seamanship were most frequently to blame. In 1865 James MacDonald, captain of the *Margaret Kerr*, appeared before the Greenock Marine Board charged with drunkenness while in command and was held to be partly responsible for the loss of his ship in the Gulf of Florida.[70] Another master, J. F. Parker of the *Barbadian*, was charged by

Kerr with 'habitual drunkenness and great neglect' during a voyage to Belize.[71]

The official log of *Lephenstrath* provides a good insight into life on board merchantmen. The ship sailed from Greenock in June 1865 with a crew of twenty. She arrived at Havana at the end of August and was delayed there until October. During this period one crew member died of 'black vomit' and another of 'yellow fever'. Two seamen deserted to American ships where wages were higher. Two others were jailed for violence, one for 'being drunk and biting off Ab. Boyle's ear without provocation'. Another was sent to 'hospital' suffering from the effects of drink and took three days to recover. The ship finally sailed to New York where some of the crew were discharged by 'mutual agreement' and others deserted. By the time she returned to Greenock, seven of her original crew of twenty had deserted, seven had been discharged, and two had died.[72] Conditions aboard the *Lephenstrath* were doubtless aggravated by the climate of Central America.

Despite his extensive shipping partnership with John Kerr, first and foremost Abram Lyle was a cooper. This business was the foundation of his wealth but little is known of its structure or performance. In April 1869 his cooperage in Nicholson Street, Greenock was totally destroyed by fire,[73] and it was feared that his insurance would not cover the loss. Nevertheless, the premises were rebuilt and Lyle's cooperage continued on the same site for many years. It is possible that part of the money recovered from insurance payments was set aside to build a new cooperage in Glasgow. In 1870 Lyle received permission from the Glasgow Dean of Guild Court to erect an extensive cooperage in Dundas Street,[74] and a year later, he was listed in the *Glasgow Trade Directory* as a cooper at the same address. His name did not appear in later directories and it would seem that the project did not come to fruition.

A striking feature of Lyle's business activities during the 1860s was his eagerness to diversify his interests so as to secure his market for barrels and his supplies of staves. His partnership with Kerr and interest in shipping throughout the 1850s nurtured this ambition. In 1859–60 Lyle set up a separate concern to import staves for making barrels. These were shipped mostly from North America, Scandinavia and Russia. As well as supplying his own needs Lyle sold staves to other coopers in the area. By 1867 his business was already substantial. In that year he imported nineteen shiploads totalling 23,895 pipe staves and 359,513 pun staves[75] and it is likely that he had become the largest stave supplier in the locality.

Of more significance was Lyle's diversification into sugar refining. In 1865, the Greenock Sugar Refinery was placed on the market by the Steel family of local shipbuilders and within a month it was purchased by a partnership consisting of Lyle, Kerr, Charles Hunter and James and Walter Grieve, all eminent local businessmen.[76] The management of the concern was entrusted to Lyle, and the author of *Family Notes* (1922) records that it 'was an immediate

Table 2.4

The Relative Size of the Glebe Sugar Refinery Company's Raw Sugar Imports
into Greenock, 1865–74

Period	Total direct imports into Greenock (tons)	Total direct imports made by the Glebe (tons)	Glebe's imports as a percentage of total imports
1865–69	135,203		
1867–69		21,796	16%
1870–74	187,654	24,132	13%

Sources: Raw Sugar Imports: J.M. Hutchinson, *Notes on the Sugar Refining Industry* (1900), p. 72
Glebe Refinery Imports: G.H.T. Harbour Dues Book

and decided success, was speedily enlarged and the output doubled (or trebled)
until it became the largest in the district'.[77]

The Glebe Refinery was much larger than most of the Greenock refineries.
Table 2.4 shows the percentage of direct raw sugar imports into Greenock
which were processed at the refinery. Although this share fell from 16 per cent
between 1867–69 to 13 per cent between 1870–74, there were fifteen refineries at
Greenock in these years and between 1867–69 the average refinery consumed
9,013 tons per annum or 6.6 per cent of the total. This calculation assumes that
the Glebe did not purchase sugar from local merchants but imported all its
needs direct from overseas.

By 1872 Lyle, with his coopering, shipping, shipowning, stave importing
and sugar refining interests, was amongst the wealthiest and most influential
of Greenock's businessmen. In just over twenty years he had built up his
considerable wealth out of the ruins of his father's cooperage business. By
diversification he had safeguarded his capital and strengthened the market for
his goods. In this respect Lyle's early career was characteristic of Greenock
business in the 1860s and 1870s. In 1880 the Select Committee on the Sugar
Industries, with reference to the Clyde, remarked that 'the refineries include a
great many of the subsidiary industries within themselves. Cooperage, for
instance, is very largely done within the refineries themselves'.[78]

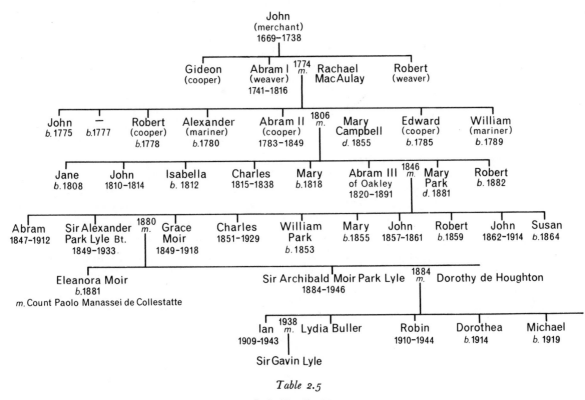

Table 2.5

Lyle Family Tree

3. 1872-1890
We were to be the Cape Line

John Kerr died at the age of forty-nine in 1872. His death was a severe and unexpected blow to Greenock. The town had prospered since the 1840s and his contribution to its development was substantial. His obituary in the *Greenock Telegraph* noted that 'he had risen gradually and almost unprecedentedly to the acquiring of a position in shipowning which was excelled by none in Greenock . . . no single individual shipowner in the Clyde, nor we are assured in the United Kingdom, possesses such an extensive fleet'. As a merchant he was both 'extremely sharp and clever'[1] and his fortune in 1872 amounted to £332,435.[2]

John Kerr's interests were wide-ranging and typical of many successful merchants of the time. On his death his share in the 'Diamond K' fleet, which then consisted of twenty-four ships, was valued at about £151,000 and the stock in trade of John Kerr and Co. was worth a further £85,000. His investment in the Glebe Sugar Refinery amounted to £29,166 and another £27,000 was invested in railway stocks. He owned £11,200 of Bank of Scotland stock and he had made a £20,000 loan to Hugh Morrison, a wealthy Glasgow clothier, besides smaller charitable loans to the Greenock Club and the Free Middle Church.[3]

For Abram Lyle the death of John Kerr meant the loss of not only a close friend but also a trusted and shrewd business partner. On the automatic termination of the partnership at Kerr's death, Lyle's share in the business was valued at £47,443 or, roughly, 25 per cent. In settlement Lyle was apportioned a half share in six of the 'Diamond K' ships and a third share in two others.[4] All these vessels had been built in the 1860s.

Under the terms of John Kerr's will, his business interests were inherited by his four sons. Since 1864 the two older sons, Alexander and Robert, had partnered their father in some ventures and in at least two ships (*Demerara II* and *Bermuda*).[5] Another son, John Kerr junior, had become a partner in John Kerr & Co., in 1871.[6] The sons' management was to be overlooked by his trustees, Abram Lyle, Charles Philip Hunter, a merchant in Greenock, Thomas Stark, a banker in the town, and William Letham, one of Kerr's senior employees.[7] Initially Abram Lyle seems to have wished to maintain the business in its old form and the management of all the vessels in which he had an interest was

Figure 3.1
A caricature of Abram Lyle III from a series of articles under the title of 'Men You Should Know' in the magazine *The Baillie*, 1879.

entrusted to Alexander and Robert Kerr. This arrangement did not last long. During 1873 Lyle became sole proprietor of four vessels in which he already held a half share, the *Queen of the Lakes*, the *Zanzibar*, the *Java* and the *Colmonell*, having a total value of £44,208. The four ships were all iron vessels of over 1,000 net tons, and the *Zanzibar*, the *Java* and the *Colmonell* had been built within the previous five years. In settlement of the deal, Lyle transferred his shares in four of the other 'Diamond K' ships to the Kerr brothers and relinquished all his interests in the Kerr business.

Abram Lyle's decision to take on the sole ownership of the four vessels was made without the help of external finance. In the later nineteenth century, banks and other financial institutions were extremely wary of making loans to shipowners, on the grounds that shipping securities were precarious. George Rae, a native of Aberdeen who became General Manager of the Liverpool-based North and South Wales Bank, shared this outlook. 'Is the periodical disbursing and manning, victualling and insuring, loading or chartering of a ship the proper business of a Bank Manager, or his Board of Directors? ... Better in my judgement sell (the ship) on her first arrival in port at almost any price, and thus avoid the pains and penalties which the pursuit of shipowning has ordinarily in store for the uninitiated'.[8] Without the hope of external help, Abram Lyle's assumption of fleet ownership was a bold and determined change of approach.

In the next two years, Lyle sought recognition that his fleet was now independent of the 'Diamond K' line. In A. P. Lyle's words 'we wanted a type of name that could make our ships out as belonging to one ownership. Ours were in future to be called by the names of capes; we were to be the Cape Line'. The *Queen of the Lakes* kept her name but the others in 1874 were renamed *Cape Cormorin I*, *Cape Horn I* and *Cape Wrath I*.

Although Lyle had become owner of some of Greenock's finest ships, his fleet was small. In 1873 he ordered a 1,782 net tons sailing ship from John Reid and Co. of Port Glasgow. She was named the *John Kerr* in memory of Lyle's close friend and partner. A. P. Lyle described the ship as a 'beautiful craft, of finest lines'; she was the largest vessel in the fleet by 300 tons, and the largest on the Greenock register. Her construction paved the way for other orders. A small vessel of 852 net tons was completed in 1874. Three others, the *Cape Sable I* (1,416 tons), *Cape Finisterre I* (882 tons) and *Cape Verde I* (1,711 tons) were built in 1874 at the yard of Thomas Wingate and Co. of Glasgow (Figure 3.2). The new ships, and the others which followed, were slow ships with 'lines' and speed sacrificed for cargo space.[9] This increase in capacity reflected the growing competition from steam ships, which by the 1870s were beginning to prove economical and fast enough to be an attractive investment for tramp shipping concerns. Nevertheless, Lyle continued to invest in sailing ships and his business flourished. The *Cape of Good Hope I* (1,399 tons) was built in 1876,

Figure 3.2

The three masted iron barque *Cape Finisterre I* built by Thomas Wingate & Co., Glasgow, for Abram Lyle & Sons, in 1874. She was sold in 1889 on the dissolution of the Company. In 1924 she was acquired by the Egyptian Government as a marine training ship and renamed *El Faroukieh*. In this photograph she is moored at Alexandria sometime after 1924. She was still lying as a hulk at that port as late as 1959.

and her sister ships, the *Cape Breton I* and *Cape St Vincent I*, followed a year later. Between 1872 and 1880 the size of the Lyle fleet had grown from four to ten ships.

It was not until 1881 that the first steamer, the *Cape Clear I* (1,501 tons), joined the Lyle fleet. The new ship, powered by compound inverted two cylinder engines, was an experiment. At her launch Lyle is reported to have said that he

Figure 3.3
The first steamship owned by Abram Lyle & Sons, the S.S. *Cape Clear I*, photographed going down the Clyde to her trials in 1881. She was built by Robert Steele & Co. of Greenock, but was not a success. In 1884 she was sold to the Union Steamship Co. of New Zealand.

saw a future for sailing ships, but not in the 'distant' future.[10] At the time many British owners made similar investments in steam – to such an extent that when the economy turned down in 1884 steamer freight rates collapsed. *The Angiers Freight Report* for that year commented, 'In almost every trade, the lowest points reached during the year at which steamers have been chartered are lower than have ever before been accepted . . . This state of affairs was brought about by the large over-production of tonnage during the three previous years, fostered by reckless credit given by the banks and builders, and over-speculation by irresponsible and inexperienced owners'.[11] In these circumstances the *Cape Clear* lost money. The Lyle family decided to cut their losses by selling her in 1884 to realise funds for other projects (Figure 3.3). Lyle's caution was characteristic of other general cargo ship-owners. In 1880, of the 280 ships registered at Greenock only twenty-nine, or about 12 per cent were steamers. Thirteen of these vessels were passenger ships owned by the Peninsular and Orient Steam Navigation Co., three by the Greenock Steamship Co., and five by Walter Grieve, a partner in the Glebe Refinery. Of established Greenock firms J. and W. Stewart and Daniel Gaff each owned three steamships,

Figure 3.4

The three masted iron sailing ship *Cape of Good Hope I*, completed in 1876 by J. & G. Thomson of Glasgow. She cost £22,234 which was an average price for such a ship in the 1870s. Thomson accepted this contract because in the severe depression of the mid-1870s they were unable to obtain orders for quality steamer tonnage.

but Baine and Johnson, Alex Currie and Scott and Co. owned only one vessel each.[12]

Although steamships had been used for passenger and mail traffic since their inception in the 1810s – first in esturial navigation and shortly afterwards on the Atlantic – they did not become economic for carrying cargo until the late 1860s. At that time the reduction of running costs and increase in efficiency of the compound engine coupled with the opening of the Suez canal in 1869 enlarged the opportunities of tramp steam shipping. These developments allowed the Harrison brothers of Liverpool to rebuild the fleet of the Charante Steam Ship Co. and Alfred Jones to open up West Africa through the African Steam Ship Co. and the British and African Steam Navigation Co.[13] By the early 1880s the advantages of steamships had become sufficiently apparent for firms like the Aberdeen Line, formerly clipper owners, and Hogarth of Glasgow, to invest in them.[14] However, in this period steamers only proved themselves profitable in carrying mixed cargoes and bulk commodities like tea and meat where rapid voyages were essential and margins high. For long voyages carrying bulk cargoes like grain and sugar the cost advantage still lay with sailing ships, like those of Lyle, which were over 1,500 tons.

Between 1872 and 1880 the size of the Lyle fleet grew from four to ten ships. Despite recent legislation to prevent overloading and poor maintenance and to promote better seamanship, losses at sea continued for Lyle. The *Queen of the Lakes* was abandoned in 1875 after her cargo shifted. In 1879, the fleet's flagship, the *John Kerr*, sailed from Middlesbrough and was never heard of again. In the following year the *Cape Sable I* disappeared with all hands on a voyage to Singapore, and the *Cape Comorin I* met a similar fate in 1882. For indemnity against these losses, Lyle depended heavily upon the Glasgow marine insurance market. Underwriters and brokers had been firmly established in Glasgow and Greenock since the eighteenth century and they successfully defended their share of Clyde marine insurance business against the encroachment of London underwriters and insurance companies in the nineteenth century.[15] Local insurance company projects were no more successful in capturing the Glasgow and Greenock underwriters' business; both the Glasgow Marine Insurance Co. (established in 1839) and the Scottish Marine Insurance Co. (established in 1840) had closed in the 1840s and the Greenock Marine Insurance Co., whose origin is unknown, was wound up in 1867.[16]

By 1880 the largest Greenock shipowner was the Peninsular and Orient, a London based company, with thirteen large vessels weighing in total 42,582 tons. The Company had extended its operations to the port in the 1870s to serve the growing emigrant traffic to the Antipodes, a consequence of the collapse of the Highland economy following the failure of the kelping industry. By 1891 over half the total Peninsular and Orient fleet of 224,327 gross tons was registered in Greenock. In 1880 A. and J. H. Carmichael owned the second largest fleet with 12,982 tons (an increase of almost 8,000 tons since 1870), John Kerr & Co. the third with 12,982 tons, and Lyles were a close fourth with 12,940 tons. In eight years the size of the Lyle fleet had caught up with the size of the Kerr brothers' fleet. The 1870s was a prosperous decade for Greenock's shipping, and total registration grew from 185 to 250 ships and tonnage from 114,236 to 228,630.[17]

The value of Lyle's fleet increased significantly in the 1870s. J. & G. Thomson of Clydebank had built the *Cape of Good Hope I, Cape St. Vincent I* and *Cape Breton* in 1876–77 quoting Lyle prices of between £15.12 (£15:2:6d) and £15.05 (£15:1s) per ton (Figure 3.4). At a mean average price of £15.10 (£15:2s) per ton the ships built for Lyles between 1873 and 1882 were worth about £138,739 (excluding the *John Kerr*). If the three surviving pre-1872 ships are added at their valuation, the fleet's total value in 1882 was about £176,339, representing a very considerable increase over the 1872 valuation of £44,208.[18]

Although Lyle continued to carry sugar throughout these years, his imported cargoes became more diverse as his vessels ventured further afield. In September 1874, the *Cape Race I* and *Cape Comorin I* arrived from the West

Indies with sugar, but the *Queen of the Lakes* docked at Greenock from Burma with a cargo of teak.[19] In 1877 the articles of agreement between the master and crew of the *Cape Horn I* stipulated that the ship would sail from Greenock to San Francisco 'and if required to any port or ports on the west coast of America or any Island or Islands on that coast or otherwise in the North and South Pacific Oceans and the Indian Ocean and China Seas and Australia and any port or ports on the Eastern coast of the United States, the West Indies or any port of North or South America to and from as freight or employment may offer for the ship'.[20] By the late 1870s Lyle's ships were already assuming the role for which the twentieth century British steam tramps were to be famous.

Lyle also switched the source of his raw sugar imports from the West Indies to the East Indies. As early as 1872, the *Colmonell* (later *Cape Wrath I*) docked at Greenock 'with the fifth cargo of Java sugar brought in here during the past three months ... A few years ago this sugar was almost unknown here ... and even in 1870 only two cargoes arrived'.[21] By 1882, Lyle's trade with the West Indies had ceased and been replaced by sugar imports from the East Indies. Six Lyle ships docked at Greenock in 1882, each loaded with 'Java sugar'.[22]

Almost every cargo of raw sugar brought to Greenock in the Cape ships was on account of Lyle. Five of the six cargoes docking in 1882 had been purchased by the firm.[23] Additional ships were rarely needed and the chartering

Figure 3.5

Industrial Greenock photographed sometime in the last quarter of the nineteenth century. The chimneys in the foreground belong to some of the fifteen sugar refineries in the town. At this period the Greenock sugar industry was at its zenith. On the right is the Cartsburn Yard of Scotts Shipbuilding & Engineering Co.

of the *Peter* with 578 tons in 1873, and the *Augustine Kobbe* with 686 tons in 1875, were exceptional.[24]

In addition to his sugar interests in the 1870s Lyle continued to bring in goods required by the coopering trade. Before 1872 staves had been a major import, but by 1874 only one such cargo was imported. In this year 'French hoops' from Nantes were increasingly important and eleven cargoes were imported in chartered vessels. Lyle ships were not employed in the trade.[25]

In 1874 coal was still the principal outward cargo – 1,707 tons were despatched to the West Indies in the *Cape Comorin I*, 1,500 went to Galle in the *Queen of the Lakes* and 400 tons went to San Francisco in the *Cape Race I* along with 315 tons of pig iron, fire bricks, starch, earthenware, agricultural implements, cement and beer.[26] In the 1870s the Lyle fleet also carried emigrants to the Colonies. The *Cape Sable I* was chartered by the New Zealand government to transport emigrants from London in 1874[27] and with similar operations in view, the *Cape Race I* was designed with ventilation throughout 'in case the ship should be chartered for carrying emigrants or coolies'.[28]

None of the cargoes exported by Lyle in 1882 were loaded in Greenock. One vessel took a cargo coastwise to London before sailing overseas whilst of the other five ships four sailed to Cardiff and one to Glasgow in ballast.[29] Lyles were searching further afield for export cargoes. It is possible that the coal and manufactured metal goods sent from Cardiff were more profitable cargo than coal sent from Greenock. However, cargoes could not always be obtained and in 1879 the *Cape Wrath I* returned to Java in ballast and again sailed from Greenock in ballast in 1886, bound for Singapore.[30]

In the 1870s, while Lyle's shipping and importing businesses flourished, the output of the Glebe Refinery continued to expand. In 1873 there were twelve refineries at Greenock and a further three under construction (Figure 3.5). The biggest, capable of a weekly output of 800 tons, was owned by John Walker and Co.; the Glebe Refinery, capable of producing 750 tons per week, was the second largest in size. These two firms dominated the Greenock industry. No other refinery could produce more than 450 tons weekly.[31] In 1872, according to John Kerr's will, the total capital invested in the Glebe Refinery was £116,668. By 1879 it was the largest refinery in Greenock[32] and by then its value may have reached £250,000. In that year the Glebe accounted for about a fifth of Greenock's output of refined sugar and possessed about a fifth of the capital invested in the industry. (Table 3.1.) It then employed 300 men to produce 1,000 tons of sugar each week. Capital invested in the next largest refinery amounted to £195,000, while in six of Greenock's eleven refineries fixed assets and utensils and stock were valued at less than £100,000.

Despite the growth in production of refined sugar from 156,000 tons in 1869 to 250,000 tons in 1880, the Greenock sugar industry was less profitable after 1872 than it had been in earlier years. From 1870 to 1874 output remained at

Table 3.1

Fixed and Moveable Capital and Output of Greenock's Sugar Refineries, 1879

Refinery	Weekly output (in tons)	Number of Employees	Fixed Capital	Moveable Capital (when working)	Total Capital (when working)
A	1,000	300	£150,000	£100,000	£250,000
B	750	250	120,000	75,000	195,000
C	650	200	120,000	65,000	185,000
D	650	200	100,000	65,000	165,000
E	600	80	80,000	60,000	140,000
F	350	60	60,000	35,000	95,000
G	350	50	50,000	35,000	85,000
H	300	100	50,000	30,000	80,000
I	320	100	30,000	35,000	65,000
J	220	60	30,000	25,000	55,000
K	not working	70	30,000	20,000	50,000
Total	5,190	1,470	820,000	545,000	1,365,000

Source: B.P.P. 1880 (332), XII, p. 588 Appendix 1.

Table 3.2

Output of the Greenock Sugar Refining Industry, 1869–78

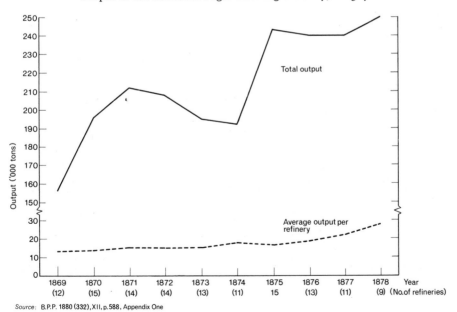

Output ('000 tons)

Total output

Average output per refinery

Year	1869	1870	1871	1872	1873	1874	1875	1876	1877	1878
(No. of refineries)	(12)	(15)	(14)	(14)	(13)	(11)	15	(13)	(11)	(9)

Source: B.P.P. 1880 (332), XII, p.588, Appendix One

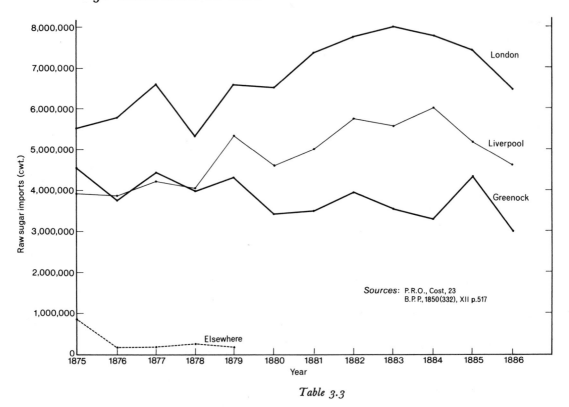

Table 3.3

Graph showing total imports of raw sugar into British ports, 1875–1886.

about 200,000 tons a year and from 1875 until after 1878 at 240,000 tons. While some firms went out of business and others closed pending an upturn in trade, output per refinery rose from 13,000 tons a year in 1869 to 27,778 in 1878 (Table 3.2). As a result the *Greenock Telegraph* was able to comment in 1877 that the depression in the sugar trade had not seriously affected the remaining Greenock firms. However, the decline in the industry had hit Greenock by 1879 and Lyle, in his position as Provost, wrote to the Home Secretary drawing his attention to the high level of local unemployment 'in consequence of the depressed state of the two principal industries here, viz shipbuilding and sugar refining'.[33] In the late 1870s and early 1880s imports of raw sugar into Greenock fluctuated markedly from year to year but the trend was unmistakably downward (Table 3.3). In 1875 imports were 4,540,328 cwt falling to 2,998,273 cwt in 1886. By comparison imports into London and Liverpool rose until 1883–84 when they too began to fall off, but never to below their 1875 level. Greenock lost its position as Britain's second sugar refining centre which it had held in 1875. By 1882 imports of raw sugar into Greenock, Liverpool and London were 3,940,190, and 5,726,964 and 9,936,255 cwt respectively.

The decline of the Greenock and the United Kingdom sugar refining industries cannot be dissociated from the general malaise which began to affect certain sectors of British industry and commerce in the early 1870s. During this period prices of many commodities fell. Between 1873 and 1876, despite a rise in consumption the price of refined sugar dropped by 13 per cent and the price of raw sugar fell by 11 per cent. This fall reflected the flooding of the British market with beet sugar and refined sugar from Europe. By 1876 Continental refiners, especially those in Germany, France and Holland, had captured about 25 per cent of the British sugar market.

During the nineteenth century Britain could depend on supplies of cheap cane sugar from her colonies and consequently sugar beet was not cultivated to any extent. European countries, apart from Holland, lacked sugar producing colonies and, rather than purchasing cane sugar from Britain, they encouraged home production of beet by a variety of tax incentives and bounties. The measures adopted in Germany were described in 1917 by George Martineau: 'The production of beet root sugar in Germany, securely defended against competition from outside, was encouraged and stimulated by its government with good judgement and moderation. The fiscal system adopted was to levy the duty, not on sugar produced, but on the weight of the roots. This created a most desirable incentive not only to the production by the farmer of the finest possible quality of root but also to the extraction from the roots by the manufacturer of the largest possible quantity of sugar'.[34] The growing of sugar beet was an ideal supplement to the subsistence agriculture practised in much of Europe during the nineteenth century.

Exports of sugar beet and refined sugar from the Continent to Britain remained at a low level until the 1870s. From then on dumping became commonplace (Table 3.4). By 1875 sugar beet made up 15 per cent of London's raw sugar imports and in 1876 it was declared in the House of Lords: 'If the doctrine was still maintained that the Government should adopt fiscal measures for other than fiscal objects and should attempt to make such measures an engine for assisting British manufacturers to compete on equal terms with their foreign rivals, the present case (of sugar) might undoubtedly be considered a very proper one for the application of such a principle'.[35] In Greenock, by 1878, feelings against unfair foreign competition ran high and it became a political question and source of agitation.[36] Imports of beet into Liverpool rose more slowly, accounting for only 16 per cent of total raw sugar imports in 1885 compared with 50 per cent at London. The year before imports into Greenock had risen sharply to make up 45 per cent of the total. Greenock was geographi-

Table 3.4

Sugar Beet Imports as a Percentage of Total Raw Sugar Imports

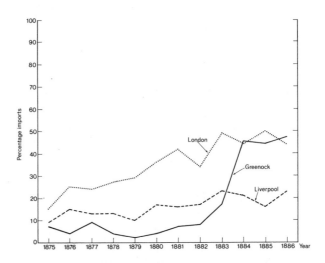

cally less favourably placed than either London or Liverpool to draw on these cheap supplies of beet. This disadvantage was compounded by the smallness of its local market. With access to cheap beet it was a simple matter for Liverpool refiners to supply the Scottish market (Table 3.3).

Lyle reacted to these changed circumstances by proposing the termination of the Glebe partnership and the construction of a large modern low cost refinery in Greenock. A. P. Lyle reflected in 1922: 'We named a sum and said to our partners "Either you buy us out at that price or we buy you out; take your choice." They elected to buy us out.'[37] In June 1881 an application was made to the Greenock Police Commissioners and to the Greenock Harbour Trust for permission to construct a refinery capable of producing 1,500 tons of sugar per week,[38] – an output 50 per cent greater than that of the Glebe Refinery in 1879 (Table 3.1). It was to be adjacent to the James Watt Dock then under construction and Lyle requested the Harbour Trustees to set apart one or two berths 'since we would have at least one vessel constantly in the dock' (Figures 3.6a and 3.6b). The plan was probably influenced by his study of American practice on a visit to the United States in 1877. The *Greenock Telegraph* reported that 'from what he had seen abroad he had come to the conclusion that public undertakings should be carried out on a complete and liberal scale and that cheese-paring and half measures should be shunned as quite unworthy of a prosperous community'.[39]

The Harbour Trustees were less than enthusiastic about Lyle's scheme. In July they replied that at this early stage of the Dock's development they were 'not prepared to fix the principle of allocating berths'; they would only agree

Figure 3.6

(a) The James Watt Dock in Greenock under construction in the late 1870s. The dock cost £500,000 and was designed to attract shipping and industry back to Greenock. The Lyles hoped to build one of the largest refineries in Britain alongside it.

(b) The formal opening of the dock in 1885 with the four masted auxiliary steel barque *Otterburn* steaming in at high water.

to do 'all in their power to make suitable arrangements at a convenient place in the James Watt Dock to facilitate the trade of Messrs. Lyle should they erec a sugar refinery near to the dock'.[40] This was a decision they were soon to regret bitterly. In August 1881 the *Greenock Telegraph* commented dolefully 'we regret to say that the Messrs. Lyle have resolved to erect their new works in the outskirts of London'.[41]

Writing in 1922, A. P. Lyle, who had been active in the firm's management in 1880, explained that the decision to move to London was not a simple matter. 'It was difficult to decide between the two places. Figures were of little help. They could tell no doubt that on the Clyde building would amount to much less and the cost per ton of refining would be decidedly lower there than on the Thames; but how could one put a money value on the *per contra* of the advantages of the huge population waiting to be served at the very factory door. The decision must rest with business flair, or on chance, more than anything else. After long interminable family debates the die was cast for London'.[42] No doubt the awareness that Greenock's natural advantage as a sugar refining centre was being eroded by cheap beet imports into the South of England also weighed heavily on their minds. In 1881 a wharf and land were purchased at Plaistow, south London and a large refinery was built.

The loss to Greenock of such an enormous undertaking was felt deeply and controversy raged over the responsibility for the failure. The Harbour Trustees were most vulnerable. They were censured in the 1881 municipal election campaign: 'The Harbour Trustees should take care that, while building new docks to entice new customers to use the port they don't by unnecessary restrictions drive away old friends'. Losses to Greenock were put at 'about £5,000 a year in harbour dues and water rates, and then the loss in workmen's wages and circulation of money consequent on removing a good going public work must be very great'.[43]

The transfer of the refining interests to London had a profound effect on the Lyles' shipowning business. It diverted their managerial talent and understandably drained funds away from shipowning. By the late 1870s Abram was taking less interest in his business affairs. His eldest sons (including A. P. Lyle), who were then in their early thirties, took an increasingly large share of responsibility. In 1881 Charles and Abram IV left to manage the London refinery; they were later followed by William and John, leaving A. P. Lyle (the author of *Family Notes*) and Robert to manage the shipping business. £150,000 was spent on building and equipping the new refinery and a loan of £100,000 was obtained from the Bank of Scotland for working capital. Due to unforeseen difficulties Lyles were obliged to ask the bank to advance £30,000 of this for fixed investment which was agreed.[44]

The relocation of the sugar refining business almost ended in disaster. In 1883, while the refinery was being built an exceptionally large sugar beet crop on the Continent led to a catastrophic fall in the price of raw sugar 'to a point which it had never entered the hearts of men to conceive'.[45] Anticipating normal prices the Lyles had invested in six cargoes of cane sugar which eventually had to be sold at a loss of about £100,000.[46] Most of their capital was locked up in the new refinery whose completion had been delayed by technical difficulties. During 1883 and 1884 bankruptcies in the sugar industry were frequent. Disturbed by the situation the Bank of Scotland called in their £100,000 loan to Lyle. The call could not have come at a worse time. Lyles' could now only raise funds by disposing of assets in a depressed market. Refineries which had been worth £300,000 a few years earlier were then realizing only £60,000 when placed on the market. In 1922 A. P. Lyle likened his family's position to 'a sailing vessel embayed on a lee coast in a gale of wind; a headland has to be weathered or she goes on the rocks; but once round it, by however narrow a margin, there is safety . . . Our barque, *Cape Race*, was once in that plight on the coast of Ireland, and the commander . . . declared that his yard arms scraped the cliffs before he rounded the point. Our case was not so perilous as that, but it was too exciting for comfort.'[47]

Although the Bank of Scotland relented and eventually extended the period allowed for repayment, some assets were disposed of. The cooperage at Greenock was closed in the mid 1880s,[48] and the *Cape Clear*, the company's only steamer was put up for sale in 1884. After 1883 the shipping business was starved of capital while all the Lyles' resources were channelled into paying off the debts on the refinery and the losses on raw sugar imports.

Despite its chequered start the London refinery was a great success. Abram and Charles Lyle managed this business with great flair. Charles, the 'practical refiner' went to London in 1881 to supervise the building of the refinery and soon afterwards he was joined by Abram IV, who was reckoned to be the most astute buyer of raw sugar in the country. Both were Chairmen in turn. William Lyle joined his brothers in London in the 1890s and became actively involved in the business. He was soon followed by John and in 1900 by Robert who had remained joint manager of the shipping business with A. P. Lyle. After Abram IV, Charles and William had retired, Robert was appointed Chairman of Abram Lyle and Sons and in 1915 his work for the wartime Sugar Commission earned him a baronetcy. In 1921 he had the distinction of leading his company into a merger with Henry Tate and Sons, which had been established in 1869 and had registered as a limited company with a capital of £1 million in 1896. The two companies were 'by a long way', the largest sugar refining businesses in the country; their weekly output was between 2,000–4,000 tons and 5,000–6,000 tons respectively.[49]

The success of the Lyle family's sugar refining business was a tribute to the business acumen of Abram Lyle III, who between 1850 and 1880 had converted his business from a small Greenock cooperage to perhaps the largest sugar refinery in Britain. This was accomplished by a series of bold and farsighted decisions. At the same time he had built up an extensive sugar and stave importing business and one of the biggest shipping fleets registered at Greenock. He had acquired other business interests. He was an active director of the Glasgow and South Western Railway Co. and of the North British and Mercantile Insurance Co. At the time of his death, he held shares in five 'single ship' companies – the Persio (£255), Caitloch (£440), Skelmorlie (£255), Alcestis (£425), Doris (£1,700) – valued at £3,075 and smaller firms, such as the London and Colonial Finance Corporation and the Bell Organ and Piano Co. He also had investments in local businesses, including boatbuilders, brass-founders, chainmakers and slaters, amounting to £24,076 in value in the year of his death. Well before his death he gave up all his interests in the family businesses and he left a relatively modest estate of £42,540.[50] In his lifetime he had made over £230,000 to his sons.[51]

Lyle retired from business at an early age, and became preoccupied with public affairs. In 1876, at the age of 56, he was elected Provost of Greenock. He was a reluctant candidate who would sooner 'have made a cask than a speech'[52] but he was persuaded to stand for election by the business community who were eager that the proposed harbour extensions were put in hand. During his election campaign opponents drew attention to the ships he had ordered from yards outside Greenock at a time of high local unemployment. He was also accused of adopting an anti-Catholic stance[53] in a town where large numbers of Irish immigrants lived in some of the worst slums in Britain (Figure 3.7). As Provost he presided successfully over several important decisions for the town, some of which were aimed at reducing the high unemployment rate. The building of Lyle Road, at a cost of £17,000, gave employment to over 200 men,[54] the Municipal Offices were rebuilt, although criticized as 'one of the most extravagant schemes ever proposed by the Council',[55] and plans for the construction of the James Watt Dock were put in hand at a cost of £500,000.[56] When Lyle's term of office ended in 1879 he retired 'with the best thanks of the community for work done of no ordinary kind' but the *Greenock Telegraph*'s editorial continued rather enigmatically that 'differences of opinion may exist with respect to the manner of procedure in certain cases, or with the objects sought to be gained by certain measures'.[57] To mark his provostship Lyle presented the town with an ornamental fountain, which still stands today in Cathcart Square.[58]

Apart from municipal office, Lyle was prominent in civic affairs in Greenock. For many years he was Chairman of the Local Marine Board which had responsibility for examining the competence of ships' officers, ensuring that ships were not overloaded, and hearing complaints made by shipowners, captains and crew. Ultimately it was responsible to the Board of Trade but under Lyle it took an independent line which, in his own words, 'surprised

Figure 3.7

From the time of Edwin Chadwick's famous report on the sanitary conditions of the Labouring Population of Great Britain in 1842, Greenock was known to have some of the worst slums in Europe. However the housing was not improved until towards the end of the nineteenth century. This photograph taken in the 1870s illustrates some of the appalling housing, mostly inhabited by immigrant Irish labour.

London and seemed to cause considerable excitement'.[59]

Lyle was a member of the United Presbyterian Church of Scotland.[60] Diligence and frugality were his guides in family life and in business. He was bearer and elder of St. Michael's United Presbyterian Church in Greenock. In keeping with his Christian duty, he was a Director of the Greenock Infirmary, to which he gave £1,500, and was connected with such diverse charitable bodies as the Training Home for Friendless Girls, the Greenock Medical Aid Society, and the Shipmasters' Provident Society. He was a leading member of the local temperance movement and at its annual meeting in 1876 declared 'he had never allowed the nasty stuff to go into his mouth'.[61] He was not, however, above joining the Loyal Toast at the town's Jubilee Banquet in the following year.[62] As Provost he was highly critical of the drink trade but at the local Wine, Spirit and Beer Trades Association's Dinner in 1878 tribute was paid in his absence to the fair minded way in which he had behaved towards the trade.[63] Compared with other Greenock merchants he lived modestly. Until the mid-1860s his home was in Nicholson Street, central Greenock and close to the cooperage. By this time Greenock's wealthy merchants were moving away from the harbour and shipyards to the western outskirts, where they built large mansions. Lyle who 'doubted the wisdom of building big homes . . . worthy of a hundred acres of park land'[64] was slow to follow. In the late 1860s he built 'Oakley', a large if unpretentious house in Eldon Road which overlooked the Clyde Estuary, and there he lived for the rest of his life. He died in 1891 at the age of seventy one.

4. 1890-1900
A Limited Company

While the Lyle brothers were devoting their time to their London sugar refinery, the shipping business was to some extent neglected and depleted. The *Cape Horn I* was lost in 1886, and the *Cape Verde I* in 1889. The *Cape Verde I*, which sank at the entrance to Melbourne harbour in June 1889, could not be raised and repaired for less than the insured value of £4,000; as a result the underwriters sold the wreck less its cargo for £1,000, and allowed Lyle 90 per cent of the insured value in settlement of the claim. The greater part of the claim fell upon Glasgow underwriters, including William Euing and Co., Alexander Kay and Co., and Thompson MacGregor and Co., but the Northern Maritime Insurance Co. of Newcastle and the Globe Insurance Co. of Liverpool also underwrote the risk.[1] Although the insurance claims investigated by the Association of Underwriters and Insurance Brokers in Glasgow confirm that Lyle was more fortunate than its competitors, these losses seriously dented the strength of the firm. Neither the *Cape Horn I* nor the *Cape Verde I* were replaced, and in 1889 the *Cape Race I* and *Cape Finisterre I* were sold. By 1890 the fleet had been reduced to four ships, each over fourteen years old.

It was not until this year that funds were available to revive the shipping company, which was reconstituted as 'The Lyle Shipping Co. Ltd.', a private limited liability company with a paid up capital of £96,100. All the Lyle brothers held equal shareholdings valued at £16,000 and James Scobie, the marine superintendent, held one share worth £100. All the firm's capital was subscribed by the Lyle family; no debenture loans or long-term bank loans were obtained. After 1894 when more capital was required a loan of £14,138 was made by Abram Lyle and Sons, the proprietors of the London refinery. In 1896 this was reduced to £10,000 when a further loan of £2,500 was made by A. P. Lyle.[2]

The conversion of the business into a limited company followed the fashion of the times. Since the Limited Liability Act of 1862 had created this possibility, many businesses had become limited companies, recognizing that as the firms grew larger and their capital requirements that much greater, ownership would have to be more widespread and the partnership concept would no longer work. In the case of shipping firms the practice of part ownership – in sixty-fourths – of a ship was giving rise to increasing problems in financing

Figure 4.1
(a) The four masted steel barque *Cape York I* in service, probably at a harbour in New Zealand. She was the first 2,000 ton sailing ship to be owned by Lyle Shipping Co. and the first all steel vessel. She was built by Barclay, Curle & Co. of Glasgow in 1890.
(b) Captain Mitchell of the *Cape York I* photographed on his quarterdeck in 1898.

new ships and also when calls had to be made on individual 'sixty-fourthers' to provide extra cash to cover voyage losses. Lyle's ships had all been wholly-owned by the one firm since 1873, and the conversion to a limited liability company was therefore merely a wise precaution.

The new company took over the assets of the old business, namely the four aging sailing ships. In August 1890 delivery of a new sailing ship, the *Cape York I* (2,030 tons), was made by Barclay Curle and Co. of Glasgow (Figures 4.1a and 4.1b). It was the first 2,000 net ton sailing ship to be owned by the Lyles and soon afterwards orders were placed with R. Duncan and Co. of Port Glasgow for two sailing ships of similar tonnage, the *Cape Clear II* (2,017 tons) and the *Cape Wrath II* (1,998 tons) for delivery in 1892. All had steel hulls which only became economic and of proven reliability in the 1890s, although they had been used since the late 1870s. Moreover the increasing availability of steam tugs in most ports allowed shipowners to operate 2,000 ton vessels without difficulty.[3] Three of the old ships were sold in 1891 and the fourth was sold in 1894. For most of the 1890s Lyles' operated just three sailing vessels. The management of the business was placed in the hands of A. P. Lyle and his brother, Robert.

The continuation of the Lyle family's shipowning business after the 1880s would seem irrational in view of their extensive commitment to sugar refining. The period between the 1870s and the First World War was not especially profitable for tramp shipping. In the forty-five years up to 1914 'the number of bad years exceeded the good by two to one' and between 1869 and 1896 freight rates fell by about 50 per cent.[4] But the fall was not continuous and this was anyway a period of falling prices and costs. The Great Depression in trade and industry affected shipping as much as other industries.

To stem declining, and at times volatile, freight rates and profitability, shipping conferences were established. These were composed of shipowners trading to a certain port or area who agreed on a minimum freight rate below which they would not trade. The first agreement was reached in 1875 between companies operating a regular service to Calcutta and the practice soon spread to the China (1875), Australian (1884), South African (1886), West African (1895), North Brazilian (1895) and River Plate (1890) trades. Those agreements were made, however, between companies operating regular services; few attempts were made at internal regulation of the tramp trade before 1914.[5] Tramp ships 'were difficult to organize not only because of the irregular nature of their trade but also because many tramp owners, like the Lyles, were also merchants and freight contractors which resulted in a certain conflict of interest'.[6] Indeed trampers undermined the conference system. The lack of success in establishing an acceptable conference rate before 1900 on the Far Eastern and African trades has been attributed to competition from tramp shipping which was as well adapted as cargo liners for moving bulk commodities such as wool, wheat and ores.[7]

The 1890s were the most unprofitable years in the history of the Lyles' shipping business. In 1891 and 1892 profits of £2,883 and £2,767 were made. In 1893 there was a loss of £970 followed by a further loss of about £5,000 in 1894. The gloom continued and by 1899 accumulated losses had reached £11,720. Moreover, no systematic depreciation policy was adopted and depreciation was treated as an allowance which could only be made if the Company's profits were sufficient. As a result the depreciation was arbitrary and no allowance was made in some years. The 'suspense account', as it was referred to in the balance sheets, totalled £14,559 in 1892 and £21,511 a year later. It was not added to in 1894 but grew to £31,477 in 1895. Thereafter it fell off to £27,794 in 1896 at which level it remained unchanged for the rest of the decade.[8]

In this decade the Lyles worked with the wrong tools. Reduction in cost benefited steamship concerns a great deal more than sailing shipowners. In 1901 J. McKechnie reviewed the improvement in marine engineering over the previous decade to the Institute of Mechanical Engineers. He was able to report that with the development of the triple expansion engine and improvements in boiler and hull design the most significant achievement 'affecting every type of ship from the tramp to the greyhound, is the reduction in the coal consumption. Ten years ago the rate for ocean voyages was 1.75 lbs per horse power per hour; today in the most modern ships it is about 1.5 lbs. Ten years ago one ton of cargo was carried 100 miles for 10 lbs of fuel, whereas now, with the great increase in the size of ships and other mechanical improvements, the same work is done for about 4 lbs of coal – a result which means a very great saving when applied to the immense fleet of over-sea carriers throughout the world.'[9] Many cargo shipowners (for example, Thomas Dunlop of Glasgow and the Brocklebanks of Liverpool), were encouraged by these apparent cost reductions to abandon sail finally in favour of steam.[10]

'Bit by bit', A. P. Lyle recalled, 'we had come to the conclusion that the day of the wind jammer was past, that steam was steadily ousting sail, and that it might be as well to realize and clear out soon before our out dated tonnage became even more of a drag on the market than it was now. So with some grief at heart we sold all our ships'[11]. The fleet was sold in 1899. The decision came not a moment too soon. The market in sailing ships was still sufficiently buoyant to realize £8 per ton but 'many of our fellow shipowners . . . held on and lost heavily'.[12]

However, the Lyles cannot be blamed for holding on to their sailing fleet. A modern comparison of the costs of steam and sailing ships has shown that until at least 1890 sail was superior to steam in some trades, but that shipowners were quick to adopt steamships when the advantages of these became clear.[13] As late as 1895 the President of Institute of the Naval Architects declared in his presidential address, 'I hope I shall not be criticized for wasting the valuable time of members of this Institution if I cast their consideration briefly to these sailing ships, which should not be allowed to disappear. I speak not only under the inspiration of sentiment, but because it seems to me on the strictest economic grounds so desirable that the cheap power of wind should be used under all suitable conditions for long voyages and for conveyance by sea of the raw materials of industry, and such articles as wheat, the conditions seem essentially suitable for the sailing ship. Professor Biles, professor of Naval Architecture at the University of Glasgow, has prepared a careful statement of cost of working six sailing ships trading to San Francisco carrying 3,000 to 3,500 tons dead-weight, as compared with a 4,000 tons cargo steamer running to the East through the Canal. The average distance per day covered by the sailing ships was 71 knots. Their working expenses averaged .014d per ton mile against .0175d in the steamer. The working expenses of the steamer per ton mile were 25 per cent greater. The first cost was £6:10s against £5 per ton, or 30 per cent in excess of the sailing ship.'[14]

It is likely that the Lyle family's shipowning business had been continued on the initiative of A. P. Lyle, Abram's second son, who remained in Scotland while all his brothers moved to London. He believed the shipping business, although less profitable, was 'more noble' than sugar refining.[15] By his own admission he was 'too Scottish for transplantation into English soil'.[16] These sentiments apart, given the uncertainty in the sugar refining industry, his brothers most likely wished to spread their risk. It is also possible that the brothers planned to link the shipping company to the London refinery by tied business.

In the last two decades before 1900, as the fleet contracted and voyages lengthened, Lyles' ships made fewer and fewer calls at Greenock. In 1886 one ship, the *Cape Wrath I*, docked and in 1889 two ships arrived. In 1891 and 1895 no Lyle ship discharged its cargo there.[17] All the Lyle ships docking at Greenock in 1886 and 1889 brought cargoes of sugar from Java but they were sailing to a greater variety of destinations. In 1889, the *Cape St. Vincent I* sailed to Melbourne and the *Cape Finisterre I* to Buenos Aires.

Between 1872 and 1900 very few of the members of the crews of Lyle ships were recruited in Greenock, or indeed in Scotland. When the *Cape Horn I* sailed for San Francisco in 1877 her crew included only three Greenock men and five other Scots. Others in the crew of twenty-eight were Welsh, Irish, English, French, Canadian, Swedish, German, Danish and Norwegian. The average age of seamen was twenty-eight and only six were older than thirty. Seamen who made up most of the ship's complement received wages of £3.50 (£3:10s) per month and ordinary seamen £2.50 (£2:10s). The mate received £8 per month, the second mate £5, the third mate £4, the carpenter £6, the sailmaker £5, and the steward £4.50 (£4:10s).[18] Some families traditionally served on Lyle ships, such as the Scobbies. Between the 1860s and 1880s James, Alexander,

Figure 4.2

No photographs survive of Lyle crews from this period, but this picture taken at Greenock in the 1890s shows a typical group of twenty-four seamen on a sailing ship. Such crews were multi-national and each seaman could only expect to earn £3.50 at the most a month.

William, Andrew (all brothers), and John (a cousin) served on Lyle ships either as masters, mates or second mates; in 1875–76 William and Andrew served on *Cape Race I* as master and mate respectively (Figure 4.2).

The experience of the *Colmonell*, later the *Cape Wrath I*, suggests that life on merchant sailing ships in the 1870s was still very arduous. Soon after sailing from Greenock, her crew became insubordinate under the effects of drink and refused to obey orders. The ironclad *H.M.S. Black Prince* was despatched to arrest the whole crew and to tow the *Colmonell* back into harbour. Nevertheless, there were some improvements in shipboard conditions. As new ships were commissioned labour saving devices were employed. The *Cape Race I*, which entered service in 1874, had 'all the appliances that science has discovered for the safety and comfort of those on board. By steam power she can be loaded, discharged or pumped, and various necessary descriptions of work will be performed by steam gear . . . Accommodation of a superior sort has been made for officers and men, including apprentices'.[19] With the introduction of steam power on sailing vessels, for driving winches and hoists, for raising anchors and sails and unloading cargoes, the amount of physical toil was greatly reduced.

However, by the turn of the century the Lyles, like many of their competitors, had found shipowning an unattractive adjunct to their principal business. For the future they decided to leave steam shipowning and management to the emerging 'professional' shipping companies. In 1899 The Lyle

Shipping Co. Ltd went into voluntary liquidation and it was formally wound up on 19 April 1900. As a measure of the poor performance in the 1890s no dividends were paid to shareholders and after the liquidation of the Company was complete in 1900, a deficit of £8,672 remained, representing a loss of approximately £1,500 to each shareholder.

5. 1900-1919
A Job for the Boys

Between April 1900 and May 1903, the Lyle family abandoned its shipowning activities. It was a time for recovery from the disappointments of the previous decade. A. P. Lyle, who had stayed behind at Greenock in the 1890s, held an equal share with his brothers in the London sugar refinery. His shareholding was worth £47,860 between 1890 and 1906. After his brother William sold most of his shares in the Company in 1906, A. P. Lyle increased his stake to £56,300. During 1902–04 the average annual profit of the London refinery was £150,000 falling to £25,000 in 1905, and recovering to over £200,000 from 1906 to the outbreak of the First World War. It has been recorded that an interim dividend of between 3 to 15 per cent was declared every three weeks or so from the turn of the century. Being prudent managers, the Lyle brothers ploughed back a large proportion of the profits into the business; so much so that when Lyle merged with Henry Tate & Sons in 1921 the Lyles were paying themselves only a quarter of the income which was being received by the Tate shareholders. The profitability of the London business would have secured A. P. Lyle an income of between £10,000 and £15,000 a year between 1903 and 1914. On his own admission he 'had as much money as I wanted, or perhaps more than was good for me'.[1]

Yet in 1900 at the age of fifty-one, A. P. Lyle was not ready to retire from business; he was keen to see the Lyle house flag flying again. His son Archie was soon to come down from Oxford, and A. P. Lyle was determined that Archie should carry on the family tradition. Under the pretext of finding his son a career, Lyle decided 'to start the shipping business afresh'.[2] A. P. Lyle was undoubtedly the driving force behind the formation of the new company. Despite his lack of enthusiasm for the day-to-day management of the business and his growing interest in public life and the pursuits of a country gentleman, he wanted the Lyle fleet to continue into the future.

Conditions in the shipping market in 1903 were very different from the position in 1890, when the first Lyle Shipping Co. had been established. Steam had ousted sail on all but coastal voyages, but steamers were far more costly to build than sailing ships. A. P. Lyle could not finance the new venture completely, as most of his capital was tied up in the London refining business. Moreover his brothers, mindful of the returns from shipping in the 1890s, 'had lost faith

in the old business'.[3] If the revived shipping interests were to be adequately
financed it was necessary to seek funds outside the family. From the outset he
refused to consider the promotion of a public company. A. P. Lyle commented:
'we had never been this type of shipowners. We had always owned the tonnage
we managed. I could not bring myself to the point of adopting this new (and
to me disagreeable) role'.[4]

Instead, he found a backer in John Birkmyre, a leading Port Glasgow
businessman. Birkmyre not only held a controlling interest of £86,500 in the
Gourock Ropework Co., one of the most celebrated firms in Greenock, but he
was also a large shareholder in various shipping and fishing companies. His
brother, Henry Birkmyre was a substantial Greenock shipowner from the mid-
nineteenth century until his death in 1900 and he, himself, had entered the
shipowning business as early as the 1860s. This interest provided a tied market
for the products of the Gourock Ropeworks (including sails and nets). By 1903
John Birkmyre held shares in at least nineteen ships or shipping and fishing
firms; these shares were valued at £25,754 in 1910.[5]

Just as A. P. Lyle wished to find a career for Archie, so Birkmyre wanted to
entrust the management of some of his shipping interests to his nephew, Peter
Macfarlane. To realize this ambition, he was prepared to advance Macfarlane
considerable sums of money against his expectations. Birkmyre and Lyle
'decided to build a fleet of steamers and carry them on under the old name and
flag of the Lyle Shipping Co. Ltd, with myself [Lyle] as the unpaid Chairman.
For the hard work we appointed Mr. James Shearer manager, while my son
Archie, and (Birkmyre's) nephew, Peter Macfarlane, were to be joint managers
with Shearer'.[6] James Shearer had borrowed a total of £3,250 from Birkmyre
by 1910 to acquire shares in the new business.

Peter Macfarlane and James Shearer came from old established Greenock
families. Between 1890 and 1900 Macfarlane's father, Captain Peter Macfarlane,
operated three ships, the *Dee*, the *Don* and the *Wynstay*.[7] With John Birkmyre,
his brother-in-law, and Robert Duncan, the Greenock shipbuilder, he was once
joint owner of the *Nyagra*. This former Cunard paddle steamer, which had been
cut down and converted to sail by Robert Duncan and Co., was bought by
John Birkmyre for Macfarlane in 1867. Captain Macfarlane may also have
been connected with the Greenock firm of J. M. Macfarlane and Co. who
owned the barque *Salab* in 1890, and who managed the Arethusa Ship Co. Ltd
four years later.[8] By 1900 the Peter Macfarlane who helped to launch the new
Lyle company was employed by the Greenock Steamship Co., in which his
uncle was a large shareholder.[9] With a paid up capital of £190,000, it was one
of the largest shipping enterprises at Greenock.[10]

James Shearer was also employed by the Greenock Steamship Co. He may
have been connected with the firm of N. and T. Shearer which owned four
small coastal vessels operating out of Greenock between the 1870s and 1890.[11]

His interests were not restricted to ship management alone. By 1919 he had become a director of the Ardgoil Engineering Co. at Gourock, a firm of steam engine manufacturers and shipbuilders with a paid up capital of £2,300.[12]

A. P. Lyle's new colleagues fully appreciated the risks involved in forming a shipping company. The years immediately prior to 1900 had been exceptionally profitable for shipowners as demand during the Boer and Spanish American Wars pushed freight rates to a high level. With the cessation of hostilities in 1901 the market collapsed and by 1902 80 per cent of British shipping was 'largely unprofitable'.[13] The depressed state of the shipping market, the disastrous results of the 1890s, and the long experience of A. P. Lyle and John Birkmyre of the industry persuaded the partners to operate the business through a series of financially independent units. The ships were to be owned by separate limited companies and managed by a management company with no direct interest in the vessels. This arrangement was frequent amongst tramp-owners of the time, as it allowed them to make individual arrangements for funding the purchase of new ships. It had the added advantage of safeguarding a fleet against a heavy loss on any one of its components. In the event of the failure of one of the ship companies, the remaining companies would be protected from the demands of its creditors.

On 27 May 1903 Lyle Shipping Co. and the Cape Antibes Steamship Co. were registered as private limited companies. Lyle Shipping Co. (the management concern) had subscribed capital of only £136, which was increased to £146 in 1907. A. P. Lyle was Chairman, James Shearer and Peter Macfarlane, Executive Directors, and John Birkmyre was a non-Executive Director. Each owned thirty-two shares while their wives and John Birkmyre held one share each. The management fee was to be £350 per annum per ship in addition to 5 per cent of profits. In return, Lyle Shipping Co. undertook to manage the voyages of the ships owned by the ship companies. Its duties included the 'fixture' of charters, the hire of captains and crewmen, the organization of voyage routes and coaling stations, the maintenance of ships and arranging insurance.

Although John Birkmyre owned only one share in the management company, he was to be the new concern's main source of finance. He and A. P. Lyle each held 37 per cent of the stock in the Cape Antibes Steamship Co., which owned the *Cape Antibes* built by W. Dobson of Newcastle in 1903. Of the rest of the shares, 20 per cent was held by Peter Macfarlane and 4.5 per cent by James Shearer. A year later the *Cape Antibes* was joined by a second steamer, the *Cape Breton II* built by Russell & Co. of Port Glasgow (Figure 5.1). This firm was controlled by Birkmyre's son-in-law, William Todd Lithgow. The new ship was owned by the Cape Breton Steamship Co. The paid up capital was £26,000 of which 90 per cent was owned equally by A. P. Lyle, Birkmyre and Macfarlane. James Shearer owned 7 per cent of the equity.

Figure 5.1

Cape Breton II, the second steamer to be built for the Lyle Shipping Co., on trials in the Firth of Clyde in 1904. She was constructed by Russell & Co., Port Glasgow at a price of £40,775.

Lyle continued to expand its fleet throughout the first decade of the twentieth century. In 1905 Russell & Co. delivered the *Cape Corso I* to the Cape Corso Steamship Co. Russell & Co., directed by W. T. Lithgow from 1870 and owned by him since 1891 had come to dominate the shipbuilding industry on the Lower Clyde. This had been achieved by the novel technique of building two standard types of sailing ship, thereby ensuring lower prices. These vessels were designed to carry bulk cargoes and to be cheap to operate and maintain. Lithgow not only attracted buyers through the cheapness and economy of his products, he also offered to take a financial stake in the vessel. Lithgow (and up to 1891, his partners in Russell & Co.) took large interests in each new ship, and then found investors to take their original speculative interest off their hands. In most cases they retained a small shareholding in each vessel as a contribution to the building profit on the ship. Between 1878 and his death in 1908, Lithgow held shares in no less than 164 vessels built in Russell & Co.'s yards. These were managed by no less than seventy different companies.[14]

Figure 5.2

Cape Finisterre II in the James Watt Dock at Greenock shortly after her completion by Russell & Co., Port Glasgow, 1907. She was torpedoed in 1917 near the Manacles Rocks, off the Cornish coast, with a loss of twenty-nine of her crew of thirty-five.

The Birkmyre family was a long-established and important customer for Lithgow's shares in Russell-built ships. The barque *Loudon Hill*, for example, built by Russell & Co. for J. R. Dickson & Co. of Glasgow in 1887, was originally financed by Lithgow. At her launch in June 1887, Lithgow held 43 of the 64 shares in the vessel, but in the subsequent disposal of his interest, shares were taken up by Henry Birkmyre, Agnes, and Maggie Birkmyre and later John, William and James Birkmyre.[15] Similarly, Lithgow and the Birkmyres combined in the ownership of Lyle Shipping Co.'s new ships. In the case of the *Cape Corso I* in 1905, Lithgow agreed to take shares to the value of £4,000, which represented 15 per cent of the equity. John Birkmyre, A. P. Lyle and Peter Macfarlane each held 24 per cent of the remaining shares, and James Shearer 11 per cent.

In 1906 the Lyles finally severed their links with Greenock and moved to Glasgow where the centre of the Clyde shipping industry had become established. One year later, a fourth single ship company was formed when the *Cape Finisterre II* joined the Lyle fleet. Paid up capital equalled £20,000 of which 22 and 23 per cent was owned by Birkmyre and Macfarlane respectively but the largest shareholding was owned by the Lyle family. A. P. Lyle took 15 per cent of the shares, his son Archie (a shareholder for the first time) owned 25 per cent and his wife owned a further 5 per cent (Table 5.1). Thereafter the practice of forming single ship companies ceased. When a fifth steamer, the *Cape Ortegal I*, entered service in 1911 it was owned by the management company (Figure 5.3).

Figure 5.3

Cape Ortegal I going down the Clyde on her maiden voyage in 1911. She served for thirty years in the Lyle fleet – longer than any other vessel before or since.

Table 5.1

Shareholdings[1] in the Steam Ship Companies, 1903–1912

	Cape Antibes 1903–12		Cape Breton 1904–12		Cape Corso 1905–12		Cape Finisterre 1907–12	
A.P. Lyle	74	(37%)	79	(30%)	66	(24%)	30	(15%)
J. Birkmyre	74	(37%)	79	(30%)	66	(24%)	44[2]	(22%)
P.C. Macfarlane	40	(20%)	80	(31%)	66	(24%)	45	(23%)
J. Shearer	9	(4.5%)	19	(7%)	29	(11%)	19	(10%)
Henry Lithgow[3]					40	(15%)		
A.M.P. Lyle							50	(25%)
Mrs. A.P. Lyle	1	(0.5%)	1	(0.4%)	1	(0.4%)	10	(5%)
Mrs. J. Birkmyre	1	(0.5%)	1	(0.4%)	1	(0.4%)	1	(0.5%)
Mrs. J. Shearer	1	(0.5%)	1	(0.4%)	1	(0.4%)	1	(0.5%)
	200		260		270		200	

[1] All shares are valued at £100

[2] Increased to 59 shares in 1910 when the paid up capital of the company was increased by £1,500

[3] Replaced by James and Henry Lithgow, 1909

Sources: S.R.O., Dissolved Company Files

Table 5.2

Sources of Long Term Capital, 1903–1907

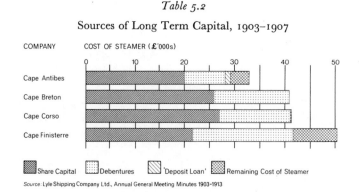

Source: Lyle Shipping Company Ltd., Annual General Meeting Minutes 1903-1913

With the exception of the *Cape Ortegal I*, the expansion of the business in the years before the First World War was largely financed by share capital taken up by the Directors. In three of the four companies this exceeded half the purchase price of the ships and often it was nearly two-thirds (Table 5.2). The issue of debentures provided the remaining capital. Most of these seem to have been taken up by Birkmyre. At the time of his death in 1910, he held debentures valued at £5,705 in the *Cape Corso I*, £4,500 in the *Cape Breton II* and £6,750 in the *Cape Finisterre II*.[16] In the case of the *Cape Finisterre II*, the deficit left after shares and debentures had been taken up amounted to £8,703. This was made up by a cash advance of £10,146 drawn from the reserves of the management company. Similar cash advances by Lyle Shipping Co. were used to protect the position of all four of the ship companies between 1904 and 1911 (Figure 5.3).

The steamers managed by Lyle Shipping Co. in this period were similar to John Masefield's 'dirty British coaster with a salt caked smoke stack'. All were 'three island' ships with well defined forecastles, poops and central islands surmounted by tall, slim funnels from which belched clouds of black smoke. The smallest, the *Cape Antibes*, was 325 feet long and displaced 2,549 gross tons while the largest, the *Cape Ortegal I*, was 405 feet in length and weighed 4,896 gross tons. All the Cape ships were powered by triple expansion three cylinder steam engines which would have given a cruising speed of about eight knots. They were unsophisticated ships; it was considered a great luxury when the *Cape Corso I* was fitted out with electric lights.[17]

By the early twentieth century Lyle Shipping Co. was a general tramp ship operator. The Company's ships plied between foreign ports and returned to Britain. The log of the *Cape Finisterre II* reveals that between May 1909 and January 1911 she sailed from Swansea to North America, then to the West Indies and then to Canada. From there she sailed to Portland, U.S.A. and then crossed the Pacific to Australia. In July 1910 she had docked at Manilla and following several short voyages in the Far East she sailed for Seattle, U.S.A. and then on to Canada. From there she returned to Australia and after two voyages between Australian ports she sailed for South Africa. In January 1911 she arrived at Colombo. There was no discernible pattern to her voyages.[18]

Before the introduction of wireless communication at the turn of the century, masters often picked up their orders by flag signals at Lloyds Signal Stations, such as those at Lands' End, Gibraltar and Hong Kong. However the contracts for many of the cargoes were arranged by ship masters on the spot, sometimes even to the extent of selling the outward cargo 'at best' and buying the return cargo. When doing business in this way some old-style masters tended to regard No. 1 Tween Deck as their own trading preserve. The introduction of the wireless allowed owners to arrange their own cargoes and the days of No. 1 Tween Deck gradually came to an end, prompting one old master to observe that 'radio is the curse of the modern day'.

The period between 1901 and 1911 has been described as the first major international shipping depression. By 1901 freight rates had fallen 50 per cent below those of the previous autumn and they were not to recover fully until 1912. In 1902 the vast majority of British shipping companies made a loss. During the commercial crisis of 1907–08 freight rates fell to the lowest level for over a hundred years and at one stage one million gross tons of British shipping were laid up.[19] By 1912 the trough of the depression was passed and 1913 and 1914 were boom years approximating to those at the turn of the century.

This depression of the shipping market was brought on by growing international competition leading to an over-supply of cargo carrying capacity and a slimming of profit margins. Between 1890 and 1910 world steam tonnage grew by 109 per cent with the German and Japanese merchant marines expanding the fastest. German competition was confined to the North Atlantic, West African and short haul European routes.[20] Greek and Scandinavian shipowners, who purchased second-hand tonnage and operated it with the advantages of cheap labour, gave especially strong competition to British tramp shipping.[21] On the Empire routes, however, Britain's position remained dominant with 80 to 90 per cent of clearances from major colonial ports in the first decade of the twentieth century.[22]

In this period the British industry was over-building, partly as a result of the shift from sail to steam. By 1913, 85 per cent of British merchant tonnage had been built since 1895, 44 per cent since 1905, and the new ships were both faster and capable of carrying more cargo per ton of ship.[23] This over-capacity was reflected in cut-throat competition, which exacerbated the downward trend in freight rates. As a result, the conference system was strengthened. In 1907 abortive attempts were made to establish a freight union among tramp owners. Trampers were often both merchants and freight contractors and the duality of their interests undermined any negotiations designed to achieve a stable and profitable freight market.

Despite these adverse conditions the Lyle fleet was profitable. The 'navigation accounts', or voyage accounts, of all four single ship companies never showed a loss. In some years net losses were only avoided by adjustment of the accounting system particularly by reducing or waiving provisions for depreciation of fixed assets. The crisis years of 1907 and 1908 yielded the worst result. In 1907–8 return on gross tangible assets was 3 per cent for the Cape Breton Co. and in the following year they were between 2 and 2.5 per cent for the Cape Antibes, Cape Corso and Cape Finisterre Companies. In this year, however, the 9.5 per cent returned on the gross tangible assets of the Cape Breton Co. reflected the volatility of shipping profits. In 1908–9, the Cape Breton Steamship Co. excepted, no allowance was made for depreciation. Otherwise between 1903 and 1910 return on gross tangible assets was between 5 and 10 per cent. Thereafter they surged ahead and between 1911 and 1913 were well above 10 per cent, and nearer 20 per cent for some of the firms (Table 5.3).

With the exception of the years 1907 to 1909 dividends paid before 1911 were always at around 5 per cent. In the crisis years they fell to 2.5 per cent and on five occasions no payments were made. Matters improved after 1912. In the year 1912–13 the Cape Corso Steamship Co. paid a dividend of 20 per cent and in the nineteen months between November 1911 and May 1913 shareholders in the Cape Finisterre Co. received a 40 per cent dividend (Table 5.3). Most profit was retained by the Company in a depreciation and reserve account which was added to at a rate frequently above 5 per cent, then taken as the standard rate of depreciation. For example, in the three years following the formation of the Cape Corso Co. its depreciation and reserve account was added to at a rate of 4.13 per cent, 6.1 per cent and 4.05 per cent of the book value of the steamer. No depreciation was allowed in the crisis year 1908–9 but arrears of depreciation were paid off at 5.6, 11.9 and 12.9 per cent in the following three years. Between 1905–06 and 1907–08 dividend payments exceeded depreciation allowance which was below 5 per cent showing that profits were being distributed at the expense of depreciation. In the years between 1909–10 and 1911–12 depreciation allowances were always above 5 per cent. In the period between 1903 and 1911 the income of the management company grew steadily as new ships came under its control. Net profits increased from £674 in 1904 to £2,042 in 1908 before falling back with the onset of the depression. Thereafter earnings improved to £3,450 in 1911 and then advanced to £13,202 and £28,441 in the following two years after the delivery of the *Cape Ortegal I*.[24] Profits were also swelled by a London agency which was established in 1911, realizing an annual profit of about £700.

In 1910, as the outlook began to improve, John Birkmyre died. Over the years since the formation of Lyle Shipping Co., he had not only helped to build up the Lyle fleet, but had also acquired interests in thirty-eight other steamers or shipping companies. Of most significance was his shareholding in

Table 5.3

Assets, Profits, Depreciation and Dividends of the Cape Steamship Companies, 1903–1913

1 Company	2 Date	3 Gross Tangible Assets	4 Profit on Navigation Account	5 4 as a percentage of 3	6 Profit after tax, interest and managers commission	7 Annual Allowance Paid to Depreciation and reserve account	8 Depreciation as a percentage of book value	9 Dividend
A	1903–4	34,934	2,414	6.9	1,726	725	2.2	5
A	1904–5	36,074	2,698	7.4	2,092	1,000	3.0	5
B	,,	46,495	2,927	6.2	2,260	1,000	2.5	5
A	1905–6	35,250	2,550	7.2	1,918	900	2.7	5
B	,,	43,812	2,006	4.6	1,152	450	1.1	2
C	,,	45,039	3,751	8.3	3,116	1,700	4.1	5
A	1906–7	37,593	3,701	9.9	2,492	1,600	4.9	6½
B	,,	48,824	4,582	9.3	3,782	2,200	5.4	5
C	,,	50,340	5,998	11.9	5,107	2,400	5.8	7½
A	1907–8	37,255	2,187	5.9	1,765	800	2.4	5
B	,,	42,441	1,289	3	964	350	0.9	—
C	,,	49,391	3,465	7	2,787	1,500	3.6	3¾
F	Reports of this company have not survived for 1907–8							
A	1908–9	34,778	718	2.1	239	—	0	—
B	,,	47,223	4,475	9.5	3,723	2,600	6.4	5
C	,,	47,436	1,164	2.5	987	—	0	—
F	,,	57,586	1,165	2	796	—	0	—
A	1909–10	37,202	2,040	5.5	1,746	1,000	3.0	2¼
B	,,	48,920	1,815	3.7	1,856	1,000	2.5	2½
C	,,	48,590	3,113	6.4	3,443	2,000	4.9	5
F	,,	57,614	1,966	3.4	1,291	1,000	2.0	—
A	1910–11	39,738	3,527	8.9	3,341	2,300	7.0	5
B	,,	49,353	3,007	6.1	2,643	2,000	6.1	2
C	,,	51,899	6,064	11.7	5,504	4,000	9.7	5
F	,,	52,122	4,208	8.1	3,072	3,000	6.0	—
A	1911–12	42,314	4,366	10.3	4.065	3,500	11.0	2½
A	1912–13	39,482	9,605	24.3	9,162	4,278	13.0	2
B	1911–13 (20 months)	53,329	14,872	27.9	15,263	7,500	18.4	11
C	1911–13 (20 months)	53,185	11,687	22	11,297	3,750	9.1	12
F	1911–13 (19 months)	53,769	20,987	39	18,583	8,800	17.5	40

1 A — Cape Antibes Steamship Co. Ltd
 B — Cape Breton Steamship Co. Ltd
 C — Cape Corso Steamship Co. Ltd
 F — Cape Finisterre Steamship Co. Ltd

Source: Lyle Shipping Co., Annual General Meeting Minutes 1903–14

the twenty-six Strath ships built by a number of Clyde yards (especially the Grangemouth and Greenock Dockyard Co.) and managed by William Burrell, who later became a multi-millionaire and built up the celebrated Burrell fine art collection. At his death Birkmyre left £431,108 (£112,093 abroad) which included shares in sixty-three ships or shipping and fishing companies valued at £45,304, but which had cost £101,426 to acquire. Peter Macfarlane owed him £23,394 (almost exactly equal to Macfarlane's total shareholding in the Lyle ship companies) and James Shearer owed £3,280.[25] Macfarlane and two other shipowners, J. H. Shankland of Greenock and J. Miller Murray of Glasgow, were appointed with four others as trustees of the Birkmyre estate. In settling Birkmyre's affairs, they decided to dispose of the shipping shares, despite the substantial fall in the market value of their investment value. In A. P. Lyle's words 'it was a bad time to sell for ships were losing money and prices were very low, but they pressed us hard to buy the shares, and we did so. To buy in a gloomy time, when everyone is in the depths of despair, is often (not always) the right thing to do, but it needs courage, or rashness, which ever term be preferred'.[26]

The Lyle family wished to safeguard their investment in the Lyle companies and avoid having to bring in new investors to take over Birkmyre's holdings. This was achieved by reconstructing the management company in 1912. Macfarlane kept his shares in the four steam ship companies and the Lithgow family retained their shares in the *Cape Corso I*. The remaining shares in the steam ship companies, valued at £69,400, were sold to Lyle Shipping Co. In return the members of the Lyle family and James Shearer received shares in Lyle Shipping Co., thereby raising its issued capital from £146 to £56,100. Birkmyre's holdings were bought out for cash. A deficit of £13,300 remained and in 1912 debentures were issued to the value of £16,600 (reduced to £13,600 in the following years) which were taken up by shareholders, principally A. P. Lyle. At intervals between 1912 and 1916 Macfarlane's shareholdings were transferred from the single ship companies to Lyle Shipping Co., increasing its paid up capital to £76,600.

In the long run, John Birkmyre's trustees may have regretted the sale of the shares. By 1911 the worst period of the shipping depression had passed and in 1912 and 1913 healthy profits were achieved. British owners benefited especially from the effects of the war between Turkey and the Balkan League between 1912 and 1913. Many Greek-owned ships, which provided the main competition for tramp shipping business, were bottled up in Mediterranean ports. The Chairman of the Baltic Exchange, London, reported that 'freights went up, everybody was busy and in consequence companies were able to pay from 15 per cent to 25 per cent dividends and put considerable sums away as reserves'.[27] As with many other companies no formal balance sheets and profit and loss accounts of Lyle Shipping Co. have survived for the war years 1914 to 1919 but it is certain that during the war years very high profits were obtained.

At the onset of hostilities in 1914 demand for shipping soared. Freight rates rose steadily. In 1915 in return for Trade Union agreements to the dilution of labour and the relaxation of restrictive practices the government acted and introduced Excess Profit Duty, first at 40 per cent and later at 80 per cent. Duty was estimated as the mean of the profits obtained during any two pre-war years in the previous five years and those just before 1914 had been good ones for shipowners. Although shipowners paid £100,000,000 of Excess Profit Duty to the government's coffers[28] the shipping market remained strong. A. P. Lyle left no doubt that his companies shared in the success: 'it was a boom, an unprecedented one. During the war large profits were earned and could not but be earned'.[29] In early 1916 the Company received an offer for its ships. Macfarlane, then serving with the army in France, received the news at the front. He wrote to his wife, 'Do not be surprised dear if you see the sale of the Lyle Shipping Co. in the papers ... Shearer wrote to me yesterday asking what I thought. It would mean that for my £23,000 in it now I should receive over £160,000 – about seven times what I put into it. I said I was only agreeable to sell *if* Lyle and Shearer thought it advisable. I am certain that the government will very soon do something to control shipping as things cannot go on as they are. Freights are rising to a fearful height. We once came home from the River Plate at 8:9d (0.44p) or ten shillings, and now the rate is £7:5s (£7.25) per ton'.[30]

Some shipowners, whose cargo space was requisitioned, were denied high profits during the war. The government paid the shipowner a 'blue book rate'; introduced in 1915, the rate was calculated on the basis of the depressed rates prevailing in 1914. The rates were not revised to keep pace with wartime inflation, until by 1918 they had become unremunerative.[31] This problem did not seriously affect Lyle Shipping Co. as their ships were requisitioned for only short periods. The only exception was the *Cape Ortegal I* on government service between 1917 and 1919.[32]

One year before war broke out James Shearer junior, the son-in-law of James Shearer senior, joined the Company as Manager and Secretary, taking over the responsibilities previously held by Peter Macfarlane. He had already established a reputation as manager for Bell Brothers, a Glasgow firm which operated ten ships in the River Plate and South American trade. Prior to that he had served with the Clyde Shipping Co. for ten years but had started his career in the Greenock offices of Thomas Skinner and Co., shipbrokers at London, Glasgow and Greenock.[33] He was an exceptionally talented ship manager and between 1914 and 1917 he and his father-in-law managed Lyle Shipping Co. by themselves. Archie Lyle and Peter Macfarlane were then serving with their regiments, Lyle in Gallipoli and Macedonia and Macfarlane on the Somme, where he became a poison gas casualty in the first week of the battle and was invalided home. His return made possible the secondment on a permanent basis of James Shearer junior to the newly formed Ministry of Shipping. For the rest of the war Shearer headed a department concerned with the fixing of government charters.[34] He was rewarded with an O.B.E.

The Lyle fleet lost three of its five steamers during the First World War. The *Cape Antibes* led an especially dangerous life. When war was declared in 1914 she was approaching Dar-es-Salaam, the principal port of the German colony of Tanganyika. Not having a wireless she was unaware of the events in Europe but luckily a Royal Naval vessel intercepted her off the port. Some months later she escaped from a Turkish port a matter of days before Turkey entered the war against the Allies. Finally, in 1915, she was mined off Archangel while carrying munitions to the hard pressed Russians. She went to the bottom within six minutes taking six of her crew with her. The other crew members rowed for twenty-four hours in an open boat before being picked up. The *Cape Finisterre II* was torpedoed off Falmouth in 1917, outward bound for Brest with a cargo for the French government. She sank within twenty seconds with the loss of thirty-five of her crew of forty-one.[35]

In the same year the *Cape Corso I* was torpedoed off Milford Haven. She was crippled and abandoned by all but six of her crew, some of whom were picked up by a Greek steamer while others 'preferred to remain where they were'. The Greek ship took the *Cape Corso I* in tow but was sunk immediately. When the German submarine surfaced the crew remaining on board the *Cape Corso I* opened fire but their ship was torpedoed again. Still it did not sink and the enemy abandoned their attack. The ship was towed to Swansea and declared a total loss.[36] Nevertheless, because of the shortage of shipping, the *Cape Corso I* was later repaired and saw twenty-five years further service with Canadian and Greek owners before being seized by the Vichy French government and later sunk by a British submarine.[37]

Of the two Lyle ships which survived the war only the *Cape Breton II* emerged unscathed despite an attempt by enemy agents to set fire to her cargo.[38] The *Cape Ortegal I* was severely damaged at Archangel in 1916 when a nearby ammunition ship blew up, causing £10,000 worth of damage which took five months to repair.[39]

It is claimed that war risk insurance failed to reimburse shipowners for their losses,[40] but A. P. Lyle had no complaint on this score.[41] However the replacement of ships was a major problem throughout the shipping and shipbuilding industries. In the early part of the war, naval construction had received priority. It was not until the unrestricted German U-boat campaign of 1917 began to decimate British and Allied shipping that the government diverted resources to merchant shipbuilding. James Lithgow, the eldest son of W. T. Lithgow, was appointed Director of Merchant Shipbuilding. With his experience of constructing standard ships, he was quick to recognize the

Figure 5.4

The Government wartime standard ship *War Bracken*, built by Caird & Co. in 1918. She was managed by Lyle Shipping Co. on behalf of the Shipping Controller from 1918–19. In this illustration she is painted with 'dazzle' camouflage which was designed to make the hull merge with the surrounding sea when viewed through the periscope of an enemy 'U' boat.

advantage of 'repetition work' in achieving the high output necessary if Britain was to replace the tonnage lost to the U-boats. Twelve standard cargo boat designs were introduced, and by the end of the war 289 of these ships had been constructed.

The government's Shipping Controller appointed 'well known firms of proven experience' to manage these ships, and Lyle Shipping Co. was one of the first selected.[42] Early in 1918, the *War Bracken* was placed under Lyle management (Figure 5.4). A second vessel, the *War Picotee* was designated for management by Lyle Shipping Co., but she was not completed until after the war, and she was sold by the government before the arrangement was ever effected.[43] The *War Bracken* was returned to the government in September 1919. In this year the war-damaged Lyle fleet was augmented by three other ships. These, the *Lipsos*, the *Oehringen* and the *Wartburg*, which in 1920 were joined by the *Marie Reppel*, were German tramps awarded to the British government as war reparations (Figure 5.5). They were managed by the Company while the government sought permanent owners.[44] In late 1919 the German vessels were returned to the government as part of the deal whereby Lord Kylsant and Lord Inchcape acquired all the ships under government control. Lyle was left with two war weary *Capes*.

Figure 5.5
The *Oehringen*, which was accepted by the Government as a war reparation from Germany as part of the Treaty of Versailles, was placed in the Lyle fleet by the Shipping Controller in 1919 and sold the following year.

By the end of the First World War the Company's balance sheet was as healthy as it had ever been. From this position of strength the Directors decided in 1919 'to start the business afresh' by liquidating the management company and all the single ship companies, paying off loan capital and transferring the unencumbered assets and reserves to a new concern. Throughout its seventeen years of existence, Lyle Shipping Co. and its associated companies had made creditable returns, often in difficult circumstances. By 1920 A. P. Lyle had reason to be proud of the re-establishment of his family's shipowning tradition.

6. 1919-1939
Showing a Firm Back

Fluctuations in world shipping and trade in the 1920s and 1930s seriously challenged the position of British shipowners. Liquidations were frequent, and a number of old-established shipping companies withdrew from the business altogether. Between three and three and a half million gross tons of British shipping was laid up between 1931 and 1933; the period from 1930 to 1935, reported the Tramp Shipping Administrative Committee, was the worst 'ever experienced by British shipping'.[1] Shipowners required special qualities and resources to meet the challenge. In the case of Lyle Shipping Co., survival after 1919 depended upon its capital position and accounting policy, its ship purchase policy, and the development of its special relationship with Sir James and Henry Lithgow.

In the year after the Armistice of November 1918, European industry rapidly rebuilt its depleted stocks. Luxury goods, which had been denied to Europe since 1914, flooded into the major international markets. As a result, the demand for shipping capacity boomed, and despite the continuation of government controls, freight rates and ship values in the British market rose to unprecedented levels. Although demand for shipping outstripped supply, the shortage was artificial. In 1919 and 1920 ships were delayed by severe port congestion which at one stage reduced available tonnage by 30 per cent.[2] Other ships were held up awaiting repairs, overhauls and conversion from war use while more were taken into government service to bring home troops, stores and equipment. But during the last years of the war heavy merchant shipping losses had imperilled the British war effort and in 1917 a massive replacement programme was put in hand in Britain and in the United States. By 1919 world tonnage exceeded its 1914 level by 1.8 million tons and new ships added daily to this total. During the boom a further 11 million tons of shipping were built.

In the spring of 1920, the freight market collapsed. Although operating costs had risen two or threefold since 1913, freight rates dropped back to their pre-war level. By 1922, the slump had forced ships off the market. A. P. Lyle, for example, reported that 'of the two boats left to us one, the *Cape Breton I*, is today laid up idle at Falmouth, the disastrous conditions into which the freight market has fallen making it a matter of less loss to lie there than to go to sea;

while the other, the *Cape Ortegal I*, is now on a voyage . . . which with luck will little more than cover her expenses'.[3]

Throughout much of the inter-war period, freight rates and voyage profits declined steadily. The tramp freight index fell from 602 in March 1920 to 112 in 1928, and tramp ship voyage profits per ton dropped from £3.8 in 1920–21 to £0.7 in 1928–29. With the onset of the economic blizzard in 1929, matters became even worse; between 1929 and 1933 the freight index fell from 115 to 85. There was no substantial improvement until after 1935. The main cause of these problems was an imbalance in the supply of and demand for shipping. This was exacerbated by the innovation of more efficient forms of marine propulsion and by improvements in the techniques of ship construction which made possible the building of faster ships capable of carrying larger cargoes.

In these changed circumstances the British shipping industry suffered more than its competitors. Between 1924 and 1929 and again in the late 1930s, world seaborne trade grew with a corresponding increase in the world's merchant fleet. Between 1914 and 1938 world tonnage increased by 47 per cent, from 45.5 million tons to 66.9 million tons while the size of the British fleet fell by 5.8 per cent from 18.9 million tons to 17.8 million tons. British tramp shipping fared worst of all, and the decline in tonnage is estimated at between 30 and 60 per cent.[4] Only Germany suffered a similar absolute decline in the size of its fleet.

There are several reasons for the relative failure of the British shipping industry. Before 1914, Britain's fleet carried half the world's trade. During the First World War, several countries exploited the opportunities created by the dislocation of British shipping. They established themselves not only as major carriers in their home trades but also penetrated the traffic with Britain's colonies, which had always been the preserve of British shipping. In the 1920s and 1930s, these wartime gains were maintained and built upon, largely because many foreign governments gave incentives to their domestic shipping industries. These included operating subsidies, flag discrimination, low interest loans to owners, grants for replacing old tonnage, and taxation relief. In the inter-war years, these incentives strengthened the fleets of the United States, Japan, and Italy, which quadrupled, trebled, and doubled in size respectively. The British government gave assistance to its own industry under the Trade Facilities Acts (1921–26), and the belated Shipping (Assistance) Act of 1935. The 1935 legislation allocated £2 million and a 'scrap and build' scheme for tramp shipping, but this effort was insufficient to counteract the determined policies of foreign governments.

Foreign competition heightened the already serious effect of the slump on the British industry. This was compounded by the collapse of overseas demand for the products of Britain's staple industries. The United Kingdom's export trade remained below its 1913 level in all but one (1923) of the inter-war years.

In the 1930s, exports rarely exceeded 80 per cent of their pre-war value, falling heavily from £729 million in 1929 to £389 million in 1932. The collapse of the coal export business was especially serious (Figure 6.1). The switch from coal to oil as the main source of industrial power caused Britain's coal exports to fall from 73.4 million tons in 1913 to 35.8 million tons in 1938. This robbed the British tramp fleet of its chief export commodity and led to a sharp rise in the number of tramp ships sailing outward in ballast. In time this handicapped the competitiveness of British shipping. This factor must not be overstressed since British tramps plied mostly between foreign ports. These difficulties were

Figure 6.1
A cargo of coal heaped up on the deck of a Lyle ship in an American port, in the late 1930s.

heightened by the construction of fleets of specialized types of ships, particularly oil tankers and refrigerated ships, with which general purpose tramp ships could not compete. Although the volume of imports into the United Kingdom grew between the wars, half the increase was contributed by tanker-borne oil imports.

Lyle Shipping Co., while it felt the impact of the depression between the wars, actually strengthened its position. In sharp contrast to the Lyles' experience in the difficult years of the 1890s, there was no question of pruning or closing down the business as a result of the collapse of the shipping market. Instead, careful attention to ship purchase and financial management allowed the Company to emerge from the depression with a strong fleet and a healthy balance sheet.

On 20 January 1920, the present Lyle Shipping Co. was incorporated as a private company, with an authorized capital of £500,000 made up of 150 management shares and 4,350 ordinary shares of £100 each. Paid up capital was £250,000.[5] The new Company acquired the assets and current liabilities of the old business, valued at £650,226 and £150,226 respectively. The major assets were the retained profits and payments received in respect of war losses. By 1920 these totalled £351,000, invested in government war loan and war bonds (£341,675), and in public companies and railway stock (£9,600). The balance of the assets largely comprised the two ships *Cape Breton II* and *Cape Ortegal I*, neither of which was in good condition. The *Cape Ortegal I* had suffered severe war damage and the *Cape Breton II* was sixteen years old. Nevertheless the liquidator of the old Company valued them at £230,000, far in excess of their historic cost (£84,388), reflecting the high market value of second hand ships during the immediate post-war boom. After the collapse of the boom, the value of the Lyle fleet was written down from £230,000 to £60,000 in 1921–22.

When the new Company's share capital was raised, £77,300 was subscribed by A. P. Lyle, £69,300 by Colonel Macfarlane, £51,000 by Archie Lyle, £23,000 by James Shearer senior, £22,600 by the Countess Nora Manessie (A. P. Lyle's daughter), £3,200 by James Shearer junior and £3,000 by James Shearer senior's four daughters. James Shearer senior, Colonel Macfarlane and Archie Lyle each owned sixty-three of the 200 issued management shares and A. P. Lyle owned the remaining eleven shares. Soon after the number of issued management shares was increased to 650: James Shearer senior, Colonel Macfarlane and Archie Lyle each received 213 while A. P. Lyle's holding remained unchanged. In addition to the issued share capital, the shareholders also provided loans totalling £250,000.

A. P. Lyle became Chairman (an office he had held in the old Company) and Colonel Macfarlane, Archie Lyle and the senior Shearer were appointed as Directors. In 1925 they were joined by James Shearer junior who received ten management shares from James Shearer senior, his father-in-law. Two years

Figure 6.2

Cape of Good Hope II, one of the first motor tramp ships to be owned by a Clyde shipping company, on her trials in 1925. As she was an experimental vessel, Sir James and Henry Lithgow agreed to take a half share in her.

later Shearer senior retired from the Company and his management shares were acquired by Archie Lyle (97), Colonel Macfarlane (86), James Shearer junior (25) and A. P. Lyle (5). Thus in 1927 the Lyle family held half the management shares in addition to over two thirds of the ordinary shares; the family's control was as firm as ever. At the death of A. P. Lyle in 1933 his entire shareholding was inherited by his grandson, Robin.[6]

The ship purchase policy of Lyle Shipping Co. was crucial to its survival in the 1920s and the 1930s. Initially, when the post-war shipping boom collapsed, the Company sold the *Cape Breton II* in 1922 for £23,000, less than one fifth of its book value in 1920.[7] The Directors also contemplated the sale of the one remaining steamer, the *Cape Ortegal I*.[8] In the event, she would remain in service for a further fourteen years. Thereafter, unlike most British tramp companies between the wars, the Company expanded its fleet. A strength of two ships totalling 8,768 tons in 1922 was increased to ten ships of 43,318 tons (including four ships which were either managed or jointly owned) by 1939.

The expansion began in 1924. As the world economy began to climb out of the immediate post-war recession, the Company purchased the twelve year old *Arakan* from the Rotterdamsche Lloyd for £40,000 (with the help of a

£25,000 advance by the Bank of Scotland). She was renamed *Cape Comorin II*. In the following year the *Cape of Good Hope II* joined the fleet. She was a new motorship of 4,963 gross tons, built by the Lithgows and powered by six cylinder four-stroke single-acting oil engines. She was jointly owned by the Company and James and Henry Lithgow, and registered in the name of the Cape of Good Hope Motorship Co. Throughout the lean years of the 1920s and 1930s, the Lithgows continued their policy of building 'on spec' when orders were scarce, and like many of these products, the *Cape of Good Hope II* was partly financed by the Lithgows' retention of shares in the new ship (Figure 6.2). The *Cape of Good Hope II* cost £108,540,[9] of which the joint owners each subscribed share capital of £10,000. The deficit was made up with a loan of £49,206 from Lyle Shipping Co., presumably supplemented by an advance of about £40,000 from the Lithgows.

The purchase of the *Cape of Good Hope II* was a cautious decision on the part of the Lyle Board. In 1924, the directors' minutes recorded that 'James and Henry Lithgow have confirmed the tentative original understanding, namely that the vessel being a certain extent experimental they were agreeable to take a half interest in the company to be formed to own the vessel'. The minutes continue that 'Messrs. Lithgows indicated that after time had been taken for a reasonable test of the ship's working and results, they presumed that if satisfactory we Lyle Shipping Co. should wish to relieve them of their half interest, but considering the impossibility of laying down at this stage hard and fast lines . . . it was agreed that the question be left open for mutual discussion and adjustment after the necessary experience and data had been obtained'.[10] In the event the ship was joint owned until lost by enemy action in 1942.

In 1926, the Lithgows offered the Company the management of two further motor ships, the *Lycia* and the *Cape York II*. The *Lycia* was a small motorship of 2,338 gross tons, built in 1924 for T. and J. Brocklebank of Liverpool by Dunlop, Bremner and Co.; the builders, with their yard at Port Glasgow, were owned by the Lithgows (Figure 6.3). The Brocklebanks and the Lithgows worked closely together and, from 1919, they jointly owned the Port Glasgow shipyard of William Hamilton and Co. The *Lycia*, which was the second motorship built in Port Glasgow, was an experimental vessel, but her engines turned out to be under-powered and she was returned to the Lithgows. The *Cape York II* (5,027 gross tons) was brand new from Lithgows' own yard and another speculative venture. She cost £99,357[11] and was powered by twin screws propelled by oil engines built by Hawthorn Leslie and Co. of Newcastle. (Figure 6.4). Both the *Lycia* and the *Cape York II* were placed by the Lithgow brothers in the ownership of the newly formed Cape York Motorship Co. Ltd which had a paid up capital of £20,000 nominally subscribed by Lyles. Although the Lyle Board loaned the Company £50,000 to help pay for the two ships, initially they declined to take an interest in them acting solely as managers.

Figure 6.3

Lycia leaving Vancouver with a cargo of timber for the British West Indies in 1934. One of the first British tramp ships equipped with diesel engines, she was built originally for T. & J. Brocklebank of Liverpool in 1924, but was rejected as being unsatisfactory.

Figure 6.4

The motorship *Cape York II* built by Lithgows Ltd, Port Glasgow, on trials in the Clyde in 1926. She was originally owned by Sir James and Henry Lithgow but passed into Lyle owner-ship in 1928.

In November 1928, however, the Lyle Shipping Co. purchased the *Cape York II* for £100,000. In April 1929 Lyles undertook to manage yet a third vessel on behalf of the Lithgows. She was the *Cape Horn II*, a new motorship of 5,643 tons, costing £124,142.[12] She was registered in the name of the Cape York Motorship Co. The diesel-engined *Cape York II* and the *Cape Horn II* could operate a medium speed of twelve knots compared with an average speed of eight knots for steamers. Moreover, the vessels were equipped with many novel devices including electric winches, electric water heaters, and electric heating in the crew accommodation. No auxiliary steam boilers were fitted in either vessel, thereby increasing cargo-space. This combination of speed and advanced equipment favourably impressed the Company's charterers and enhanced its reputation.

In the 1920s the Lyle Shipping Co. preferred to purchase second-hand rather than new ships. After the purchase of the *Arakan* in 1924, the eight-year-old *Verbania* (5,021 gross tons) was bought from Cunard in 1926 and was renamed the *Cape Cornwall*. (Figure 6.5.) Her purchase at a price of £25,000 was financed by the sale of £26,311 worth of wartime investments.[13] Two years later the *Balfour* was bought from the Canadian Pacific Railway Co. (managers Canadian Pacific Steamship Ltd) and renamed *Cape Verde II*. She had been built by the Lithgow-controlled Robert Duncan and Co. at Port Glasgow in 1917, under the emergency war loss replacement programme. She was acquired by Lyles for £40,000 and the purchase was again financed by the sale of investments.[14]

Although profitability suffered during the immediate post war recession, the setback was only temporary. Profits grew steadily from £17,852 in 1922–23 to £27,748 in 1927–28 before falling back to £25,443 in the following year. Profit as a percentage of gross tangible assets rose from between 5 and 5.4 per cent between 1923 and 1925 to a minimum of 6 per cent from 1927 until 1929. Dividend payments also improved from 5 per cent annually between 1923 and 1925 to 10 per cent between 1927 and 1929. The Company continued to provide for depreciation out of profits, but the accounting policy adopted was not always consistent. The great fall in the market value of new and second hand ships which preceded the collapse of the post war boom forced the Company to write down the value of the fleet from £230,000 in 1920–21 to £60,000 in 1922–23. This provision was made by writing off the loan of £250,000 made to the Company by shareholders in 1920. Thereafter no further provision for depreciation was made until 1924–25 when the fleet's value was written down by 6 per cent, followed by 5.7 per cent in the next year. These two allowances were more than adequate when compared with the then normal practice of depreciating ships by 5 per cent per annum. Between 1926 and 1928 depreciation was made at an average rate of 3.5 per cent and in 1928–29, no allowance was made. The diminution of these allowances was not the result of a shortage of funds, but was probably an adjustment or compensation for the higher rates of previous years.

Towards the end of 1929, following the Wall Street crash, the world economy entered a long depression which continued until 1934. Lyle Shipping Co., like its competitors, was badly affected. Voyage profits fell drastically, and the Company's energy was devoted to survival. Voyage profits dropped by £5,000 to £6,871 in 1929–30. In the following year a deficit of £8,191 was recorded on the navigation account. Careful management reduced this to £2,091 in 1931–32, but small deficits were again reported in the following two years. Only in 1934–35 was the navigation account in the black with a modest surplus of £1,852.

Nevertheless, the Company did not suffer any overall annual losses during the period of the slump. Company profits fell from £15,548 in 1929–30 to £254 in 1930–31. In the following year they improved to £7,000 but in the next two years were below £3,600. No substantial improvement was made until 1935–36 when profits stood at £15,846. Dividend payments fell from 10 per cent in 1928–29 to 2.5 per cent in the following year. Thereafter shareholders received no return on their investment until 1936–37. As a measure of the depth of the crisis the Directors waived their fees of £400 per annum between 1931 and 1935. In virtually every year of the depression the Board was unable to make proper provision for depreciation. In the short-term recovery in the years 1930–32 depreciation of over 5 per cent of fleet value was made, but allowances were below 3 per cent in the following three years when the crisis deepened. (Table 6.1).

The Board's policy since 1919, and especially their prudent capital expenditure and the maintenance of a healthy reserve account, allowed Lyle Shipping Co. to meet the crisis. During the 1920s, as new tonnage was added to the fleet, the reserves were gradually reduced from £268,476 in 1923 to £123,637 in 1929–30. This sum was invested in stock which, despite the prevailing market conditions, gave a return of £7–8,000 between 1929 and 1934. Investment income was supplemented by fees of about £3,500 per annum paid by the Lithgows for the management of their ships. T. and J. Harrison, the Liverpool shipping company, were similarly protected by their investment income, and throughout the depression its Chairman could refer with satisfaction to the investments as 'a useful fighting fund'.[15]

In 1934, as world trade began to recover, the Lyle Board undertook the urgent task of modernizing the Company's fleet. The average age of the steamers was then 19.5 years. The first new purchase was a thirteen-year-old steamer,

Figure 6.5 (*overleaf*)
Cape Cornwall arriving at Muroran, Japan, with a cargo of timber after sustaining severe storm damage while on a crossing of the North Pacific in January 1934.

Table 6.1

Financial Structure of the Company, 1921–1939

Year	Gross tangible assets	Net tangible assets	Profit before interest and tax	Net current assets[1]	Profit as a percentage of gross tangible assets	Book value of fleet	Depreciation as a percentage of the fleet value	Dividend
1920–1	£692,452	£507,175	£127,130	£377,119	18.4	£230,000	3.0	—
1921–2	£357,149	£276,651	£38,852	£216,593	10.9	£60,000	74.9	2½%
1922–3	£328,031	£281,857	£17,875	£243,766	5.4	£38,035	36.7	5%
1923–4	£319,771	£285,137	£15,926	£242,704	5.0	£38,035	0	5%
1924–5	£351,268	£303,584	£18,870	£225,323	5.4	£75,030	6.0	5%
1925–6	£404,025	£303,680	£16,352	£183,886	4.0	£70,530	5.7	7½%
1926–7	£423,299	£328,048	£27,833	£174,755	6.6	£104,030	3.4	10%
1927–8	£464,790	£325,345	£27,748	£52,612	6.0	£140,461	3.6	10%
1928–9	£432,769	£324,198	£25,443	£86,465	5.9	£135,461	3.7	10%
1929–30	£396,591	£316,173	£15,548	£78,427	3.9	£135,461	6.6	2½%
1930–1	£379,510	£307,085	£254	£38,815	—	£126,461	7.1	—
1931–2	£397,694	£330,434	£7,003	£53,119	1.8	£126,461	5.5	—
1932–3	£390,743	£310,988	£2,529	£53,044	0.6	£119,461	2.5	—
1933–4	£378,544	£255,219	£3,560	−£55,617	0.9	£170,108	2.1	—
1934–5	£376,606	£256,879	£5,769	−£56,883	1.5	£172,467	2.9	—
1935–6	£326,964	£267,949	£15,846	−£5,833	4.8	£147,659	9.5	—
1936–7	£372,706	£278,385	£26,587	−£60,807	7.1	£195,880	5.1	5%
1937–8[2]	—	—	—			—	—	—
1938–9	£419,772	£341,452	£32,413	£110,293	7.7	£160,997	6.9	7½%

[1] Between 1921 and 1930 investments in and loans to subsidiaries have been included in current assets.

[2] No accounts survive for 1937–38.

Source: Lyle Shipping Co. Ltd, Annual Reports

the *Cycle* (4,520 gross tons), owned by the Australian Steamship Proprietory Co. (managers Howard Smith Ltd). Lyle Shipping Co. paid £14,000 for the ship.[16] Renamed the *Cape Wrath III*, she was delivered at Sydney and replaced the slightly older *Cape Cornwall* which was sold to Chinese ship breakers.

At the same time the Lyle Board was arranging to acquire and operate more modern tonnage. In 1928, immediately before the onset of the slump, Pardoe-Thomas and Co. of Newport, Monmouthshire, acting in their capacity as managers of the Ottoman Line Ltd, the Newport Normandy Line Ltd, the Newport Provence Line Ltd, and Newport Liners Ltd, ordered five steamers from Lithgows. The ships were the *Knight Almoner*, (4,443 gross tons), the *Knight Batchelor* (4,398 gross tons), the *Knight of St. George* (3,807 gross tons), the *Knight of St. Michael* (3,807 gross tons) and the *Knight of St. John* (3,807 gross tons). (Figure 6.7.) The last three were built to the same design. All were conventional steamers and the total value of the order was £228,489.[17] With the onset of the depression Pardoe-Thomas found itself over-committed. The construction of the *Knight Batchelor* was suspended but the other ships were completed in 1929

Figure 6.6
Cape Wrath III in service in the 1930s. She was built as the *Cycle* by Armstrong Whitworth & Co. at Newcastle-on-Tyne in 1921, and purchased by Lyle Shipping Co., in 1934.

Figure 6.7
Knight of St. John built by Lithgows Ltd for Newport Liners Ltd, steaming in the Clyde shortly after her completion in 1930. She was acquired by Lyle Shipping Co. in 1934 and renamed *Cape Race II*.

Figure 6.8
Cape Howe I, originally the *Knight Almoner*, leaving the Clyde in the 1930s.

and 1930. They were mortgaged to James Shearer senior and Bertie Pardoe-Thomas. In March 1933 the mortgage was transferred to James Shearer and John MacCulloch (of Lithgows Ltd). Shearer and MacCulloch were appointed joint receivers on behalf of Lithgows soon afterwards. In February 1934, with the Lithgows' agreement, the Company purchased the four ships at a knocked down price of £126,000 or £31,500 per ship[18] and renamed them *Cape Howe I* (Figure 6.8), *Cape Corso II*, *Cape Nelson I* and *Cape Race II*. Lithgows Ltd also gave the Company an option to purchase the *Knight Batchelor*, which then remained unfinished on the stocks.[19] Even in 1934 when ship prices were at basement level the deal was a bargain. The magazine *Fairplay* priced a new ready single deck steamer of 7,500 tons deadweight at £37,000 or £4.9 per ton.[20] The 'Knights' had cost the Company just £4.5 per ton. Soon after ship prices rose as world trade picked up and the freight market improved. *Fairplay* quoted the 1935 price of a newly completed 7,500 deadweight tons tramp ship at £52,000, an increase of £15,000 in the twelve months since the Company made its purchase.[21] By 1936 the price had risen by a further £8,000.[22]

To finance the purchase of the 'Knights' Lithgows advanced Lyle a loan of £50,000, repayable over five years at 3 per cent interest for the first six months.[23] Other funds were raised by the sale of investments to the value of £40,000 and disposal of the older ships. In 1934 the *Cape Comorin II* was sold to Italian ship breakers for £6,950.[24] The *Cape Verde II* was acquired by Chinese owners, later passing into Japanese hands; in 1943 the old ship was sunk at Singapore by British forces. Last to go was the *Cape Ortegal I*, one of the Company's steamers which had given twenty-five years service through war and peace, the longest of any 'Cape' before or since. In 1936 she was sold to Cornish owners for £8,250[25] and was broken up in 1939. The renewal of the Lyle fleet between 1934 and 1935 made it difficult for the Company to derive benefit from the 'scrap and build' scheme introduced as part of the Shipping (Assistance) Act of 1935.

Lyle Shipping Co. emerged from the slump in a position of strength. The firm was manager and part owner of a fleet of relatively modern motorships and it fully owned one old and four modern steamers. With this refurbished fleet it was well placed to take advantage of the improvement in world trade. Between 1933 and 1939 voyage profits rose from £1,805 to £33,444. Overall Company profits rose from £3,560 in 1933–34 to £5,769 in 1934–35 and then increased steadily to £32,413 in 1938–39, and the return on gross tangible assets increased from 0.9 to 7.7 per cent, a marked improvement on the returns recorded at the end of the 1920s (see Table 6.1). The Directors began to draw their fees again in 1935–36. After the slump dividend payments were sacrificed in order to make good arrears in depreciation provisions. In 1935–36, the first year since 1929–30 when substantial profits were made, an allowance for depreciation at the rate of 9.5 per cent was made, and in 1936–37 and 1938–39 annual depreciation was maintained at over 5 per cent. Dividend payments were resumed in 1937 when shareholders received a return of 5 per cent, their first income for seven years.

With a return to profitability the Lyle Board decided to replace the *Cape Wrath III*, the last old steamer in the fleet. In 1937 she was sold after only three years in the Company's service. She had never been a success. Her consumption of coal was high and after less than twelve months service the Directors had contemplated her disposal.[26] She was sold to Latvian owners and in 1942 was torpedoed and sunk in the Windward Passage.

The Lyle Board replaced the *Cape Wrath III* with the *Cape Sable II* (Figure 6.9). This steamer had been ordered from Lithgows Ltd by Pardoe-Thomas and Co. as the *Knight Batchelor* (see page 81). In 1936, mindful of the growing demand for new tonnage, the increase in steel prices and the improvement in shipyard wages, Lyle Shipping Co. took up its option and purchased her for £63,040.[27] £20,400 of war stock was sold to help finance the deal.[28]

Figure 6.9
(a) Plans of the *Cape Sable II*, constructed by Lithgows Ltd, in 1936. She was ordered by Pardoe Thomas & Co. of Newport as the *Knight Batchelor* and purchased by Lyle Shipping Co., while on the stocks.
(b) *Cape Sable II* leaving the ways at Lithgows Ltd's Port Glasgow yard.

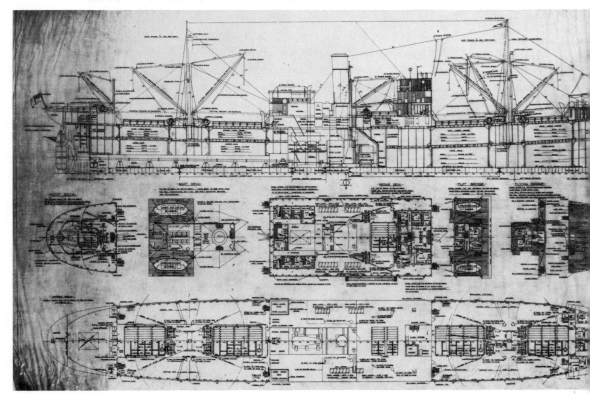

In 1939, in anticipation of war and an increase of demand for shipping, the Company placed orders with Lithgows Ltd for two new oil-fired vessels, the *Cape Wrath IV* and the *Cape Rodney I*.[29] In August of the same year, the Company undertook to manage a new motorship, the *Cape Clear III* (5,085 gross tons), for the Lithgow brothers. She cost £144,067 and was registered in the name of the Cape York Motorship Co. In late 1939 a further motorship, the *Cape Verde III* (6,914 gross tons) was ordered from the Lithgows at a cost of £168,313.

In the 1930s the sale of investments to pay for new tonnage reduced the reserves of Lyle Shipping Co. from £123,037 in 1929 to £30,000 in 1936–37. When substantial profits were recorded at the end of the 1930s the reserves were rebuilt. At the same time the improved performance of the subsidiary companies allowed them to repay £50,000 of their loans from Lyle Shipping Co. By 1938–39 £189,287 was invested in government securities and public companies. The Company's portfolio included shares of I.C.I., Shell Transport and Trading Co., Phoenix Assurance Co., Commercial Union Assurance Co., Scottish Iron

and Steel Co., Stewarts and Lloyd Ltd, and J. and P. Coats Ltd. As in the 1920s the investments bolstered the Company's overall profitability.

In the 1930s, profits were augmented by arranging long term charters of individual ships (time charters) to move large cargoes at a fixed price over a period of months or even years. It was uncommon for any Lyle ship to be laid up for longer than a few days. For much of her life the *Lycia* was time-chartered to the Canadian Transport Co. and plied between Western Canada and the West Indies carrying timber in one direction and sugar in the other.[30] During the 1930s the ex-Pardoe Thomas ships were time-chartered for several years by the Booth Line of Liverpool, which operated services to South America. The vessels, particularly the *Cape Sable II*, were found to be ideal for the Brazilian small port coastal trade. Similarly in the 1930s the *Cape Wrath III* carried cargoes of phosphate on time-charter from Christmas Island in the Indian Ocean to Durban and Capetown before returning to Britain via Dutch ports.[31] Lyle ships also sailed on one of the main tramping routes, carrying coal from Britain to the River Plate and returning with grain.

In 1937 the *Cape Horn II* was chartered to the Union Steamship Co. of New Zealand for twelve months and traded between the North Pacific ports and Australia. In 1938 this was extended for a further year on more advantageous terms. James Shearer, the Company's Manager, wrote to the Lithgows, the ship's owners, that 'their ideas of rates for her were 4s 6d ($£0.22\frac{1}{2}$) but I am pleased to say that by our showing a firm back they were eventually edged up to 5s ($£0.25$) . . . This is an excellent fixture and far beyond anything which I know of having been done recently'. Shearer went on to suggest the news was sent to Henry Lithgow who was on holiday 'as there are more knocks than bouquets these days'.[32]

During the 1930s companies with which time charters were negotiated also included Adelaide Steamship Co., the Anglo Canadian Ship Co., the Blue Star Line and the Isthmian Steamship Line. These cargo liner companies, like the Booth Line and the Union Steamship Co., sought to provide comprehensive shipping facilities extending to dry cargo shipments on the services they operated.[33] They could achieve this most profitably not by buying trampships, but by time chartering them from tramp shipping companies such as Lyle.

British shipowners in the inter-war years have been admonished for failing to adapt to the conditions prevailing after 1918. 'Adaptability was the key to survival . . . and the failure of British shipowners to respond rapidly to the new competition was one of the reasons for the stagnation of the industry'.[34] The greatest technological advance at this time was the introduction of the diesel engine. By 1939 only a quarter of the British fleet used diesel propulsion compared with, for example, half the Scandinavian or Dutch fleets. Motor ships had several advantages over steamers – for example a lower fuel consumption ratio, a greater steaming range, a greater cargo capacity and a saving in the amount

Figure 6.10

The motorship *Cape York II* being re-engined at Rotterdam in 1926. Her original and largely experimental diesel engines, built by R.W. Hawthorn Leslie & Co. Ltd of Newcastle, had proved unsatisfactory and broke down on numerous occasions.

of boiler water carried. However the building cost per deadweight ton of motorships far exceeded the cost of building a coal burner, with the result that the profits derived from the motorships operational advantages were considerably discounted by higher capital charges.

Lyle Shipping Co. owned only one diesel ship until 1939 in addition to its half interest in the *Cape of Good Hope II* and its management of the *Lycia* and the *Cape Horn II* (see pages 74 and 76). This was not a disadvantage. Operating conventional steamers, often of considerable age, the Company made larger than average profits in most years. Nor did their experience of diesel propulsion induce them to turn away from steam. The *Cape York II* consistently broke down, and in 1936, she was re-engined by the Rotterdam Dry Dock Co. at a cost of £6,800.[35] (Figure 6.10.)

Differing bunker consumption of coal burners and motorships combined with different coal and diesel oil prices around the world called for different options in voyage estimating and planning. This is graphically illustrated by the voyage estimates for cargoes of rice shipped in the early 1930s from Thailand to Cuba. 'For the first cargo that came on the market ... Lyles had a coal burning steamer in position ... Bangkok/Havana via Suez being 12,024 miles and via Panama 11,768 gave a difference of 256 (miles) in favour of going trans-Pacific. A further item in favour of the Panama route was that the canal transit costs would have been substantially lower than Suez. Everything pointed to trans-Pacific until it came to the bunkering programme and resultant deadweight for cargo. The voyage via Suez was then figured based on the numerous available bunkering ports on that route, and she was fixed via Suez as clearly the much more profitable. Within a few weeks another similar cargo came on the market, but this time it was a motorship that was in position. The first estimate on her was done via Suez following the pattern of the coal burner, but sure enough with the motorship's greater range and with diesel in Miri at $7 the second estimate showed without question she should go trans-Pacific; so with the same cargoes, the same loading and discharging ports, the coal burner went one way half around the world and the motorship the other'.[36]

After 1920 the day-to-day running of Lyle Shipping Co. fell more and more under the control of James Shearer junior. In 1920 he returned from the Ministry of Shipping to resume his duties as Secretary and Manager. During the war he had acquired a wide knowledge of the British shipping industry and the men who controlled it. At the same time, he had become a close friend of Henry Lithgow. His importance in the running of the post-war Company was recognized by the Lyle Board, and he was appointed a Director in 1925. His ability was widely acknowledged and, in 1938, the Scottish shipowners elected Shearer as their representative on the London-based Tramp Shipping Administrative Committee. The Committee had been established in 1935 under the aegis of the British Council of Shipping, and was subsequently responsible for introducing a minimum rate scheme for tramp shipping. In 1942 Shearer was asked to accept the Vice-Presidency of the Chamber of Shipping of the United Kingdom with a view to his becoming President in 1943. He declined because of the pressure of his work in Glasgow. (Figure 6.11).

James Shearer was totally preoccupied with his work. He had a penetrating mind and a shrewdness which enabled him to dominate every aspect of the Company's activities. In addition, he abhorred wastage and slackness. He took a keen interest in the seagoing personnel and was scrupulous in his review

Figure 6.11

James Shearer, junior, 1880–1964, secretary and subsequently Managing Director of the company. Without his able management the Company would probably not have survived the inter-war years.

of the progress of individual voyages. With the support of his fellow Directors, he impressed on the Company's masters that they represented Lyle in foreign ports and by their conduct and example could attract business. The masters appreciated this trust and as a result were keen to safeguard and promote the Company's interests overseas. They would endeavour to keep their vessels at sea as much as possible, taking steps to avoid delays in port and became expert in judging conditions when selecting the best weather route for a voyage. Captain Love, a former Lyle master, recalled in 1977:

'Every trick in the tramp ship masters' book was known to them. A favourite was to make a nuisance of themselves screaming for attention night and day in the ear of anybody who would listen, to such an extent that the port

Figure 6.12
(a) King Neptune and his attendants prepare to welcome a new member to their kingdom as the *Cape of Good Hope II* crosses the Equator sometime in the 1930s.
(b) A group photograph taken aboard the *Cape York II* on Jubilee Day 1935, from left to right, W. Campbell, steward, W.S. Keith, mate, S. Bradley, second engineer, J. Cuthbert, second mate, W.B. King, chief engineer and F.H. Saunders, wireless operator.

authorities and business gentlemen would combine to give the master every attention to get him back out on the seaward side of the break-water. This principle worked as long as the vessel did not return to that port too soon. A ship whilst in port made no money unless on time charter, during which time of course the ship's master would use another chapter of his book'.

James Shearer wrote regular detailed letters to the masters, who were often away for up to two years. Men who should know recall that 'an owner was never seen yet by sheer personality expressed in letters; he seemed to be in an office 15,000 miles from Glasgow'. At the time it was difficult for directors to communicate with charterers by wireless and impossible for them to pay regular overseas visits.

For most of the inter-war years conditions for seamen on board tramp ships were generally poor. Until the late 1930s the engineering crew lived in one cabin beside the engine room while the rest of the crew inhabited a large mess in the forecastle. In these rooms the men ate, slept and relaxed. Food was prepared in a central galley by a certificated cook and ships were known either as 'hungry ships' or 'good food ships'. Lyle had a good reputation for feeding their crews well, even though bacon and eggs were restricted to the weekends, while H. Hogarth & Sons Ltd, a Glasgow tramp ship company with strong links with Lyles, were known as the 'Hungry Hogarths'. Each crewman was issued weekly with tea, sugar and condensed milk and he brewed his own tea in the galley. Alcohol was not permitted on board ships but captains were authorized to take aboard one case each of whisky, rum and port wine for consumption on appropriate occasions. All crewmen slept on iron bunks with drawers fitted below to contain their belongings. A wardrobe was sometimes provided. Until 1928 seamen were required to buy their own blankets together with a 'straw donkey' or mattress obtained from ship chandlers at a price of about 2s 6d (12½p) (Figures 6.12(a) and (b).) Despite its improvements in living conditions the Company continued to be known by its traditional nickname 'Lousy Lyles'.

In the inter-war years the Lyle family played a lesser role in the Company's affairs. In 1920 A. P. Lyle was seventy-one and he retired to his country estate at Glendelvine, Perthshire, which he had purchased in 1905. In 1923 he contributed £50,000 towards the cost of the Scottish War Memorial in Edinburgh at a time when funds were hard to come by. In the following year he was rewarded with a baronetcy. His son, Archie, who became Sir Archibald Lyle on his father's death in 1933, preferred the life of a country gentleman and public servant to that of business man. He was well known as a 'respected laird, gallant soldier and versatile sportsman'. He won a Military Cross during the First World War and from 1923-28 commanded the Scottish Horse, a territorial regiment.[37] Although he was Chairman of Lyle Shipping Co., he left the management of the concern in the capable hands of James Shearer. Colonel

Figure 6.13
Colonel Peter Macfarlane, Director and later Chairman of Lyle Shipping Co., photographed in the uniform of the Royal Artillery during the Second World War.

Macfarlane did not have an executive role after the First World War but continued to take a keen interest in the Company, its ships and their crews; the Company remembers him as 'the Sailor Colonel'. (Figure 6.13.)

The record of Lyle Shipping Co. from 1920 to 1939 represented a considerable achievement. Where others failed, the Company succeeded. Astute management, fortified by the support of the Lithgow brothers, allowed the Company to withstand the knocks and win the bouquets.

7. 1939-1952
The Burdens of War

The Lyle fleet's losses during the Second World War were heavier than the losses between 1914 and 1918. Of the ten ships in the Company's fleet at the outbreak of war, nine had been lost by 1945. Moreover, five of the twenty-two ships which passed into the Company's service during the war years were sunk before the end of hostilities. The experience of Lyle Shipping Co. was similar to that of many of its competitors. During the first three years of the war, the Atlantic was one of the main battlegrounds, where the Axis powers were determined to cut Britain's supply routes and starve it into submission. The Allies were equally determined to preserve these routes, and their eventual victory depended in great measure on the heroism and fortitude of their merchant seamen.

Immediately upon the outbreak of war the Lyle fleet was depleted by the requisitioning of the *Lycia* and the *Cape Howe I* for service in the Royal Navy. At the opening of hostilities they were joined by the *Cape Sable II*. This ship and the *Cape Howe I*, renamed H.M.S. *Prunella* and H.M.S. *Cyprus*, were converted into 'Q' ships (merchant ships with concealed armament) for use in the campaign against the 'U' boat (Figure 7.1). They were equipped with Asdic gear, four torpedo tubes, depth charge throwers, and six 4.7 inch guns, and crewed by 230 men compared with the normal trading complement of 36 seafarers. A few days before the declaration of war the *Cape Sable II* was ordered to discharge her cargo of phosphate at Kotka in Finland and proceed to Portsmouth to be handed over to the Royal Navy. While sailing through the Baltic on her way to Newcastle she was interrogated by a German destroyer and later mock-attacked by German fighter planes at 0600 on 3 September when her crew were still uncertain whether Britain was at war. They were left in no doubt at 1100 when a message was received that war had been declared, and immediately the direction-finding aids were closed down to prevent detection by enemy aircraft. As a result the ship lost its way in fog, but arrived safely off the Tyne instead of the Forth, its intended destination. By coincidence its escort to Portsmouth was provided by the newly converted *Cape Howe I*. The crew were dismayed by this choice since they had always considered the *Cape Howe I* an inferior ship. This was confirmed shortly after leaving Newcastle when the *Cape Howe I* was unable to maintain company with her charge. The

Figure 7.1
The *Cape Sable II* photographed in the Mediterranean during the Second World War. In 1939 she was converted for war use and is seen here with a four inch gun and an oerlikon gun mounted aft. Her life rafts are prominent.

Figure 7.2
Cape Sable II painting ship at San Pedro, in the 1940s.

crew of the *Cape Sable II* saw the *Cape Howe I* entering the Portsmouth break-water as their train departed to take them to Scotland on leave.

The *Cape Sable II* (H.M.S. *Cyprus*) and the *Cape Howe I* (H.M.S. *Prunella*) were clumsy in their new role as 'Q' ships. In June 1940 H.M.S. *Prunella* was torpedoed and sunk off Iceland, while hunting German submarines. H.M.S. *Cyprus*, having proved herself ineffective as an Armed Merchant Cruiser, was refitted as a merchant ship in 1942. She was not returned to Lyles until 1946. (Figure 7.2) The *Lycia*, transferred to the Miscellaneous Naval Service, was used for general purpose duties before being sunk early in 1941 as a blockship to protect Scapa Flow where the battleship *Royal Oak* had been sunk at her moorings in 1939.

Figure 7.3
(a) *Cape Wrath IV* entering Havana, Cuba, during the Second World War.
(b) *Cape Wrath IV*, a dual fired steamship, built and joint owned by Lithgows, photographed on her trials in 1940. A gun is mounted in the stern and the large white cross was used for convoy station keeping at night when vessels steamed without lights.

Figure 7.4

Cape Hawke I and *Cape Rodney II* during a post war refit in the fitting out basin of D. & W. Henderson Ltd, Glasgow.

Shortly after the beginning of hostilities the Ministry of War Transport opened negotiations with the United States of America for purchase of ships to relieve Britain's pressing shortage of tonnage. Early in 1940 agreement was reached and a large batch of ships was purchased by the Ministry. Four of these vessels, the *Empire Buffalo*, the *Empire Mermaid*, the *Empire Puma* and the *Empire Steelhead*, were placed under Lyle's management to compensate the Company for its requisitioned ships. These had been ordered during the First World War by the United States Shipping Board as part of its emergency war loss replacement programme and completed in 1919 and 1920, and by 1940 they were semi-obsolete.

Meanwhile, in the expectation of the large profits which had been made during the First World War, Lyle Shipping Co. had come to an agreement with Sir James and Henry Lithgow for the purchase of four ships to be built at Lithgow's Port Glasgow yard. In June 1940 the Lyle fleet was reinforced by the delivery of the first of these vessels, the *Cape Wrath IV* (Figure 7.3(a) and (b)). She was followed by her sister ship the *Cape Rodney I* in September 1940, at a cost of £111,831 (Figure 7.4). Both these vessels were allocated to the Cape of Good Hope Motorship Co. and were jointly owned by the Lithgow brothers and Lyle Shipping Co. A condition of this arrangement was the owners' reimbursement of the management company for any trading losses incurred.

In March 1941 the *Cape Hawke I* and *Cape Verde III* were completed. The *Cape Hawke I*, which cost £163,607, was wholly owned by the Lithgows and registered in the name of the Cape York Motorship Co. The *Cape Verde III*, which had been ordered in December 1939, cost £168,313 and was jointly owned with the Lithgows. She was placed in the Cape of Good Hope Motorship Co. under similar guarantees.

From the beginning of the war the Company's ships, like other merchant vessels, were armed. Initially, the armament typically consisted of four Ross rifles. In about 1941 Holman projectors for throwing hand grenades into the path of enemy aircraft were installed. Later that year Bofors guns were fitted. The *Cape Corso II* was the first ship to be so armed and her crew were able to repulse many enemy aircraft attacks when sailing on the United Kingdom, Gibraltar and North African routes. Such armament provided little protection from U-boat attacks.

The additions to the Cape fleet between 1939–41 barely kept pace with war losses. The *Cape York II* was sunk during an enemy aerial torpedo attack off Peterhead in August 1940, but without loss of crew. During 1941 three further ships were lost through enemy action. In February the *Cape Nelson I* was torpedoed near Iceland with the loss of four of her crew. In March the *Empire Mermaid* was torpedoed off the Hebrides and sank two days later while being towed into port. Twenty-three of her crew perished, making this the Company's first serious war casualty. In August the new *Cape Rodney I* was sunk by a

German U-boat off Ushant. All her crew were picked up.

In 1942 the enemy U-boat campaign reached its zenith when, following the entry of Japan into the war, Allied strength was stretched to its limit. In March 1942 the *Cape Horn II* caught fire while on passage to Suez with a cargo of 4–5,000 tons of ammunition and war materials. Despite the danger her crew fought the blaze for six hours until 'nearly all the after deck was red hot and buckling, the deck cargo was ablaze and fire had spread into the starboard side of the bridge deck'. Her crew then abandoned ship and were picked up by the *Clifton Hall*. Twenty minutes later the *Cape Horn II* 'blew up with a terrific explosion' and sank stern first five minutes later.[1] In May the *Empire Buffalo* was torpedoed and sunk in the Caribbean with the loss of twelve crewmen. The rest were in the water for twenty-one hours before being picked up. Soon afterwards the *Cape of Good Hope II* was torpedoed at a position North East of the Virgin Islands, on passage from New York to the Persian Gulf. Although her two boats were at sea for twelve and seventeen days before reaching land, all her crew was saved. Later in May, even worse news followed. The *Cape Corso II* was sunk by aerial torpedo North West of North Cape. She had been carrying munitions to the North Russian port of Murmansk and the freezing Arctic water claimed the lives of fifty of her crew of fifty-six. In July the *Cape Verde III*, the most recent addition to the fleet, was torpedoed near Trinidad. Two of her crew perished. The *Cape Race II* was lost off Iceland in August while on passage from America to Hull. All her crew were saved.

These losses were made good by ships placed under Lyle management by the Ministry of War Transport. In the nine months following the loss of the *Cape Race II* in August 1942, nine steamers were allocated to Lyle's management – *Ocean Traveller*, *Fort Wedderburne*, *Empire Day*, *Fort Steele*, *Fort Lajoie*, *Empire Claymore* (soon to be transferred to the Belgian government), *Fort Anne*, *Empire Farmer* and *Fort Cumberland*. All were new steamers of between 6,500 and 7,500 deadweight tons and were built as part of the Allied emergency wartime building programme. The *Ocean Traveller* and the three Empires were built in British yards and owned by the Ministry of War Transport. The Forts were 'Liberty' ships, built in Canada for the Canadian government or in the United States for the War Shipping Administration. The 'Liberty' ships were bareboat chartered to the British Ministry of War Transport, which placed them under the management of British companies.

In 1943 the tide of the Battle of the Atlantic turned in favour of the Allies. The Royal Navy, assisted by the United States Navy, formed special hunting groups to track down the U-boat 'wolf packs', with spectacular results. In addition the construction of auxiliary aircraft carriers (Figure 7.5), based on merchant ship hulls, and R.A.F. Coastal Command's increased strength in long range aircraft (equipped with depth charges since 1942) gave convoys much needed air cover in the middle of the Atlantic, where ship losses were

Figure 7.5
The *Empire MacAndrew* at anchor off Greenock sometime during the Second World War. She had a standard merchant ship hull but was completed as an auxiliary aircraft carrier. After the war she was converted to commercial use and was purchased by Lyle Shipping Co. in 1951 and renamed *Cape Grafton I*.

heaviest. As a measure of this success Lyle Shipping Co. lost no ships during 1943.

The Company was not so fortunate in 1944. The *Empire Day* was torpedoed off Zanzibar and sank almost immediately. Her crew took to the boats but the chief officer was taken aboard the German submarine and later perished when the U-boat was hunted down by Allied warships. In August 1944 the *Cape Clear III* sank after colliding with the American steamship *Henry Dearborn* in the Gulf of Suez. These losses, the last which Lyle Shipping Co. suffered in the Second World War, were soon made good. Two American-built Liberty Ships, the *Samtana* and *Samspeed* (Figure 7.6), bareboated to the Ministry of War Transport by the United States War Shipping Administration, were placed under Lyle management. In 1945 *Empire Nairobi* was placed under the Company's control together with the *Empire Teme* (formerly *Ilona Siemers*), a war

Figure 7.6
The liberty ship *Samspeed* seen in the Clyde sometime after the Second World War. In 1947
she was purchased by Lyle Shipping Co. and renamed *Cape York III*.

prize seized by the Allies at Lübeck. Meanwhile in 1944 the old *Empire Puma*,
the last of the four First World War ships in the Company's service, had been
transferred to Michalinos and Co. In 1945 the *Fort Anne* was transferred to the
Hain Steamship Co. and the *Empire Farmer* was sold to the French government.
By the close of hostilities the Lyle fleet consisted of three Cape steamers
(excluding the *Cape Sable II* which was still requisitioned by the government),
seven war built vessels managed on behalf of the government and the *Empire
Teme*, the war prize placed temporarily in Lyle's care. The fleet in 1945
exceeded the size of the 1939 fleet by one vessel.

    As a result of its management work on behalf of the government, the cash
position of Lyle Shipping Co. was considerably strengthened. During the war
the Company's reserves built up rapidly as payments were received for war
losses (based on book value and a compensation for replacement value) and as
retained profits were accumulated. In 1939 the Company's 'cash-in-hand'

amounted to £78,573: by 1945 it equalled £564,883. In the same period the value of the Company's investments rose from £103,859 to £509,200.

The extraordinary conditions in the ship purchase market made it difficult for the Company to employ these funds to buy new or second-hand tonnage. The government controlled Britain's shipyards as effectively as it did the country's shipping industry. In the hope of obtaining 'further financial interest in shipping property' Lyle approached the Lithgows in 1941,[2] with a view to purchasing a stake in the *Cape Hawke I*, which the shipbuilders wholly owned, but Sir James Lithgow (then Controller of Merchant Shipbuilding) was 'not disposed to sell anything at present'.[3] However in September 1941 government permission was obtained to build the *Cape Howe II*, a 7,000 ton steamship, on joint account with the Lithgows at a cost of £162,000. The ship was delivered in 1943 (Figure 7.7). This was the only ship acquired by Lyle Shipping Co. between 1940 and late 1945. As part of its plan for transition to peacetime working in 1942 the government had placed a number of its Empire steamers on the market, for delivery at the end of the war. Lyle Shipping Co. offered to purchase the *Empire Day*, built in 1941, for £185,000 but the ship sank.[4]

The anticipation of large wartime profits which had led Lyles to step up the shipbuilding programme in late 1939 did not materialize. The government had also learned from the experience of the First World War, and from September

Figure 7.7
Cape Howe II painted battleship grey for war services and armed with a stern gun and special mountings for the rapid launching of life rafts in case of a sudden fatal attack.

1939 imposed a licensing system to enable it to obtain the quality of tonnage it required and to control the level of freight rates. At its monthly meeting in December 1939 the Lyle Board considered 'the increasing control of British merchant shipping by the government's frequent refusal to license ships and to the tendency for them to direct ships to certain loading ports at regular rates of freight fixed by the Ministry of Shipping'.[5] Despite these measures, however, the government was unable to call up sufficient tonnage to trade on dangerous routes at the rates it was prepared to pay, especially when shipowners could obtain higher rates on non-government service. On 4 January 1940, the government abandoned the licensing system in favour of direct requisitions. The Lyle Directors noted that requisitioning was 'now taking the place of the licensing and directed system and that a great many ships had already been requisitioned'. They foresaw that 'the system will soon be extended until all British ships are so treated'.[6]

Although certain sections of the shipping community were dissatisfied with the position, requisitioning had been extended to the entire British merchant fleet by August 1940. For the remainder of the war, the Ship Management Division of the Ministry of War Transport supervised the employment of tramp shipping, chartered foreign shipping, purchased new tonnage, and controlled the City Central Chartering Office.[7] All British ships were chartered by the government at freight rates which allowed owners a profit of 5 per cent on the agreed value of each ship, plus a depreciation allowance of 5 per cent. The depreciation provision compared favourably with the experience of most shipowners in the pre-war years. The shipowners received a fee based on average management costs in previous years; the fee was not intended to yield a profit. As it was beyond the resources of most tramp shipowners to arrange for the additional wartime duties of assembling and loading cargoes, control of their ships was given to the more organized liner companies. The ships owned by Lyle Shipping Co. and its subsidiaries were not affected by the transfer. The Company's achievement between the wars, together with the influence of James Shearer and Sir James Lithgow (with his government connections), ensured that the Company retained its ship management function throughout the war years.

Between 1939 and 1945 stringent government control allowed the Lyle Shipping Co. to record only modest profits. A Lyle prospectus published in 1953 recorded the 'very adverse effect on earnings' from wartime controls. Although the number of ships owned by Lyle Shipping Co. and its subsidiaries fell from ten to four between 1939 and 1945, net voyage profits dropped by 81 per cent from £41,995 to a mere £8,158. In the same year the book value of the Lyle owned ships fell from £150,000 to £40,000 as a result of wartime losses and the favourable depreciation allowance. The drop in voyage profits was only partially offset by a rise in income from management fees. During the war years, as the government placed more ships in the Lyle fleet, the fees received rose from £9,532 in 1940 to £14,804 in 1945. Despite the growth of the Company's investments from £103,859 to £557,839 (mostly war bonds) and its cash balances from £78,575 to £216,302, interest payments only increased from £8,286 in 1939–40 to £10,031 in 1944–45. This was due to the rigorous government control of other industries and of the capital markets.

Increases in investment income, interest on bank loans and management fees failed entirely to compensate for the decline in voyage profits. Despite an increase in the Company's gross tangible assets from £440,908 to £1,267,089 between 1939–40 and 1944–45, Lyle Shipping Co.'s profits before tax and the payment of interest fell from £50,618 to £23,986. The growth in the Company's gross tangible assets resulted from the excess of compensation payments for war losses over book values, and by a rise in turnover. Consequently, profits as a percentage of gross tangible assets fell from 11.5 per cent in 1939–40 to 1.9 per cent in 1944–45. The government permitted dividends of 7.5 per cent to be paid in all the war years and provision for depreciation to be made at the rate of 5 per cent (Table 7.1).

At the end of the war the return to peacetime conditions was more expeditious than in 1919. By the close of 1945 most of the government's restrictions on tramp shipping had been considerably relaxed. The years following the Allied victory were boom years, reflecting the efficacy of strict wartime controls and the American government's rapid reconstruction of Western Europe. Between 1924 and 1945 profits per ton of ship made by a cross-section of tramp shipping companies rose above £2 in only one year (1938). In nine of the twenty-two years they were below £1. In 1946 profits per ton of ship rose to £2.93 and then to £7.18, £7.77, £5.82 and £4.16 in the following four years up until 1950 (Table 7.2). The prolonged boom confirmed the worst fears of the shipowners who recalled the fortunes lost by reckless speculation during the 1918–20 boom. Their uncertainty was increased by long delivery dates quoted by shipbuilders adding to the risk that new tonnage would be completed after the boom had passed. After 1945 shipbuilders order books were swelled by orders for liners and tankers which were in short supply and by an inflow of orders from overseas.

The problems which confronted the Lyle Board in 1945 were similar to those which its predecessor had faced in 1918. During the war the fleet had been virtually wiped out and as a result insurance payments had accumulated. By 1946 the Company's investments and cash balances stood at £1,074,083. The Board had to decide if these should be used to finance new construction. In 1918 fortuitously, the Lyle Board had erred on the side of caution and had benefited accordingly. By contrast, in 1945 it pursued a vigorous investment programme and would reap similar rewards.

In late 1945 the Company agreed with the Lithgow brothers to take a half interest, at a cost of £132,545, in the motorship, *Cape Ortegal II* (Figure 7.8).

Table 7.1

Financial Structure of the Company, 1939–1952

Year	Gross tangible assets	Net tangible assets	Profit before tax and interest	Net current assets	Profit as a percentage of gross tangible assets	Depreciation as a percentage of book value	Book value of fleet	Percentage Dividend
1939–40	£440,908	£345,241	£50,618	£125,159	11.5	7.3	£150,000	7½
1940–1	580,524	389,443	53,219	100,304	9.2	13.6	110,000	7½
1941–2	804,061	421,134	36,703	123,927	4.6	17.1	87,500	7½
1942–3[1]	—	—	32,158	—	—	—	—	7½
1943–4	1,041,240	784,054	22,158	599,861	2.1	5.7	42,400	7½
1944–5	1,267,089	767,982	23,986	587,330	1.9	6.6	40,000	7½
1945–6	1,800,793	713,906	28,898	535,927	1.6	6.7	37,500	7½
1946–7	1,831,487	1,231,346	146,425	541,279	8.0	5.9	330,000	10
1947–8	1,935,306	576,400	210,743	543,127	10.9	4.7	667,052	10
1948–9	1,269,289	842,590	116,795	217,184	9.2	0	408,000	10
1949–50	1,189,104	763,404	45,300	322,376	3.8	18.1	369,277	10
1950–1	1,154,104	868,966	64,666	405,595	5.6	0	941,283	15
1951–2	2,222,579	1,866,193	406,432	997,918	18.3	54.0	660,911	15

[1] A balance sheet was not made up in 1942–3

Source: Lyle Shipping Co., Annual Reports, 1940–52

Table 7.2

Comparative Profitability of the Lyle Shipping Co., 1940–50

Year	Number of tramp ships in sample	Tonnage of sample of tramps	Voyage profits made by sample of tramps	Profit per ton of ship made by tramp ship sample	Tonnage of Lyle-owned ships	Voyage profit of Lyle-owned ships[1]	Lyle voyage profit per ton of ship
1940	289	1,373,310	£1,736,263	£1.26	15,819	£45,364	£2.87
1941	214	1,034,249	£1,924,369	£1.86	12,012	£28,239	£2.35
1942	206	986,705	£1,575,303	£1.60	4,398	£18,909	£4.3
1943	210	1,019,550	£1,553,067	£1.52	4,398	£7,884	£1.79
1944	235	1,127,744	£1,355,389	£1.20	4,398	£8,158	£1.85
1945	171	858,302	£1,457,883	£1.69	4,398	£13,796	£3.1
1946	131	739,479	£2,169,300	£2.93	26,044	£120,850	£4.64
1947	153	848,487	£6,088,667	£7.18	26,044	£182,415	£7.0
1948	155	883,766	£6,863,104	£7.77	33,218	£139,856	£4.2
1949	150	856,186	£4,984,542	£5.82	40,681	£27,354	£0.67
1950	165	986,082	£4,100,991	£4.16	40,641	£51,283	£1.26

[1] In 1949 and 1950 'voyage profits' also include fees received for the management of ships.

Source: Fairplay's Annual Summary of British Shipping Finance and Lyle Shipping Co., Annual Reports.

Figure 7.8
Cape Ortegal II, built in 1946 by Lithgows Ltd, leaving Capetown heavily laden.

The Lithgows were keen to build a further ship, but the Company was less enthusiastic. The Lyle Directors would only agree to the venture if the Lithgows sold them half its interest in the *Cape Hawke I*, which it had placed under Lyle management in 1941. James Shearer wrote to Henry Lithgow 'we feel that as a matter of long policy, with so many uncertain commercial factors and chiefly the American and British Government surplus tonnage, a better balance would be preserved in the value of our fleet if we had something to mix with the new ships thereby assisting towards a lower average'.[8] He continued that 'from the angle of risks, coupled with the keeping down of capital costs, the bringing in of the half ownership of the *Cape Hawke I* would be of considerable value'. The Lithgows agreed, the Lyle Shipping Co. obtained a half interest in its *Hawke I* for £62,000,[9] and the construction of the new motorship, later named *Cape Rodney II*, was put in hand at a cost of £241,179. This price reflected the rise in building costs during the Second World War. By the end of 1945 the Company had committed itself to expenditure of £315,314. It is doubtful

Figure 7.9
The motorship, *Cape Grenville I*, on trials in the Clyde in 1949.

Figure 7.10
Cape Franklin I, built in Canada in 1943 as the *Fort Cumberland* and purchased by Lyle Shipping
Co. in 1950, passing the *Pauline Friederick* in the English Channel in the early 1950s.

whether such large investment would have been undertaken had the Lithgows not been prepared to share the risks.

The Company's acquisition of older tonnage was more ambitious, and the Cape fleet continued to trade at close to its wartime strength. At the end of the war the Lyle Shipping Co. managed nine steamers owned by the British, Canadian or United States governments. The *Empire Nairobi* and *Empire Teme* were returned to the British government in 1946 but the other ships continued under the Company's management until 1947 or 1948. In this way the fleet's strength was maintained in the immediate post-war years. However, between 1946 and 1952, encouraged by the continued buoyancy of the freight market, the Lyle Board purchased four of these ships when their return to their owners was due, together with three other war-built ships which had not been under Lyle control. In early 1947 the Company bought the *Samtana* and *Samspeed* from the Ministry of War Transport for a total price of £300,000.[10] They were relatively modern ships and their purchase price at £20 per gross ton was a bargain. They were renamed *Cape Verde IV* and *Cape York III*. Likewise three months later the *Ocean Traveller*, managed by the Lyle Shipping Co. since 1942, was acquired from the Ministry of War Transport for £115,500.[11] She was renamed *Cape Corso III*. In January 1948 the *Ocean Vulcan*, which had previously been managed by Idwal Williams and Co., was purchased from the Ministry for £182,000 and renamed *Cape Nelson II*.[12] In 1947 the Lithgows and the Lyle Shipping Co., mindful of the 'not unfavourable outlook' agreed to build on joint account a new motorship at a cost of £311,684 for delivery in late 1949.[13] The vessel, which displaced 7,463 gross tons, was named *Cape Grenville I* (Figure 7.9). Two years later, in 1950, the *Fort Cumberland*, which had been under the Company's management since 1943, was purchased for £83,500 and renamed *Cape Franklin I*[14] (Figure 7.10). She carried several cargoes of buses from Bristol to Havana (Figures 7.11(a) and (b)).

This rapid increase in the Company's ship purchase commitments accelerated when ships in the Cape fleet were transferred from part-ownership to full ownership in 1950. After the death of Henry Lithgow (Figure 7.12) in 1948, his trustees were obliged to pay death duties of £2,790,909 on his estate. So as to avoid incurring interest on that sum the trustees borrowed £1,935,000 from companies with which Henry Lithgow had been associated. This loan included £130,000 from the Lyle Shipping Co. and its subsidiaries. By the end of March 1950 the Company's loan had been cancelled by the transfer of Henry's 50 per cent share in the Cape of Good Hope Motorship Co. and the Lithgows' interests in all but two of the five motorships in the Lyle fleet (the *Cape Hawke* and the *Cape Ortegal II*). The remaining shares of Sir James Lithgow, a staunch ally of the Lyle Shipping Co., were sold to Lithgows Ltd on his death in 1952.

The reconstruction of the Lyle fleet after the war did not, however, provide the Company with the type of modern fleet which could sustain a competitive

Figure 7.11

(a) *Bristol* buses for Cuba being loaded on board the *Cape Franklin I* at the Royal Edward Dock, Avonmouth, March 1951.

(b) *Cape Franklin I*, fully laden with a further cargo of buses for Cuba, being towed out of Avonmouth docks by the tug *Kingsnorth* in September 1951.

Figure 7.12
Lady Lithgow launching the *Cape Clear III* from Lithgows Ltd's Port Glasgow Yard in 1939, watched by Colonel P.C. Macfarlane (left) and Henry Lithgow (right).

challenge in the overstocked shipping market of the post-war years. By the end of the 1940s the diesel engine had long established its superiority over steam power. This, together with anticipation of 'the considerable sums which the war-built (steam) ships would cost for upkeep and repair in the coming years',[15] forced the Company to initiate a limited renewal programme. In 1951 the *Cape Verde IV* (formerly *Samtana*) and the *Cape York III* (formerly *Samspeed*) were placed on the market. Panamanian owners made an offer of £515,000 for the *Cape Verde IV*, but the deal fell through, although the Company received £50,000 in compensation,[16] and the ship was retained in the fleet until 1957. Late in 1951 the *Cape York III* was sold to Italian owners for £560,000.[17] At the same time the *Cape Corso III* was put up for sale but no buyer could be found.[18] The Company had missed its chance. By early 1952 the second-hand ship sale market was inactive, Greek and Italian buyers apparently having exhausted their funds.[19]

Despite the failure to sell a second vessel, Lyle Shipping Co. bought two motorships, *Derryheen* and *Derryclare*, from McCowen and Gross Ltd for £1,170,000 in early 1952.[20] Although these vessels had been built in 1943 and 1946 respectively they were powered by Doxford diesel engines. They were renamed *Cape Clear IV* and *Cape Grafton I* and proved themselves most flexible and economic in operation. Between 1946 and 1952 the book value of the Lyle fleet had risen from £37,500 to £660,000.

In 1951 the modernization of the Cape fleet was taken a step further. The high freight rates current after the outbreak of the Korean War in June 1950 caused many owners throughout the shipping world to order new tonnage. British shipbuilders' order books lengthened, and Sir James Lithgow advised the Lyle Directors to reserve berths in his yards if they wanted new tonnage completed by the mid-1950s. Berths for two motorships were accepted, but no formal orders were placed until 1953. In 1950 the Lyle Board expanded its ship management business. The steamers *Table Bay* and *Durban Bay* were taken under management on behalf of the Western Canada Steamship Co. High crew costs made it prohibitively expensive for their owners to operate them under the Canadian flag, as Canadian law required that only Canadian nationals could be employed.

After 1945 Lyles benefited fully from the rise in freight rates. Profits, before tax and interest, advanced from £28,898 in 1945–46 to £146,425 in 1946–47. The upward trend continued in 1947–48 when profits reached £210,743. Thereafter, they fell back to £45,300 in 1949–50, before rising again to reach £406,432 in 1951–52. Return on gross tangible assets increased from less than 2 per cent during the war years to 8 per cent in 1946–47 and then to 10.9 per cent in 1947–48 before falling off to 3.8 per cent in 1949–50. In 1950–51 returns improved and by 1951–52 reached 18.3 per cent, the highest level recorded since 1920. As a result of this high profitability dividends of 10 per cent were paid between 1946–47 and 1949–50, rising to 15 per cent in the following two years (see Table 7.1).

Voyage profits and management fees increased from £28,282 in 1945–46 to £144,639 in the following year. In 1947–48 they stood at £213,414 before falling to £27,354 in 1949–50 when freight rates suddenly collapsed. With the outbreak of the Korean War in June 1950 the market recovered to meet increased world demand and by 1952 voyage profits and management fees had risen to £423,118. Income from investments also improved after the war but it did not make a substantial contribution to profits as these assets were progressively reduced from £509,200 in 1945–46 to £120,734 in 1949–50 to release funds to rebuild the fleet and to purchase the Lithgows' shares. Income rose from £10,630 in 1945–46 to £17,233 in 1948–49 but dipped thereafter to £12,636 in 1951–52. As neither the balance sheets of the Cape of Good Hope Co. nor the Cape York Motorship Co. survive, it is impossible to determine their contribution to the profits of the parent Company.

During the war years the Company's profitability compared favourably with that of other tramp ship companies. Between 1940 and 1946 profits per ton of ship owned by Lyles were consistently above the profits of a large sample of tramp ships operated by other owners. Between 1946 and 1950 the position was reversed and in 1949 and 1950 the comparative performance of Lyles was markedly poorer. Profits per ton obtained by other owners were £5.82 and £4.16 while the Company's profits equalled just £0.67 and £1.26 (see Table 7.2).

With its enlarged peacetime fleet, and with its profitability under pressure, the internal financing of the Company's assets could not be maintained indefinitely. In 1951, the Lyle Board considered a public flotation of the Company's shares. In the late 1940s when freight rates were buoyant the market value of ships rose to a level well in excess of book value. The *Cape York III*, for example, had been purchased for about £150,000 in 1947 and was sold five years later for £560,000. As a result, the potential death duty liabilities on shareholders' estates rose to such an extent that the Company could not have remained as a private limited concern in the event of the death of a major shareholder. In 1950 this was an urgent consideration. Despite the appointment to the Board of younger men – Captain (later Lieutenant Colonel) Michael Lyle, son of Sir Archibald Lyle, A. Keith Macfarlane, son of Colonel Macfarlane, William Nicholson, who had worked in Lyle's office since 1927, (all appointed in 1946), and Thomas Shearer, son of James Shearer (appointed in 1950) – two of the Company's principal shareholders, Colonel Macfarlane and James Shearer, were then over seventy years old.

The experience of the Lyle family had provided a foretaste of the difficulties which might arise. During the war Sir Archibald Lyle's eldest sons, Ian and Robin, were killed in action and Sir Archibald himself died in 1946. After suffering such grievous losses, the Lyle family was required to make a crippling financial sacrifice. The family paid death duties on all three lives totalling a seven figure sum. The risk of incurring further death duties made it impossible for the Company to continue the business on its traditional basis; the tax structure had become a decisive obstacle to the establishment or progress of heavily capitalized private concerns, especially where the owners were too old to take out large life assurance cover. Although the Lyle family retained Sir Archibald's shares in the business, Mrs. Bankier (Robin Lyle's widow) sold many of the shares which her husband had inherited from his grandfather, Sir Alexander Lyle. Existing shareholders, or their relatives, purchased these shares but their resources were insufficient to acquire a larger batch, especially at their inflated price of over £200 per £100 share in the early 1950s.

The Board examined four solutions to this problem. The Company could 'go public'; it could be sold as an entity to a shipping company in need of modern tonnage; the fleet could be sold and the business liquidated, which would provide shareholders with their highest return; or one of the subsidiary companies could be retained and the rest of the Company sold. Advice was sought from Sir Ian Bolton, a distinguished Scottish accountant and one of Henry Lithgow's trustees. Glasgow Industrial Finance Ltd was asked to examine the feasibility of floating 30 per cent of the Company's equity and in the end this solution was adopted.

At an extraordinary general meeting of the Company in January 1953 a resolution was passed for the capitalisation from reserves of £750,000. This was used for paying up 500,000 unissued ordinary shares of 50p (10s) each and 500,000 preference shares of £1 each. These were then allocated to shareholders in the proportion of one new ordinary share and one preference share for each ordinary share held. In February the remaining ordinary shares were offered for sale at £1.02½ (£1:0:6d) per share and the preference shares were offered for sale at their par value of £1. Mr. (later Sir) Iain Stewart, the Managing Director of the Glasgow engineering company Thermotank Ltd, was invited to join the Board as an outside non-executive Director with the approval of Glasgow Industrial Finance Ltd. It is a tribute to Lyle Shipping Co.'s management that the share issue was six times over-subscribed and was apportioned in no less than 13,000 lots. The influence of the Lyle, Macfarlane and Shearer families remained dominant. After the sale, they still held 328,440, 240,880 and 74,200 ordinary shares respectively[21] and so retained voting control of the Company.

In 1903, when the public flotation of the first Lyle Shipping Co. had been considered, A. P. Lyle had rejected the option on the grounds that 'we had never been this type of shipowners. We had always owned the tonnage we managed'.[22] Fifty years later, after a massive expansion in its business commitments, Lyle did both own and manage the fleet of Cape ships. However, it had become essential to widen the capital base of the Company to safeguard its survival. The experiences of the Second World War and its aftermath were crucial to this transition. The Company had taken on heavy responsibilities of ownership and management during the war, and had then chosen to maintain and extend its commitments after the war. Yet retained profits and the link with the Lithgows could not be expected to support this burden in the long-term, as the fall in profits and the death of Henry Lithgow in 1948 had demonstrated. If the Company was to maintain its ownership of the Cape fleet and to exploit its increased management expertise, the introduction of external capital was a logical step.

While the restructuring of the Company had become a high priority by 1952, a question mark hung over the prospects of the Lyle fleet. During the immediate post-war years high freight rates had induced many tramp ship-owners throughout the world to order new tonnage. Between 1948 and 1950 the total world dry cargo fleet grew from some 54.2 million deadweight tons to 60.8 million deadweight tons. Yet British owners, with a caution born of their experiences in the inter-war years, did not expand or modernize their fleets at anything like the rate of their competitors, and the United Kingdom dry cargo fleet only increased from 13.6 million deadweight tons to 13.9 million dead-

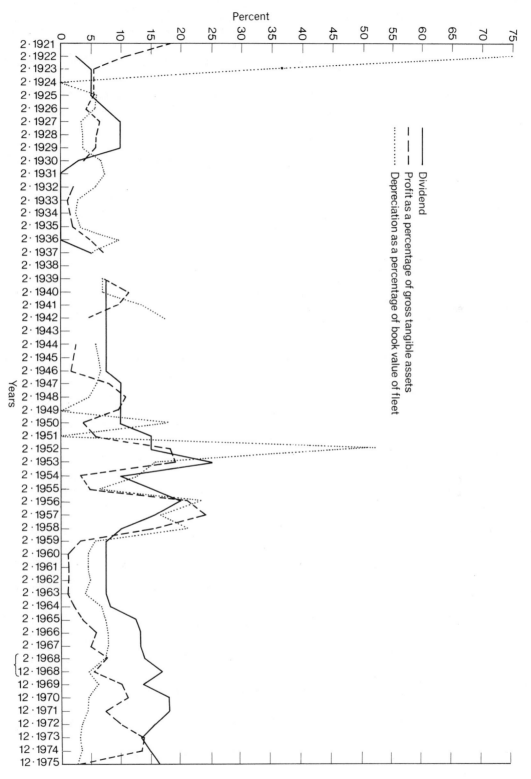

Percent

Dividend

Profit as a percentage of gross tangible assets

Depreciation as a percentage of book value of fleet

Years

Table 7.3

weight tons. Lyle Shipping Co. pursued a more vigorous course than most of its British competitors, but the overseas competition, especially from Norway, set a demanding pace in the shipbuilding and chartering markets. As the new Company opened for business in January 1953, the outcome of this international contest for shipping business was giving all British owners serious cause for concern.

8. 1953-1963
A Shipping Revolution

In its first years as a public company, Lyle Shipping Co. witnessed major structural changes in world seaborne trade. Between 1950 and 1960 the total dry cargo carried rose from about 300 million tonnes a year to almost 550 million tonnes, while the world trade in crude petroleum increased from about 225 million tonnes to nearly 550 million tonnes. These developments were accompanied by a shift in the pattern of dry cargo trade. The coal trade, which had been the staple export of the United Kingdom since the late nineteenth century, was totally eclipsed by the rapid growth of the petroleum trade. As a result the European share of imports and exports of dry cargo, which accounted for 48 per cent of the world trade in 1938, fell to 33 per cent by 1967 and that of Asia and the Far East grew from 16 per cent to 28 per cent, partly reflecting the expansion of the Japanese economy.

These changes were paralleled by profound alterations in the world shipping industry. Although the United Kingdom fleet increased from about 17 million gross tons in 1939 to just over 20 million tons in the 1960s, its share of the industry as a whole fell from 28 per cent in 1939 to 11.5 per cent in 1968.[1] Apart from the sharp rise in the size of the Liberian fleet, the fleets of Japan and Norway dramatically increased in size and importance during the period. In the Far East, for example, the growth of the Japanese Mitsui Line posed a serious threat to the old-established conference system in the mid-1950s. In addition in the dry cargo market many of the developing countries established their own fleets, often requiring exporters to ship 50 per cent of their goods in domestic tonnage.

The structure of the shipping industry also changed. The old distinctions between liner companies (operating regular runs on fixed routes carrying passengers and parcels of general cargo) and tramping companies (operating no fixed routes and carrying mainly commodity cargoes) became less obvious. The introduction of reliable air transport, especially from the late 1950s, considerably reduced the passenger market for liners notably in the North American and Indian routes. More seriously, air freight robbed the cargo liner companies of their most profitable payloads. This combination of circumstances allowed

Table 8.1

World Seaborne Trade by Weight, 1937–1974

Year	Dry Cargo[1] mn. metric tonnes	Tanker Cargo[2] mn. metric tonnes	Total mn. metric tonnes
1937	375	105	480
1950	299	225	524
1955	450	380	800
1960	540	540	1,080
1964	720	790	1,510
1965	775	862	1,637
1966	820	950	1,770
1967	858	1,017	1,875
1968	930	1,141	2,071
1969	999	1,276	2,275
1970	1,123	1,440	2,563
1971	1,136	1,526	2,661
1972	1,180	1,654	2,834
1973	1,364	1,867	3,231
1974	1,410	1,838	3,248

Source: United Nations Statistics

[1] Includes some liquid cargo other than petroleum.

[2] Crude petroleum and refined petroleum products excluding bunkers and those products not generally carried by tanker, namely paraffin wax, petroleum coke, asphalt and lubricating oil which are included as dry cargo.

Table 8.2

Geographical Distribution of World Seaborne Trade by Weight

Area	1938	1967
Europe	48%	33%
N. America	20%	19%
Asia	16%	28%
S. America	8%	9%
Africa	6%	9%
Australia	2%	2%

Source: United Nations Statistics

Notes. 1. N. America comprises the U.S.A. and Canada; S. America includes the central American and Caribbean countries.

2. Europe includes Turkey and the U.S.S.R.

3. Asia includes the Near East but excludes China, Mongolia, North Korea and North Vietnam, for which statistics are not available.

tramp ships to operate as auxiliary cargo liners. As a result liner companies
chartered far more tramp ships than ever before and some set up their own
wholly-owned tramping subsidiaries.

At the same time the rationalism of other industries and the drive towards
greater efficiency of operations had a major impact on world shipping practice.
The emergence of large industrial groups (like Rank, Hovis, McDougall Ltd,
and Tate and Lyle in the United Kingdom) led to streamlining of their shipping
requirements, with the emphasis on larger shipments which could be speedily
loaded and unloaded at newly established bulk terminals with extensive
storage facilities. Some commodities, particularly sugar, which had previously
been shipped in bags, switched to bulk shipments to take advantage of the extra
efficiency. This increased the average loading rate of sugar from 300 tons per
day in some ports to 20,000 tons per day in ports with bulk loading equipment. Special power-operated cranes with grabs, either fitted on the ship or
installed on the quayside, also helped to decrease greatly the discharging
time.[2]

However, the economies achieved by specialized loading and discharging
equipment depended on the individual ports visited. As late as 1965 *Cape
Wrath V* was discharging a cargo of oats in Italy into small, open carts pulled
by emaciated donkeys. On that occasion the master, mindful of the costs of
many days' delay, took the donkeys' condition to heart and helped them to help
themselves. Consequently, as discharging progressed the donkeys became
plumper and fitter, and worked harder. The out-turn of cargo showed a loss
of 10 tons but this was considered by the master as good business and he
consequently made no demur when accused of landing his cargo short
weight.

The concept of a single-deck ship was not new, and some owners had successfully operated single deckers over many years. The growing popularity of
bulk-carriers followed upon the decline in the use of 'tween-deck designs for
carrying profitable payloads of small parcels of goods. The increased efficiency
of operations brought about the decline of the 'tween-decker and its replacement by the single-deck bulkcarrier, whose wider hatches, and unobstructed
box-like holds substantially reduced loading and discharging times and thus
made more efficient use of the expensive ship and port facilities. The larger size
of shipments also led to larger ships with lower freight costs per ton.

In addition the larger industrial groupings buying on contract from pro-
ducers displaced many of the old merchant companies which had traditionally
purchased commodities on the 'spot' market. This had a far reaching effect on
the character of the tramp shipping market during the 1950s. Although
companies like Lyle had negotiated time charters with liner companies since the
1920s, the majority of tramp steamers still undertook extended voyages picking
up cargoes from merchants and brokers on the spot market. A typical voyage

Figure 8.1

Lake Minnewanka entering Capetown with a cargo of timber in the late 1950s. This vessel was owned by Western Canada Steamships Ltd, and managed by Lyle Shipping Co. between 1954 and 1960

might have been to ballast from the United Kingdom to the River Plate to load grain for Japan, followed by a ballast voyage to Canada to load lumber and paper products for Australia. More grain might be loaded there for India, followed by a ballast voyage to Aden to load salt for Japan, and another ballast voyage to Fiji to load sugar home to the United Kingdom where the crew would be changed. In the 1950s the predominance of spot fixtures was overtaken by time charters with liner shipping companies or directly with cargo owners, even for as long as ten years, and more importantly for the future to contracts of affreightment whereby 'a ship operator undertakes to carry great quantities of a product on a particular route or routes (in several consignments) over a period of time using ships of his own choice which are not necessarily specified in the contract'.[3] In the prevailing market conditions these developments gave charterers keener rates for the larger total quantities involved and also allowed them to be certain of their shipment costs long in advance to help their pricing to their own customers. However, as a corollary, they then needed to deal with reliable shipping companies whose fleets were large enough to ensure them a regular service.

During the early 1950s, although the Lyle Board realized that the creation of a modern and flexible fleet was essential to the long-term profitability of the Company, it failed, like many of its competitors, to recognize the revolution in shipping operations or to capitalize fully on the rapid post-war expansion of world shipping services. Many British owners, recalling the sudden fall in freight rates in 1920, found it hard to believe that the dry cargo market would continue to expand; consequently, while the world dry cargo fleet grew from 60.8 million deadweight tons in 1952 to 81.9 million deadweight tons in 1958, the United Kingdom fleet only expanded from 13.9 million to 14.2 million.[4] The same attitude of caution affected their decisions on the type of ship to operate. James Shearer and Colonel Macfarlane at Lyle shared this caution and the younger Directors were unable to persuade them to alter their views.

In February 1953 the Cape fleet consisted of thirteen ships, in addition to the *Table Bay* and the *Durban Bay* which had been managed on behalf of the Western Steamship Co. of Canada since 1950. This was the largest number of ships yet operated by Lyle Shipping Co., but the fleet was not modern; only six of the vessels were motorships. Ten ships were nine or more years old and, with the exception of the *Cape Sable II* which had been completed in 1936, all had been built during the Second World War. Two additional war-built steamers, the *Cape Adan* and *Cape Melan* owned by the Canadian firm of Lunham and Moore Ltd, were placed under Lyle management in 1954. This was only a short-term expedient, and both ships were sold in the following two years. Also in 1954, the Western Canada Steamship Co. placed the *Lake Minnewanka* under Lyle management but sold this ship later in the year, together with the *Durban Bay* (Figure 8.1). The *Table Bay* was operated by the Company until 1957, and in 1956 was joined by the motorship *Lake Pennask*, built in 1953 and recently purchased by the Canadian company. She was managed until 1962. These ships, which passed under Lyle management when freight rates were buoyant, gave a very profitable return to their owners, but only brought a small fixed management fee to Lyle.

The changed character of the tramp market began to be reflected in the scope of Lyle's business and the Company's innovative use of contracts of affreightment in a period of depressed freights. In the 1950s the amount of business done with the British Phosphate Commissioners increased significantly. Annual contracts began to be negotiated involving both contracts of affreightment and time charters. In 1954 the *Cape Grenville I* was chartered to the Commissioners for nine months and in the same year under a second contract Lyle agreed to carry six cargoes of phosphate from Nauru or Christmas Island to the

United Kingdom; a further contract was negotiated with other charterers for the carriage of coke in the opposite direction, from Europe to New Caledonia. In 1958 the Company contracted with the Commissioners to carry eighteen cargoes of phosphate from Nauru or Ocean Island to Australia or New Zealand. Other cargoes carried included sugar, coal, grain, lumber, paper products, wool and salt. During the 1950s time charters continued to be arranged with liner companies including the Pacific Steam Navigation Company, the Port Line, the New Zealand Shipping Co., Shaw Savill and Albion, the Palm Line and others such as the Great Lakes Shipping Corporation and Coastal Tankers Ltd. Other time charters were negotiated with companies with no shipowning interests, such as Ralli Brothers, Dreyfus and Le Nickel S.A. In the early 1950s James Shearer also reached an agreement with the Donaldson Line which had insufficient vessels to maintain its North Pacific Service and called on Lyle to fill any gaps.

During the second half of 1956 Lyle, for the first time, entered into long-term time charter commitments securing the Company's future earnings. In the early part of the year Sandy (later Sir Alexander) Glen of H. Clarkson & Co., the London firm of shipbrokers, approached his friend William Nicholson to enquire if Lyle Shipping Co. would consider building ore carriers for 'time charter' to BISC (Ore) Ltd, the shipping subsidiary of the British Iron and Steel Corporation which was responsible for arranging the importation of ore for the British steel industry. The idea of carrying ore in the Company's ships was an anathema to James Shearer, 'who considered an owner had to be in dire straits before committing himself to charter his ships for a cargo of ore. When he examined the figures and saw the benefit of a solid income over a long period, his attitude changed'.[5] During June the Board approached BISC (Ore) Ltd and proposed to form a joint holding company to build and own ore carriers.

By opening negotiations with BISC (Ore) Ltd, the Lyle Board was following the example set by others. As early as 1949 Sir James Lithgow through Lithgows Ltd, in conjunction with Charles Connell & Co., the Glasgow shipbuilders, and J. & J. Denholm Ltd, the Glasgow shipowners, had formed Scottish Ore Carriers Ltd to ensure supplies of raw materials to Colvilles Ltd, the West of Scotland steel making combine. The time charters negotiated between Colvilles and Scottish Ore Carriers had been taken over by BISC (Ore) on its formation in 1950. During that year because of the high demand for shipping as a result of the Korean War, the Corporation found itself unable to charter sufficient tonnage to meet the steel industry's requirements, and from then on, taking Sir James Lithgow's lead, negotiated a large number of time charters with various British shipping companies. Some shipping firms and shipbuilders entered into charters for between ten and fifteen years and profited handsomely from the resulting stabilization of their earnings. From 1958 to 1969 ore-carrying was the most profitable sector of the British deep sea carrying trade providing an

Table 8.3

Pre-Tax Profits of British Deep-Sea Shipping Companies after Depreciation, as a Percentage of Capital Employed

Years ended 31 March	Liners			Tramps			Tankers*
	Passenger	Passenger/ Cargo	Cargo	General purpose	Ore Carriers	Other Carriers	
1958	4.6	9.7	15.0	15.7	9.5	16.7	7.1
1959	7.2	4.7	5.8	3.3	4.3	0.0	2.8
1960	6.7	3.2	2.9	−0.6	5.0	−1.2	2.1
1961	3.7	4.0	4.2	0.1	4.3	−1.1	3.5
1962	−2.7	−0.3	1.4	−0.4	7.2	−3.2	4.8
1963	−3.8	−1.9	0.8	−2.6	9.4	0.0	6.3
1964	−2.6	0.2	2.3	−1.5	10.7	0.0	4.5
1965	0.2	2.3	4.0	0.9	12.2	5.0	5.1
1966	0.1	0.2	3.3	2.3	13.9	4.8	4.5
1967	−6.9	−4.1	1.8	2.5	12.3	4.2	4.0
1968	−1.5	0.0	1.9	2.5	15.7	6.2	2.9
1969	0.3	8.0	5.2	4.8	18.7	8.7	3.0

* excluding tankers owned by oil companies

average return on capital before tax of some 10 per cent per annum compared with some 3 per cent for bulkcarriers and some 4 per cent for tankers (Table 8.3). By 1966, 600,000 gross tons or twenty per cent of a sample of 3,200,000 gross tons of United Kingdom owned tramp ships taken by the British Chamber of Shipping was on time charter to BISC (Ore) Ltd.[6]

The credit squeeze of 1956 made it impossible for BISC (Ore) Ltd to finance a jointly owned company, but a chartering agreement for two vessels went forward when Lyle Shipping Co. agreed to shoulder the whole ownership of the two ships. Under the terms of the contract the two new carriers (increased to three in 1957) were to be chartered for a period of fifteen years to BISC (Ore) Ltd. They would sail in ballast out of the United Kingdom and return with ore, principally from Seven Islands in the St. Lawrence, Lower Buchanan in Liberia, Vittoria in Brazil, Murmansk in the USSR, and various North African ports. The agreement was protected by an escalation clause, whereby the charter hire was to be increased to cover any inflation in costs. These charters were to prove as remunerative to Lyle Shipping Co. in the 1960s as to the other companies sharing in this market.

For the Company and the British tramp shipping industry the BISC (Ore) charters marked the beginning of a new trend in shipping practice. For Lyle this was the first time that vessels had been designed and built against a specific time charter. As the ships were to be used solely for carrying ore into specially designed bulk terminals, equipped with purpose-built off-loading

Figure 8.2
Cape York IV photographed in the English Channel. She was completed in 1955 and was one of the last conventional 'tween deck tramp ships built by Lyle Shipping Company.

facilities, no cargo gear was needed. Large open hatches covered the simple box-like holds, and the ships' bottoms were specially strengthened to carry the heavy ore.

Although Lyle entered the ore carrying business later than some, it was able to take advantage of technical developments in ship construction. In the mid-1950s the average size of ore carrier chartered to BISC (Ore) Ltd was 9,000 deadweight tons, a size which was becoming unremunerative to operators. Consequently, in 1956, Lyle ordered from Lithgows Ltd two 16,000 deadweight ton ore carriers for delivery in 1962 and 1964. These schedules were subsequently brought forward to 1959 and 1961 owing to the cancellation of orders. In March 1957, the Company ordered a third ore carrier from Lithgows Ltd and this ship was completed in 1962. The three ore carriers differed in design.

Figure 8.3

Cape Franklin II, built by Lithgows Ltd, on trials in the Firth of Clyde in 1959. She was the first ore carrier to be owned by Lyle Shipping Co. and the first vessel in the fleet to have her engines positioned aft.

The first two, the *Cape Franklin II* and the *Cape Nelson III*, were 524.5 feet long and displaced 15,500 and 16,450 deadweight tons respectively (Figure 8.2). The *Cape Franklin II* had her engines placed aft and her bridge placed amidships, while the design of the *Cape Nelson III* was recast with both engines and bridge at the stern of the ship. She was the first truly modern vessel to enter the post-war fleet. The *Cape Howe III* with a similar layout to the *Cape Nelson III* was a much larger ship, with a capacity of 27,500 deadweight tons and measuring 608 feet in length. With the *Welsh Herald* and the *Gothland*, she was one of three large ore carriers chartered to BISC (Ore) Ltd at the time and remained the largest vessel in the Lyle fleet until the *Cape Otway* was completed in 1976.

Proposals for a similar chartering project were put to the Board in 1956. John Kilgour & Co., the Company's London shipbrokers, advised that if Lyle Shipping Co. built a 19,000 deadweight ton oil tanker a long term charter could be arranged for the vessel on very advantageous terms.[7] Although the British tanker fleet expanded by 96.6 per cent between 1948 and 1960, invest-ment in tankers did not prove attractive to many tramp companies. From the inter-war period the United Kingdom industry had been dominated by the oil companies, particularly Anglo-Persian Petroleum Ltd (later British Petroleum Ltd). For example, in 1968, 75 per cent of the United Kingdom owned and registered tanker fleet belonged to oil companies and only about 9 per cent to tramp companies.[8] This made it difficult for independent owners to find time charters and deterred small companies like Lyle Shipping Co. from buying tankers. Before the approach from Kilgour, the Lyle Board had already considered entering the tanker trade when the *Derryclare* and *Derryheen* were purchased from McCowen and Gross Ltd in 1951. An opportunity then existed for the purchase of a tanker under construction for McCowen and Gross, at a cost of £710,000.[9] In both 1951 and 1957 the Lyle Directors decided against extending their interest into this field believing that 'oil and water did not mix'. It was anticipated that the higher wages rates paid to tanker crews might lead to conflict with the crews of the Company's tramp ships.

Whereas the ore carriers reflected the changed conditions in shipping, Lyle's other investments in ships in the 1950s lagged behind the trend. The *Cape York IV* and *Cape Horn III*, which had been ordered from Lithgows Ltd in 1953 at a total price of £1,200,000, were commissioned in 1955 and 1957 respectively. Both vessels were conventional three island tramps with their engines and superstructure placed amidships. Yet the Lyle Board was already aware of the advantage of aft-located engines and superstructures, which were finding increasing favour with foreign owners. This arrangement did away with the shaft tunnel which was liable to costly damage during loading and discharging, increased discharging time, obstructed cargoes such as timber, reduced the cubic capacity available for cargo, but improved the ballasted trim of the ship. In addition the long propeller shaft was costly to manufacture and install and lost power in transmission. A delay in the construction of the *Cape Horn III* provided an opportunity to reconsider her design. Lithgows redrew her plans with her bridge and her engines positioned aft, but the original plan was reinstated when two of the Company's senior masters 'both expressed the [widely held] view that the high superstructure plus the funnel aft and the raised forecastle head forward would make the ship very unmanageable as far as docking is concerned'. They were unable to recommend the design to their Directors.[10] The cost of the *Cape York IV* and *Cape Horn III* was offset by the sale in 1956 of the *Cape Franklin I* (built in 1943), and in 1957 of the thirteen-year-old *Cape Verde IV*, which realized £515,000 (Figure 8.3).

In 1956 the Company took a further step aimed at modernizing its fleet. Initially the Board asked Lithgows Ltd to consider building a jointly owned ship, but they declined as their yards were then reserved for orders until 1965.[11] Unable to obtain berths with their traditional builders, the Lyle Board turned to William Denny Bros. Ltd of Dumbarton, who undertook to build two 14,500 deadweight tons 14 knot dry cargo ships, powered by steam turbines, for delivery in 1960 (Figure 8.4). The value of the order was £2,400,000 and follow-

Figure 8.4
The *Cape Sable III* photographed while on trials in 1960. She is notable as one of the few steam turbine tramp ships ever built. Her engines proved unsuccessful and she was disposed of in 1966.

on orders were placed for two further ships in March.[12] These first two ships, the *Cape Sable III* and *Cape Wrath V* were well above the average size of tramp ships then being operated by the British mercantile marine; foreign going tramp ships averaged only about 10,000 deadweight tons in 1959. In making this investment Lyle was ready to take advantage of an expected fluctuation in the size of parcels of goods which were acceptable to shippers and receivers.

Following the design of the *Cape Franklin II*, the *Cape Sable III* and *Cape Wrath V* had their engines placed aft and their bridge amidships. Although planned as dry cargo ships they were initially fitted out to carry motor cars from the United Kingdom to the North Pacific, returning with grain from North America. In 1958 a twelve month contract for the carriage of one cargo of motor cars per month was reached with the British Society of Motor Manufacturers and Traders Ltd. Later that year the contract was extended for two further years.[13] However, the chartering policy of the Society favoured cargo liner operators. With the decline in British car exports to the North Pacific Lyle's share of the business ceased. This meant that the outlay made on equipping the holds of the *Cape Sable III* and *Cape Wrath V* with special wooden false decks which had been designed and patented by Lyle to enable them to carry

1,000 cars was not recouped. Generally, however, the *Cape Sable III* and *Cape Wrath V* were unsuccessful; their engines proved uneconomical, and both ships were sold at a substantial loss in 1966 after only six years service.[14]

The ore carriers and the dry cargo vessels represented a heavy capital outlay, which could not be provided for out of reserves. The four dry cargo ships alone cost almost £5 million and the three ore carriers cost over £3 million. At an early stage it was agreed to finance the ore carriers by borrowing and, in 1957, £500,000 was capitalized from reserves, thereby increasing the Company's borrowing powers. The Bank of Scotland was approached and in April 1957 agreed to allow a maximum overdraft of £2 million to finance the construction of the first two ore carriers. The loan, which was secured on the ships, was to be reduced annually and liquidated over seven years.[15] This was made possible by the fifteen year charters agreed with BISC (Ore) Ltd and was the first occasion that the Company had borrowed from a financial institution to cover the building of new ships.

Between June 1956 and March 1957 Lyle Shipping Co. had undertaken to build no less than seven ships. This confidence in the future was probably based on the exceptionally large profits recorded in the previous three years rather than on the uncertainty experienced in the decade as a whole. In 1952–53, the year in which the Company went public, voyage profits reached £752,906 before depreciation, and investment 'and other' income added a further £20,563. This profit represented a return of 25.6 per cent on gross tangible assets worth £3,021,071. After the Korean War, two lean years followed. Between September 1953 and March 1954 freight rates declined sharply, especially in the North Pacific market where the Company was heavily committed. Voyage profits fell by over £500,000 to £47,519 and in the last half of the year were insufficient to cover normal depreciation. Net profit before tax and depreciation fell to £90,109 and return on gross tangible assets declined to almost 20 per cent. Consequently, a dividend of 10 per cent was paid which fell far short of the 17.5 per cent dividend forecast before going public (Table 8.1).

In the following year, 1954–55, trading conditions improved substantially and voyage profits almost doubled. The return on gross tangible assets improved by only 1.63 per cent, but this result was affected by the disruption of shipping during port strikes both at home and abroad. In the following three years, 1955–56 to 1957–58, the Company took full advantage of the buoyancy of the shipping market in the period after the closure of the Suez Canal and in the subsequent period of political uncertainty. Voyage profits rose to £1,055,488 in 1955–56 and then to £1,478,071 between 1956–57 before falling back to £1,074,497 in the following year. In 1955–56 and 1956–57 return on gross tangible assets reached 29 per cent, two of the largest returns in the Company's history, and in the following year it was 22.9 per cent. Healthy profits enabled the investment portfolio to be increased from £305,180 in 1952–53 to

£2,129,920 in 1957–58. In 1956–57 the Company had also made short-term loans of £500,000, which were increased to £850,000 in the next year. Thus investment income and interest again made a considerable contribution to the Company's profits, rising from £20,563 in 1952–53 to £137,654 in 1957–58. Compared with voyage profits of £1,074,497 in 1957–58, however, this factor was not as important as it had been in the 1920s and 1930s (see pages 77 and 85).

After the re-opening of the Suez Canal in 1957 freight rates fell sharply and competition in the international dry cargo market intensified. Lyle Shipping Co., and other United Kingdom tramp owners, found that it was becoming less easy to trade their old war-built vessels in competition with modern tonnage operated under foreign flags and also British tonnage bought cheaply by foreign owners. Consequently, many old ships were realized at a time when the market values of second-hand tramps had fallen far. Lyle Shipping Co. sold its steam ships first. In March 1958 the *Cape Wrath IV* was sold for £120,000.[16] In the following November the *Cape Sable II*, which had been in the fleet since 1936, was sold for £56,500 (compared with an asking price of £130,000 in the previous year).[17] In April 1959 the *Cape Corso III* and *Cape Nelson II* 'which cannot make money given the present frieght rates' were also put on the ·market.[18] In June the *Cape Corso III* was sold for £57,500, and in December the *Cape Nelson II* for £72,500.[19]

Unlike foreign shipping companies which had seized the opportunity to invest in bulkcarriers and had then been able to sell conventional tramp ships during the boom, Lyle and several other British tramp shipping companies had missed their chance. The total world dry bulkcarrier fleet grew from 7.8 million deadweight tons in 1958 to 19.9 million deadweight tons in 1962 and reached 37.9 million deadweight tons in 1966, while the United Kingdom fleet only increased from 1.5 million deadweight tons to 3.8 million deadweight tons during the same period.[20] Moreover, by the end of the 1950s, the British tramp fleet was generally older, smaller and slower than those of foreign rivals. In 1957 the largest British tramp was under 12,000 deadweight tons. In 1960 only one tramp of over 12,000 deadweight tons operated under the British flag and the modal size of most new ships built was between 10,000 and 12,000 deadweight tons. In contrast, at the end of 1960 the world tramp fleet included 229 bulkcarriers of above 14,000 deadweight tons.[21]

Several factors contributed to this relative disadvantage. British owners were reluctant to switch their business away from British shipyards which had full order books, and the high level of British taxation of companies which were not investing in fixed capital anyway made it difficult to build up reserves to meet the costs of new tonnage. Addressing the 1956 Annual General Meeting, Colonel Macfarlane argued 'how helpful and how sensible it would be if the Chancellor of the Exchequer were to put even a proportion of this money (taken in taxation) into a "kitty" for new ships . . . Only by some such means will British shipowners be able to keep abreast of their competitors on the high seas and avoid being completely outdated by ships sailing under flags of convenience whose owners do not have to bear the crippling burden of British taxation'.[22]

The tax burden was the cause of widespread anxiety throughout the shipping industry, and the existing arrangements gave little help to shipowners who wished to replace or invest in new tonnage. Since 1944 'initial depreciation allowances' had given owners tax relief on up to 40 per cent of their original capital expenditure, but the allowances in no way helped to cover the costs of borrowing funds to build new vessels. This position was partly rectified in 1954, when the Government introduced 'investment allowances' of up to 120 per cent of the original capital expenditure. These allowances for shipowners continued to be available after February 1956, when the 'initial depreciation allowances' were reinstated for other types of assets. Nevertheless, the 1954 allowances gave little overall benefit to British shipowners, and were insignificant in comparison to the direct subsidies paid by certain foreign governments to their shipping businesses. For example Norwegian shipowners were permitted to allow the total capital costs of new tonnage against their tax liability and as a result most of them preferred to invest in new ships rather than pay tax.

In the view of the Royal Commission on Taxation Profits and Income in 1955, the United Kingdom shipping industry remained 'one of the extreme illustrations of the difficulty of replacing fixed assets in times of rising costs'. Lyle Shipping Co., with its conservative building policy, qualified for allow-

Table 8.4

Tax Paid by Lyle Shipping Co., 1952–1960

Year ending	Profit tax	Excess profit tax	Income tax	Estimated tax relief on investment allowances transferred to depreciation
2.1952*	£167,500	£42,500	£346,921	
2.1953*	28,000		234,430	
2.1954*	12,500		36,950	
2.1955*	18,500		14,520	
2.1956	50,000		297,950	£51,500
2.1957	100,000		575,887	72,500
2.1958	59,500		288,190	55,500
2.1959	3,000		58,964	
2.1960			5,999	

* Consolidated Profit and Loss Account

ances of £179,000 between 1956 and 1958. Despite lower rates for retained profits, this relief failed to offset the punitive taxation which helped to destroy the old system of financing new investment out of income; between 1952 and 1959, Lyle Shipping Co. paid £2,340,811 in tax (Table 8.2). Thereafter, especially after the Labour Government's introduction of 'free' depreciation for ships purchased after April 1965, more generous allowances combined with low profits exempted the Company from the payment of any tax on earned income.

As a result of the low freight rates after 1957, the widespread introduction of bulkcarriers by foreign companies in the late 1950s and early 1960s and the decline of liner chartering, the operation of 'tween-deck tramp ships for bulk cargoes became uneconomic.[23] Lyle then entered a period of severe financial pressure. Between 1957–58 and 1958–59 voyage profits of Lyle Shipping Co. fell by almost £1 million and made no substantial improvement until 1962–63. When allowance is made for depreciation, voyage profits were only £2,187 in 1958–59 and £6,025 in the following year. Thereafter they improved but did not exceed £100,000 until 1964–65 when voyage profits rose to £228,805. Dividend payments fell from 10 per cent in 1957–58 to 5 per cent in 1958–59 and did not rise above this ceiling until 1964–65 (Table 8.3). They were only kept at this level by the annual distribution of £25,000 from the capital reserve. In the Chairman's report to the 1958 Annual General Meeting, Colonel Macfarlane, who had been with the Company since 1903, stated that 'tramp shipping, without doubt is experiencing one of the worst depressions I can remember'.[24] In 1960 he recorded that the depression 'is still with us' and it was not until 1965 that his successor as Chairman, Dr. Percival Agnew, could refer to a good result.

The Company's finances were bolstered by further sales of outmoded ships. In July 1961 the *Cape Howe II*, the last of the Company's steamers, was sold for £105,000. By this time the two new dry cargo ships and the first of the ore carriers had been completed and later in 1961 the second ore carrier was delivered. Between 1962 and 1965 the six remaining ships, which had been built during the war or to wartime designs, were disposed of. In November 1962 the *Cape Clear IV* was sold for £80,000 and in January 1963 the *Cape Hawke I* was disposed of for £57,000. The *Cape Grafton I* and *Cape Rodney II* were sold later in 1963 and the *Cape Ortegal II*, the last ship to be joint owned with Lithgows Ltd, was sold in the following year. In 1965, the last of the old ships, the *Cape Grenville I*, was purchased by foreign owners.

After 1957 the fall off in profitability and the rise in excess tonnage in the world fleet combined with the depressed freight market severely affected the Company's ship replacement programme. The orders for the two further conventional dry cargo ships, placed with William Denny Bros. Ltd in March 1957, were converted to options and later cancelled.[25] Financing the building of the

Table 8.5

Financial Structure of the Company, 1952–63

Year[1]	Gross tangible assets £	Net tangible assets £	Profit before tax and interest £	Net current assets £	Profit as a percentage of gross tangible assets	Book value of fixed assets £	Value of depreciation allowance £	Depreciation as a percentage of fixed assets	Percentage Dividend	Cash value of dividend[2] £
1952–53	3,021,011	2,553,521	577,244	1,312,415	19.11	1,241,106	196,225	15.8	25	48,677
1953–54	2,681,960	2,376,667	90,109	1,272,960	3.36	1,103,706	143,083	12.96	10	45,375
1954–55	2,883,774	2,410,540	139,060	1,079,409	4.82	1,331,131	155,662	6.61	15	61,000
1955–56	3,690,315	2,980,266	787,034	1,548,616	21.33	1,431,650	316,194	22.09	20	76,187
1956–57	3,290,774	4,460,021	1,276,578	2,738,321	24.13	1,681,700	278,012	16.53	15½	86,250
1957–58	5,510,303	4,549,447	874,652	2,911,447	15.87	1,598,000	336,943	21.08	10	76,188
1958–59	4,976,612	4,559,522	152,608	1,764,250	3.06	2,755,272	152,365	5.54	7½	74,312*
1959–60	6,114,077	4,617,598	55,501	181,598	0.90	4,436,000	204,133	4.60	7½	75,531*
1960–61	6,246,792	4,561,670	74,048	− 797,600	1.19	5,339,170	245,452	4.60	7½	75,531*
1961–62	7,263,239	4,607,687	86,655	−1,586,428	1.19	6,174,015	294,999	4.78	7½	75,531*
1962–63	8,177,986	4,551,656	90,939	−2,546,444	1.11	7,078,000	281,394	3.97	7½	75,531*

[1] For 1952–56 the consolidated Balance Sheets of Lyle Shipping Company and its subsidiary companies have been used.
[2] Figures marked * include a capital distribution of 2.5% (£25,000) on Ordinary and 'A' Non-voting Ordinary Shares.
Source: Lyle Shipping Co. Ltd: Annual Reports, 1952–63.

third ore carrier, the *Cape Howe III*, became more difficult. In late 1958 the Lyle Board requested the Bank of Scotland to increase the Company's overdraft facilities to £3 million, but the Bank declined to increase the facilities to more than £2.5 million.[26] The Company's internal finances were severely strained, and dividend payments were restricted. 'In view of the exceedingly low level of freight rates ... and the Company's heavy capital commitments for new tonnage',[27] no interim dividends were paid between 1958–59 and 1964–65. Heavy calls were made on the Company's reserve funds, and short-term loans were called in during 1959–60. Between 1957–58 and 1962–63, despite a fall in the Company's investments to below their book value, shares were sold to produce funds and the total value of investments fell from £2,061,540 to £576,885. The cash position was bolstered in March 1960 by the receipt of a rebate of £100,000 from Lithgows Ltd on the first ore carrier, the *Cape Franklin II*.[28] Following the cancellation of orders for ships at the end of the 1950s, Lithgows Ltd had managed to obtain prices from sub-contractors well below their estimates. Lithgows Ltd agreed to pass part of these savings on to the Company by making the rebate.

The financial strain on the Company was at its greatest in April 1962 when a further three instalments remained to be paid to Lithgows Ltd on the last and largest of the three ore carriers. The Lyle Board again applied to the Bank of Scotland for an increase in the overdraft facility to £3 million, but the Bank would permit an extension to only £2,800,000.[29] Rather than sell more investments at below their purchase price the firm negotiated with Lithgows Ltd who agreed to defer payment until completion of the ship. In September 1962, when an analysis was made of the Company's financial position, it was revealed that although 'the Company was certainly hampered at the moment by a lack of liquid assets, future commitments could be met by the sale of investments still held and when the third ore carrier came into service at the end of the year the overdraft burden would gradually begin to lighten'.[30] In these circumstances it was agreed that no further action needed to be taken. By November of the same year all the instalments on the *Cape Howe III* had been paid to Lithgows Ltd without the sale of any more investments.

Between February 1957 and February 1963 the size of the Lyle fleet fell from twelve to eleven ships, and in the same period, the last of the managed ships passed out of Lyle hands. However, in the same period the fleet's tonnage increased from 103,504 to 146,649 and the average age of the ships fell from 12.9 to 8.6 years. The age of the fleet was soon reduced by the sale of the *Cape Grafton I*, *Cape Rodney II*, *Cape Ortegal II* and *Cape Grenville I* and by mid-1965 the Lyle fleet had been reduced to seven ships equalling 108,604 tons. Although none of the Company's ships was then more than ten years old, two were steam turbine ships and two were conventional 'tween-deckers; all four were unsatisfactory and out of date. Only the three ore carriers with their time charters exactly fitted modern requirements.

For most of the 1950s the Company remained under the management of the old school. James Shearer remained at the helm until 1958 when, at the age of 78, ill health forced him to resign as Managing Director. He remained a Director until 1964 and died that year shortly after his retirement. William Nicholson replaced him as Managing Director and had the unenviable task of piloting the Company through the years of uncertainty and change at the end of the decade. But his room for manoeuvre was circumscribed by the traditional outlook of the Company. Colonel Macfarlane carried on as Chairman until 1965, resigning in his eighty-seventh year. He was appointed to the honorary position of President and he died in 1968; his son, A. Keith Macfarlane had died in 1963. In the 1960s there was no obvious replacement to Colonel Macfarlane and, in 1962, Dr. J. Percival Agnew was invited to join the Board. A distinguished figure in Glasgow business life, he had been the Company's auditor and financial adviser for many years and in 1965 he was appointed Chairman. The departure of James Shearer and the two Macfarlanes created opportunities for the younger Directors, William Nicholson, Tom Shearer and, in particular, Herbert Walkinshaw who had joined the Board in 1960. In the 1960s the influence of this new generation of managers began to assert itself.

In the first decade of its life as a public company, Lyle Shipping Co. had faced testing difficulties. The financial pressures of the late 1950s made it clear that the flotation of the Company was not a magic cure to the problems of funding ship replacement or sustaining consistent profitability. As the 1950s drew to a close, the prospects for successful tramp shipping depended not only upon a firm capital base and the Company's credit-worthiness, it also hinged upon the type of re-equipment chosen to meet the demands of the rapidly changing shipping market. By 1963, Lyle Shipping Co. had made moves towards the expansion of its contract and time charter business and the re-juvenation of its fleet. Yet with the United Kingdom's share of world shipping in a long decline, and in a period of rapidly changing commercial requirements in shipping, a question mark hung over the long-term prospects for the conventional ships which remained in the fleet.

9. 1963-1977
The Making of a Bulkcarrier Fleet

During the 1960s new types of merchant ship were evolved to meet changing patterns in demand and the introduction of containerization produced further significant changes. In the early 1950s there were basically three types of ship – the liner (cargo and passenger), the tramp ship and the oil tanker. By the end of the 1960s there were super-tankers, ore-bulk-oil (OBO) carriers, bulkcarriers, containerships, lighter aboard ship (LASH) vessels, specialist ships for the carriage of gas and chemicals, product carriers, roll-on-roll-off (RORO) ships and many other new types. The size of ships also increased so that by the mid-1970s there were tankers of 500,000 deadweight tons and dry cargo ships well in excess of 200,000 tons. The British shipping industry reacted to this changing technology with a remarkable vigour which it had not displayed before in the twentieth century. The 1970 Rochdale Committee of Enquiry into Shipping underlined the rapidity of the changes taking place. 'At the beginning of our enquiry it was obvious that the wind of change was beginning to blow through the industry. At that time it seemed little more than a zephyr; it has become a gale. The effects both in the physical equipment now being used . . . and on the attitude of mind of many of those responsible for its operation is profound'.[1] Between 1967 and 1977 British shipping companies invested £4,000 million in new tonnage, or more than £1 million per day. In 1977 the average age of ships in the British mercantile marine was less than six years, making it the most modern fleet in the world.

By the early 1960s British tramp shipowners were increasingly aware of the need to replace their conventional cargo vessels with bulkcarrier ships. The increases in efficiency had meant that in the thirty years after the Second World War freight rates on average did not increase despite the rate of inflation: this situation was tolerable only for those shipping companies which modernized their fleets. British tramp ship companies, which faced strong competition from foreign owners and from cargo liner operators, then began to order bulkcarriers. In 1963 P. and O. and Anglo Norness Shipping Co. formed Associated Bulk Carriers Ltd, which was registered in Bermuda, to operate as the chartering company for the new bulkcarrier fleet of P. and O.-owned Hain-Nourse Ltd. Two years later, Bibby Brothers and Co., Bowring Steamship Co., H. Clarkson and Co., and Houlder Brothers combined to form Seabridge Shipping Ltd for the trading of large bulkcarriers. Between 1965 and 1968 over half the British-registered bulkcarriers of over 30,000 deadweight tons were built for these two consortia.[2]

Lyle Shipping Co., led by its Managing Director, William Nicholson, was as alive to the challenge of the future as its larger competitors. In November 1962 the Board proposed to the British Phosphate Commissioners, one of their established customers, that Lyle should build a bulkcarrier for time charter to the Commissioners for a minimum of five years.[3] The proposition was rejected. In the following year the Lyle Directors, undeterred by their disappointment, examined in great depth the future prospects for tramp shipping and considered the purchase of bulkcarriers to replace the older tonnage in the fleet. The Directors authorized an investigation to determine what size of vessel the Company could best afford and operate economically in the light of its past history.

In the 1960s, the world cargo liner trade was rapidly switching to container services and many British companies were taking the lead in their provision. In 1965 British and Commonwealth Shipping Co., Furness, Withy and Co., Ocean Steam Ship Co., and P. and O. combined to form Overseas Containers Ltd. Shortly afterwards, in 1966, Associated Containers Transportation Ltd, was set up by Ben Line Steamers Ltd; Blue Star Line Ltd; Cunard Steam-Ship Co.; Ellerman Lines Ltd; and T. and J. Harrison Ltd. As these two groups controlled more than 80 per cent of United Kingdom deep sea cargo liners, it was obvious that they would come to dominate this new trade.[4] In these circumstances the Lyle Board was dissuaded from investing in the very costly container ships and associated shore installations, particularly containers. Moreover, the Directors guessed that the introduction of containers might benefit the bulk-carrying trades, as some commodities, like timber and concentrates, formerly carried in 'parcels' on cargo-liners, were not suited to containerization and could be more conveniently carried in specially equipped small bulkcarriers. Similarly, later in the 1960s, the high capital cost of LASH vessels and the uncertainty of British trade union reaction deterred the Directors from recommending investment in such ships.

These investigations confirmed the Lyle Board in its determination to pursue the development of a bulkcarrier fleet. It was decided not to invest in bulkcarriers of between 40,000 to 70,000 deadweight tons which could pass through the Panama Canal, as it was reckoned that this 'Panamax' size would be selected by a majority of world owners and would therefore be difficult to charter. Furthermore, the cost of these ships would severely limit the number Lyle could afford to build and would bring the Company into direct competition for cargoes not only with larger concerns but also against the much larger vessels with their greater economic efficiency. Finally, a decision was made in favour of 'handy sized' bulkcarriers of about 530 feet in length, with a draught of not more than 32 feet, and a breadth of 75 feet (to allow trading through the

St. Lawrence Seaway). It was realized that this size of ship could serve a great number of smaller ports which could not accommodate the larger ships, especially in the Pacific area where the Company had traded for many years and where prospects were heightened by the renaissance of Japan. For example, they were the maximum size of ship which could enter such places as Port Pirie in South Australia from which cargoes of zinc and lead concentrates had for many years been carried to Europe under annual contracts with Australian Mining & Smelting (a subsidiary of Conzinc Riotinto Australia).

Bulkcarriers of this size indicated a deadweight capacity of about 20,000 tons and this was markedly more expensive for shippers per ton of freight than bulkcarriers of over 50,000 deadweight tons. In 1970 it was estimated that savings from using very large bulkcarriers as compared with average sized general purpose ships, could be as high as 75 per cent.[5] The Lyle Board, however, was confident that, on the basis of the Company's previous experience, the handy sized bulkcarrier offered greater chance of full employment regardless of the activity of the freight market. They were convinced that the trading potential of the larger size of bulkcarrier was limited. This analysis proved to be accurate as, by the late 1960s, the bigger bulkcarriers of Panamax size and larger were found to be much more difficult to trade profitably through a recession. The high capital costs involved for charterers in shipping larger cargoes and storing them at both ends proved a disincentive to large shipments.

Having chosen their vessel type, the Lyle directors were faced with the task of funding the construction of a new fleet. Traditionally, British owners financed the expansion or replacement of their fleets from internal funds, from retained profits and from depreciation. Between 1959 and 1969, over four-fifths of the £600 million spent on new ships by British owners was found in this way. In the case of Lyle Shipping Co., however, the existing overdraft and limited reserves precluded internal financing, and initially the old link with Lithgows Ltd again came to the aid of Lyle's investment plans. In June 1963 Lithgows Ltd approached the Lyle Board suggesting that an order be placed for a 16 knot 16,000 deadweight ton bulkcarrier for delivery in 1965 at a cost of £1,275,000. As an alternative a 14 knot 30,000 deadweight ton carrier costing £1,460,000 was proposed.[6] Both these projects were eligible for an 80 per cent loan under the Shipbuilding Credit Scheme introduced by the Conservative Government in that year to stimulate the depressed shipbuilding industry. Government consent and the Bank of Scotland's permission were obtained, the Company's borrowing powers were increased from £3 million to £4.5 million, and on 15 November the Company placed its order with Lithgows Ltd for a 17,520 deadweight ton bulkcarrier, at a contracted price of £1,125,000. This ship, the *Cape Rodney III*, joined the fleet in 1965 (Figure 9.1). The final cost of the vessel was £1,348,000 (Table 9.1).

In spite of this heavy loan, efforts were made to obtain more tonnage to

Figure 9.1
Cape Rodney III, the first bulkcarrier built for Lyle Shipping Co. and the third of the company's ships to have both engines and bridge located aft. Built in 1965 she is seen here at Venice.

fulfil the Company's obligation to its charterers. In September 1963, Philip, Hill and Erlanger, the finance house, was approached with a view to making contact with an insurance company or finance house to purchase and place on bareboat charter to Lyles a 'spec' vessel being built by William Denny Bros. Ltd. This firm advised that Lambert Bros., a firm of established shipowners, were prepared to purchase a ship and bareboat it to Lyle Shipping Co. for ten years, on condition that it was a new vessel.[7] The negotiations came to nothing. The merchant bankers, Samuel Montagu and Co., were then asked to purchase the Denny ship and charter it to the Company, but they declined.[8] Barclay Curle and Co., the Glasgow shipbuilders, who had few orders and were in difficulties, were approached by the Lyle Board to ascertain if they would build a bulk-carrier and bareboat it to the Company for fifteen years.[9] Again the proposal foundered. In February 1964 the Bank of Scotland was asked to finance a second bulkcarrier similar to the one being built for Lyle Shipping Co. at Lithgows Ltd, but the proposals were not adopted.[10]

In March 1964 'in view of the Company's very heavy overdraft', which then stood at £2,800,000, several shipyards were approached in an effort to finance the building of a bulkcarrier.[11] The Company first approached Lithgows Ltd with the option of taking a 50 per cent interest in the ship. Despite attempts by

Table 9.1

Cost and Funding of Ships Purchased by Lyle Shipping Co., 1965–1976

Date		Gross cost £000	Investment grant £000	Investment grant as a percentage of gross cost	Foreign loans as a percentage of gross cost
1965	Cape Rodney III	1,348	3	0.2	
1966	Cape St. Vincent II		Not available		
1967	Cape Clear V	1,474	337	22.9	20
1968	Cape Wrath VI	1,782	422	23.7	80
1968	Cape Sable IV	1,794	427	23.8	30[1]
1969	Cape York V	1,922	387	20.1	20[1]
1971	Cape Horn IV	2,096[2]	410	19.5	80
1971	Cape Hawke II	2,137[2]	425	19.9	80
1971	Cape Grafton II	2,171[2]	430	19.8	80
1972	Cape Leeuwin	2,227	432	19.4	70
1973	Cape Grenville II	2,792[3]	548	19.6	80
1976	Cape Rodney IV	4,635	912	19.7	80[4]
1976	Cape Ortegal III	4,625	910	19.7	80[4]

[1] Excluding Bank of Scotland loan
[2] Excluding re-engining costs which were £489,000 for *Cape Horn*, £513,000 for *Cape Hawke*, and £495,000 for *Cape Grafton*.
[3] Including re-engining cost
[4] British government loan

Lithgows' Managing Director, Mr. Ross Belch, to persuade a London finance house to undertake the venture, the Lithgow Board reluctantly turned down the offer.[12] John Brown and Co. and Austin and Pickersgill Ltd of Sunderland, were then drawn into negotiations. John Brown showed considerable interest and offered to build an 18,000 ton bulkcarrier for charter to the Company. An agreement was negotiated in 1964 by which a newly-built bulkcarrier was bare-boated to the Company for five years. The ship, the *Cape St. Vincent II* of 20,022 deadweight tons, was commissioned in 1966 (Figures 9.2(a), (b), (c)) and was owned by William Dennison Ltd, a subsidiary of John Brown & Co. Lyle Shipping Co. had an option to purchase the total equity of William Dennison, and this was completed in 1972 when the ship was sold at a profit.

As part of this renewal programme the Lyle Board resolved not only to finish selling the vessels built to wartime design but also to put on the market the more modern but technically inefficient 'tween-deckers. In 1965 the Company sold the *Cape Grenville I*, the last vessel in the fleet constructed to a wartime design, and the *Cape York IV*, built in 1955. The *Cape York IV* realized £380,000.[13] In the following year the *Cape Sable III* and *Cape Wrath V*, which had been built as recently as 1960, were put up for sale. They had never been successful ships

Figure 9.2
(a) *Cape St. Vincent II* under construction in the west yard of John Brown & Co. (Clydebank)
Ltd in March 1966.
(b) *Cape St. Vincent II* going down the ways in the late summer of 1966.
(c) (page 142). *Cape St. Vincent II* on trials in 1966. The cranes and hatch covers are being tested.
This vessel was owned by John Brown and chartered to Lyle Shipping Co.

and were a drain on the Company's profits. The last conventional steamer, the *Cape Horn III*, was sold in 1967 for £380,000.[14]

Initially, these vessels were replaced by only two new bulkcarriers, and the Company anticipated difficulties in servicing its established shippers. As a temporary expedient before further ships could be ordered, the modern Norwegian bulkcarrier *Cape Rona* (formerly *Rona Castle*) of 18,160 tons was taken on a five year charter in February 1965. She was joined in early 1966 by the bulkcarriers *Cape Dalemos* of 17,130 tons (formerly *Dimitros A Lemos*) and the *Cape Marina* of 23,967 tons (formerly *Marina Grande*) which were chartered for two and three years respectively. With the rise in tramp voyage freight rates the charters of the *Cape Rona* and the *Cape Marina* proved to be very profitable, but the *Cape Dalemos* did not perform satisfactorily and her charter was quickly terminated by mutual agreement. The two successful charters gave much needed flexibility to the Cape fleet. Moreover, they gave the Board time to find the funds to cover further construction.

Meanwhile the Lyle Board, spurred on by success in obtaining finance to build the original bulkcarriers *Cape Rodney III* and *Cape St. Vincent III*, had been making further efforts to acquire more vessels of the same type. In 1965 Lyle Shipping Co. approached Scott's Shipbuilding and Engineering Co. of Greenock and proposed that a new bulkcarrier, similar to the *Cape St. Vincent II* should be built and owned by Scott's and placed on bareboat charter to Lyle Shipping Co. As an inducement the Lyle Board offered to lend Scott's £300,000 on the completion of the ship to be repaid over fifteen years. At one stage the deal looked promising, but it finally collapsed.[15] In September 1965 Barclay Curle and Co. were again asked if they would build and own one, or possibly two, 18,000 ton bulkcarriers and charter them to the Company. Again no agreement could be reached.[16] In late 1965 a similar proposition was put to Swan Hunter, and Wigham Richardson Ltd of Newcastle-upon-Tyne, Barclay Curle's parent company. They agreed in principle, but their terms were too stringent to be acceptable to the Company.[17]

With mounting disappointment at the unwillingness of British shipbuilders to meet their requirements, despite the provision of loans of some £56 million to British yards under the Shipbuilding Credit Scheme, the Lyle Directors considered placing orders in overseas yards. Many British cargo lines and tramp shipping companies were considering a similar switch, but Lyle Shipping Co. were ahead of most of their competitors in taking positive action. The management, from its experience in the charter market, was impressed by the quality and design of ships being built, by the low prices of new tonnage and by the business efficiency of Scandinavian shipbuilders. As a result Herbert Walkinshaw and Tom Shearer made a 'survey' of Norwegian and Swedish yards in November 1965 and recommended that the Company should request tenders from Scandinavian shipbuilders.

Figure 9.3
Cape Clear V fully laden with timber, photographed in the English Channel in 1969.

In December the Board resolved to order a 19,900 deadweight ton bulk-carrier, the *Cape Clear V* (Figure 9.3) at a contract price of £1,148,850 from the yard of Haugesund Mekaniske Verksted A/S of Haugesund, Norway, on condition that a 50 per cent loan repayable over five years was forthcoming from a British finance house. This was Haugesund's first British order and they agreed to obtain a kroner loan of 20 per cent of the purchase price from Norwegian banks.[18] The deal almost foundered when Hambros Bank Ltd declined to advance the necessary £½ million, but the Bank of Scotland stepped in and agreed to extend the Company's overdraft facility. The rest of the finance was to be found from Lyle's own resources and investment allowances set against tax. The extensions to the government scheme made in 1962, notably the free depreciation rule, came into operation at the beginning of the 1965 financial year and Lyle was able to benefit accordingly[19] (see page 131). In January 1966 the scheme was augmented by the Labour Government's introduction of investment grants of 20 per cent of capital expenditure, or 40 per cent in regional development areas. Consequently, Lyle was eligible for a grant of £337,000 on the vessel's total contract price of £1,474,000 (Table 9.1).

The decision to build abroad had not been taken lightly. Dr. Agnew, in his statement to the 1966 Annual General Meeting, referred to the 'full specification for the price quoted, guaranteed delivery dates and, above all, the credit terms made available' as being the principal factors influencing the Directors. He went on 'your directors would prefer to build in Britain but until British prices become competitive, delivery dates guaranteed and credit terms become available to British owners building in British yards, one cannot expect any company to disregard the obvious benefits which are to be obtained by building abroad'.[20] This view reflected disquiet in the United Kingdom shipping industry as a whole. By the mid-1960s credit facilities available to British owners ordering from British yards had become generally less favourable than the facilities offered by foreign yards, yet foreign owners could obtain better credit from British yards than British owners. Following Lyle's footsteps other British shipping companies, including Shell and P. & O., ordered tonnage from Norwegian yards and Norwegian owners were to some extent displaced. In their turn, certain Norwegian owners took advantage of the good credit facilities offered by British shipbuilders and ordered bulkcarriers from United Kingdom yards. This anomaly was removed by the Shipbuilding Industry Act of 1967, which empowered the Ministry of Technology to guarantee bank loans to British owners buying from British yards. By 1967, nevertheless, a significant number of British orders had already been switched to foreign yards.

For its part, the Lyle Board was delighted with the Haugesund deal, initiated by Herbert Walkinshaw and Tom Shearer, and resolved to continue the policy.[21] In January 1966, with the support of British government investment grants, the Company ordered two slightly larger bulkcarriers of 22,000 deadweight tons each. The order was placed with Marines Hovedverft of Horten, Norway (later renamed A/S Horten Verft), and delivery was scheduled for 1968; as at Haugesund, Lyle's order was the first British contract undertaken at Horten. The ships were later named *Cape Sable VI* and *Cape Wrath IV*. Horten advanced the Company 60 per cent of the cost of the first vessel repayable in kroner over a number of years, and a further 20 per cent was advanced by the Second Loan Institute of Oslo. The Institute also agreed to advance 20 per cent of the cost of the second ship (later increased to 30 per cent) and the Bank of Scotland agreed to meet any further requirement.[22] Both contracts attracted British government investment grants of almost 24 per cent of the final price. The *Cape Wrath VI* cost £1,782,000 and the *Cape Sable IV* £1,794,000 (Table 9.1).

A fourth ship was projected in March 1966, but it was found more difficult to arrange finance. Furthermore, the order was delayed when the Bank of Scotland refused to grant the necessary increase in the Company's overdraft facility in view of its heavy commitments on new buildings. The Bank eventually relented and the vessel was ordered in November 1966 as freight rates began to move up. The delay cost the Company £150,000 on the purchase price, which at £1,922,000 was over £100,000 more than her two predecessors. This ship, delivered in 1969, was named *Cape York V*. In September 1967 a fourth order was placed with Horten but the ship was later delivered to the Glasgow ship-owners, H. Hogarth & Sons, with whom Lyle had developed close relations. The completion of these four ships amounted to a rebuilding of the Company's fleet. 'The result will be that by 1969 (the) Company will own a group of ships possessing good speed, above average cargo handling capacity and . . . numerically the largest group of this particular type under the British Flag'.[23]

The favourable credit available to the Company on its orders from Norwegian yards had been an essential contribution to this ambitious building programme, but the changed attitude of the U.K. government removed some of the obstacles to expansion. Whereas the government's fiscal policy had stifled British shipping in the 1950s and provided little incentive, the investment grants introduced by the 1963–70 Labour governments in January 1966 were valuable encouragement to British owners. As a reflationary measure the standard rate of 20 per cent of the capital expenditure, and 40 per cent in the regional development areas, was raised in 1967 and 1968 to 25 per cent and 50 per cent respectively. From April 1965, ships owned by British companies also enjoyed tax free depreciation for capital expenditure net of grant. (When the investment grants were terminated in October 1970, they were replaced by depreciation allowances on gross capital expenditure.) These measures ensured that owners did not require to draw heavily on cash resources when ordering new tonnage but only needed to be confident that their trading income would cover the repayment of loans. As a result of this change of official attitude, between 1966 and 1976 Lyle Shipping Co. attracted £5.6 million in investment grants and made provision for only £3.9 million in taxation.

In building a fleet of bulkcarriers and planning to operate them in a highly competitive world market Lyle Shipping Co., like most other tramp shipping concerns, became more technically aware. Previously tramp owners, unlike cargo liner operators, had left much of the design of their vessels to the ship-builders, but with the advent of bulkcarriers and the changes they brought to the world dry cargo market they were forced to examine every improvement likely to reduce costs. Lyle's main research drive was directed towards obtaining the maximum deadweight tonnage possible within their chosen dimensions of about 530 feet in length, a draught of 32 feet, and a beam of 75 feet. In achieving this ambition the Company found Norwegian shipbuilders more amenable than their counterparts in meeting their requirements. Using the builders' standard hull forms the Company managed gradually to raise the deadweight tonnage of its bulkcarriers from 17,520 tons in *Cape Rodney III* (delivered in 1965) to 21,900 tons in *Cape York V* (delivered in 1969), and to 23,700 tons in the later Haugesund ships (delivered in 1971 to 1973).

Apart from the advance in hull design there were other technical problems to be conquered. The nature of many of the ports in which it was planned to operate the bulkcarriers made it necessary to equip them with deck cranes with power grabs. These cranes had been evolved to replace traditional derricks and allowed for highly efficient cargo handling where quayside cranes were unavailable. For example, Lyle could tender for charters to The British Phosphate Commissioners to carry phosphate to the smaller Australian ports, because its ships were equipped with modern and efficient cranes with grabs. The development of this novel equipment to suit Lyle's requirements caused many problems and it was not until the 1970s that an effective grab was fitted in all the Company's bulkcarriers. In addition a variety of other new features were introduced and improved with the object of cutting down manning levels in a period of rapid wage rises. These included special mooring devices, power operated hatchcovers, remote controlled ballasting arrangements and machinery which would operate safely unattended. By these means the strength of the crew of the Company's bulkcarriers was reduced from 36 in the *Cape Rodney III* to 26 in the vessels delivered in the early 1970s.

During the mid-1960s the Company continued its policy of negotiating a mix of time charters, contracts of affreightment and spot charters. However, contracts of affreightment became more important since they inevitably gave a greater degree of flexibility. The Company's most important customer continued to be the British Phosphate Commissioners. An annual contract of about twelve cargoes of phosphate was negotiated until 1966. In the following year a three year contract was signed whereby Lyle undertook to move fifty-four cargoes totalling 750,000 tons of phosphates, at the time the largest contract to have been won by the Company.[24] Other contracts of affreightment negotiated in the 1960s included the movement of sixteen cargoes of sugar from Durban to Japan during eleven months in 1963, eight cargoes of pyritic cinders from Adelaide to Japan in 1963 and nine cargoes of coal from Sydney to Japan between February 1964 and January 1965. The two new bulkcarriers and the three chartered bulkcarriers were similarly employed on such contracts. The three ore carriers, the only other vessels in the Cape fleet by the end of 1967, remained on time charter to BISC (Ore) Ltd.

As the Norwegian bulkcarriers were being built, the Lyle Directors came to the conclusion that to increase the Company's competitiveness in negotiating for time charters and contracts of affreightment, and to improve the operating efficiency of the Cape fleet, it would be advantageous to find a trading partner. The need for such an arrangement became more pressing as foreign competition intensified, operating costs increased, and other British owners (following the example of Seabridge Shipping Ltd) organized themselves into consortia or joint management partnerships. The main competition to Lyle and other British companies operating similar sized bulkcarriers came from Norwegian

groups which had been established in the early 1960s and by aggressive marketing and good commercial intelligence succeeded in gaining a large share of the
world bulk dry cargo trade.

During 1966 Lyle Shipping Co. opened discussions with H. Hogarth and
Sons, a well-known Glasgow company with a long history in tramp shipping.
The original business had been established by James Goodwin and Hugh
Hogarth as ship stores merchants at Ardrossan in 1862, shortly afterwards
becoming shipowners. After the separation of the original partnership in 1878,
Hugh Hogarth had moved his business to Glasgow, where the Hogarth
Shipping Co. was formed to take on the ownership of Hogarth's ships in 1898.
Management for the Company's ships was provided by H. Hogarth and Sons,
which was set up in 1901 and reconstructed in 1952. By 1966, the capital base
and fleet of H. Hogarth & Sons were comparable to those of Lyle; Hogarth
was also engaged in similar fleet replacement, and traded in the same commodities in the same parts of the world as Lyle Shipping Co.[25] The Directors of
Hogarth, who included Herbert Walkinshaw's brother John, had also followed
Lyle in ordering several ships of the same class and from the same Norwegian
yards. However, unlike Lyle, Hogarth was an unquoted company, still closely
controlled by the Hogarth family.

The first trading contract between Lyle and Hogarth had taken place in
September 1964, when a joint contract was arranged to carry five cargoes of
phosphates from Tampa to Australia.[26] In September 1966 formal proposals
were put forward for closer co-operation between the two companies. Although
both Lyle and Hogarth were to remain as separate and distinct entities, the
day-to-day control of the two fleets was to be merged and carried on by a
management company. The scheme was designed to allow greater flexibility of
operation and thus strengthen the competitiveness of the two companies. These
advantages would be augmented by economies of scale including savings in
running costs, especially in the purchase of fuel and ship stores.

From the start of the negotiations it was recognized that the greatest draw-
back would be in the 'reconciliation of personalities and uprooting and trans-
planting staff ashore and afloat'.[27] For Hogarth this consideration proved temporarily to be insurmountable and the plan was shelved for twelve months.
However, in May 1968 the scheme came to fruition when Scottish Ship
Management was formed with a share capital of £10,000, equally divided
between Lyle and Hogarth. In its conception S.S.M. was to prove a unique
venture. Although S.S.M. was not a shipowning company, it took on all the
employees of both Lyle and Hogarth, apart from a small staff serving each
Board of Directors, and thus acquired the experience and expertise of both
owning Companies. Under the scheme the bulkcarriers of the two Companies
were to be operated as a group to give greater flexibility and economies of scale.
The freight income of the vessels in the group would continue to be payable to

Figure 9.4
Baron Wemyss a Norwegian built bulkcarrier owned by H. Hogarth & Sons Ltd. With this Company Lyle Shipping Co. formed Scottish Ship Management Ltd in 1968 to manage their joint fleets.

the respective owners but financial adjustments, in accordance with a pooling agreement, would be made to ensure that a vessel which was allocated a less profitable charter to allow another vessel to receive a profitable one was adequately compensated. A special S.S.M. house flag and funnel insignia were designed to help give the new fleet a common identity. Lyle Shipping Co. was represented on the Board of Scottish Ship Management by Herbert Walkinshaw and Tom Shearer, while H. Hogarth and Sons was represented by John Walkinshaw and Walter Scott. Herbert Walkinshaw was later to be appointed its first Managing Director. To affirm the corporate identity of the new grouping, both Lyle and Hogarth moved into adjacent premises at 48 Buchanan Street, Glasgow, where office space was also provided for S.S.M. This had the added advantage of effecting further savings in establishment charges (Figure 9.4).

In May 1967, shortly before the formation of Scottish Ship Management Ltd, the first of the Norwegian built bulkcarriers, *Cape Clear V*, was delivered to Lyle; later in 1967 Hogarth also took delivery of its first bulkcarrier, *Baron Forbes*. Simultaneously Lambert Brothers Shipping Co., a London shipping concern, agreed to order four bulkcarriers of the same design as those owned by Hogarth and Lyle and place them under management of Scottish Ship Management.[28] Lambert Brothers, which became a subsidiary of the Hill Samuel Group Ltd in 1968, withdrew from the venture in 1976.

In June 1969 a further decision was taken to expand the new fleet when, on the basis of a favourable financial forecast for the period 1968–75, Lyle Shipping Co. ordered four more bulkcarriers, the *Cape Horn IV*, *Cape Race III*, *Cape Hawke II* and *Cape Grafton II* for delivery in 1971. (Figures 9.5(a) and (b)) Three orders. were placed with the Haugesund company and one with Kaldnes M/V A/S of Tonsberg. The ships of 23,500 deadweight tons and 534 feet in length were slightly larger than those of the earlier class. The *Cape Race III*, of similar size, was placed on a ten year charter to Alcan (Bermuda) Ltd to carry bauxite from

Figure 9.5
(a) *Cape Horn IV* loading cargo at Avonmouth, shortly after her commissioning in 1971.
(b) *Cape Grafton II*, a bulkcarrier completed by the Norwegian builders Haugesund Mekaniske
Verksted. She is seen here heavily laden passing the Sydney Opera House.

the Caribbean to Canada and was built to specifications set by this company. The ship's hull was strengthened for icework, principally for winter trading to the St. Lawrence river. All four orders were financed by 80 per cent loans from Norwegian sources (repayable like their predecessors in kroner) and 20 per cent investment grants from the British government. All four vessels cost about £2 million each (Table 9.1).

Further additions to the fleet followed when the *Cape Leeuwin* was completed at Horten in 1972 (Figure 9.6), and the bulkcarrier *Cape Grenville II* was completed by Haugesund in 1973. The total cost of the two ships was £5,019,000, which was financed by Norwegian loans amounting to 80 and 70 per cent of the final cost respectively, supplemented by 20 per cent British government investment grants (Table 9.1). During the same period Hogarth built a similar

Figure 9.6
Cape Leeuwin berthed at Avonmouth Docks in 1973, a year after her completion.

number of identical bulkcarriers and the joint fleet of handy-sized bulkcarriers was unique in Britain, as was the concept of S.S.M.

Implicit in the thinking of both Lyle Shipping Co. and H. Hogarth and Sons in bringing S.S.M. into being, and Lambert's decision to join the consortium, was the revolution in marketing techniques which had accompanied the advent of the bulkcarriers. The means of winning time charters and more particularly contracts of affreightment were, as the Rochdale Committee of Enquiry into Shipping noted in 1970, 'quite different from those traditionally employed on the charter market'. Moreover, as the Committee rightly pointed out, such arrangements were a pre-requisite for shipping companies like Lyle and Hogarth if they were to be able to meet the repayments on their new bulkcarriers; 'few owners can contemplate having one or more of such costly vessels entirely dependent upon the vagaries of the spot charter market.' A large fleet of similar ships and reliability were essential to win the new 'contracts of affreightment'.

Consequently, immediately after its formation, S.S.M. mounted a concerted effort to market the services that could be provided by the recently built fleet. In particular, S.S.M. sought to increase its share of the Australian trade, which was largely dominated by Norwegian companies. At the time this was the fastest growing trading area. Between 1959 and 1974 dry cargo loaded and unloaded in the world's ports increased by 185 per cent while in Australia and Japan it rose by 795 per cent and 662 per cent respectively.[29] Ironically S.S.M. with its well-equipped Norwegian-built bulkcarriers was able to compete successfully against Norwegian shipowners and secure contracts for the movement of pyrites, concentrates, coal and timber in addition to further contracts from the British Phosphate Commissioners. This achievement also owed much to the high standing of S.S.M. masters and crews in the eyes of charterers.

The adoption of bulkcarriers brought other far-reaching changes to established shipping practice. At the same time as S.S.M. was seeking new customers for its ships, it was also concerned with the important task of manning them with suitable crews. The ships were faster and spent much less time in port than the old 'tween deckers. Existing officers and crew had to adjust to the new conditions and new entries had to be trained to use the novel equipment. In this they were helped by the provision of training programmes and a greatly expanded recruitment of cadet officers, who first qualified in nautical colleges. For the first time senior officers were occasionally allowed to take their wives with them, a privilege which would be extended further in the 1970s. Moreover the duration of periods of duty was reduced from the two years of the early 1960s to four or five months and repatriation by air became commonplace. In addition to higher salaries, better pensions and longer periods of paid leave, officers and men also benefited from a transformation in their living conditions. Each crew member was allocated his own cabin and subsequently his own shower and washing facilities, and every ship was fitted with a swimming pool, gymnasium, television and a bar. Bars were first installed in Lyle ships in 1962 and the Company can probably claim to be the first non-passenger/cargo operator to adopt them.

The two original Clyde built ships and the Norwegian vessels provided Lyle Shipping Co. with the type of bulkcarrier fleet which the Directors had envisaged in 1963. Yet the building of the fleet was not without its setbacks. Three of the ships ordered in 1969, along with four Hogarth vessels and all four Lambert ships ordered at the same time, were each fitted with a pair of medium speed diesel engines designed and built by Ruston and Hornsby Ltd of Lincoln, and developed jointly with the National Research and Development Corporation. Ruston and Hornsby, which had been taken over by the English Electric Co. in 1966, became part of the General Electric Co. in 1969.

From the outset the Ruston and Hornsby engines proved to be extremely unreliable, continuously breaking down at sea. It transpired that they had been little tested under seagoing conditions. Before the *Cape Grenville II* was launched in 1972 the problem had become so acute that the Lyle management decided to fit this ship with an engine of a different design. Since the engineroom had been designed to accommodate two medium speed diesels it was not possible to instal a conventional slow-speed diesel engine, and after considerable thought, discussion and investigation the Dutch medium speed engine built by Stork Werkspoor was eventually chosen. As this engine proved satisfactory under seagoing conditions Lyle, Hogarth and Lambert agreed to abandon the Ruston and Hornsby engines and replace them with Stork Werkspoor diesels. Between 1973-74 the entire production capacity of the shipyard and engineering works of Amsterdamsche Droogdock Maatschappij were taken over and one by one the eleven ships were re-engined. It was an enormous task which was undertaken at great cost and inconvenience to the three companies and their chartering customers. As a measure of the difficulties involved an opening had to be cut in the bulkhead of each ship through which the old engines were removed and through which the new engines were railed in. An additional difficulty of re-engining was scheduling the ships so as to reach the Dutch yard at the right time with the minimum amount of wasted time or ballast voyages. Re-engining also cost six weeks of earnings at a time of good freight rates. Moreover, when the ships first showed signs of serious engine problems in late 1971/early 1972, the prevailing low freight rates caused anxiety about the effect of the engine problems on the cash position. Lyle Shipping Co. called for compensation from the General Electric Co. but only a small payment was offered. In his statement in the annual report for 1972 Dr. Agnew revealed that 'some part of the cost of re-engining is being borne by the original engine builders and reasonable financial terms have been agreed. Nevertheless, a certain part of the burden in terms of capital cost and loss of earnings will fall on the Company.' Dr. Agnew, then Lyle's Chairman, commented at the time that 'this whole episode was probably the biggest blow the Company has ever sustained'. The technical problems continued when the Kamewa propeller hubs cracked and had to be replaced. Then even the Stork Werkspoor engines developed fractures in the bed-plates which were attributed to faulty design, and this had to be rectified.

A further anxiety was the exchange losses which the Company suffered in repaying its Norwegian loans. With the rapid devaluation of the pound sterling, particularly since 1973, the repayment of the loans became increasingly expensive. The originally advantageous rates of interest were more than offset by the depreciation of sterling and the appreciation of the kroner. Between 1972 and 1975 losses of £2 million were incurred on repayment of loans, with a further loss of over £1 million in 1976 and at the end of 1976 losses of £3 million remained unrealized.

In 1970, with the currency problem in mind, and attracted by British government incentives in the shape of 80 per cent loans under the Industrial Development (Ships) Act 1969 supplemented by 20 per cent investment grants, the Lyle Board placed an order for two 'Cardiff' class bulkcarriers with Upper Clyde Shipbuilders Ltd. At the same time Hogarth placed contracts for two similar vessels with U.C.S. Despite repeated reassurances to the Lyle Board from the U.C.S. management that the Company's finances were sound, U.C.S. went into liquidation in 1971, before construction could begin. Lyle Shipping Co. lost its deposit of some £400,000, pending completion of the liquidation and resolution of the disagreement between the U.C.S. Committee of Inspection and the government over the government's obligations towards the creditors of U.C.S. Lyle and Hogarth's orders were subsequently converted to 26,000 dead-weight ton bulkcarriers and transferred to Govan Shipbuilders Ltd (formed out of the U.C.S. Govan and Scotstoun yards) in order that the companies could realize the favourable government grants they had originally been promised. The Lyle vessels, the *Cape Ortegal III* and *Cape Rodney IV* were finally delivered in 1976 at a total cost for each ship of about £4.6 million, less the investment grant of 20 per cent.

Meanwhile the Lyle Directors, disappointed for a second time in their attempts to build in Britain, had, in late 1975, ordered a bulkcarrier of 31,992 deadweight tons from Mitsui Engineering and Shipbuilding Co. of Japan. This vessel, the *Cape Otway*, was much larger than the Company's standard bulk-carrier and was constructed to fulfil a ten year charter negotiated by S.S.M. with the British Phosphate Commissioners for the transport of phosphate from the South Pacific to Australasia. The Lyle Board's decision to build in a Japanese yard arose from the fact that none of the British yards contacted were prepared to alter their standard design to comply with the particular features required by the charterers within the price and delivery period stipulated. The ship was delivered on schedule in 1976, the same year as the two Govan ships.

While the additions to the fleet were in progress, older ships were sold. As the charters to the British Steel Corporation (BISC (Ore) Ltd) ran out, the ore carriers were put on the market. The *Cape Franklin II* was sold in 1974, the *Cape Nelson III* in 1976, and the *Cape Howe III* will follow in early 1978. The original bulkcarriers, *Cape Rodney III* and *Cape St. Vincent II*, which were smaller and less profitable than the newer bulkcarriers in the fleet, were sold in 1970 and 1972 respectively, for a total of £2¼ million or about £1½ million over their book value. Two of the Norwegian-built ships were sold, the *Cape Clear V* in 1973 and the *Cape Wrath VI* in 1976, when they realized over £5 million, £3 million over book value, and £2 million over original cost. These vessels were put up for sale when they were about eight years old, an age at which the Board reckoned a ship to have reached its optimum second-hand price. By realizing funds in this way, the Company was able to reduce the outstanding kroner loans obtained to finance Norwegian-built bulkcarriers (Table 9.1).

In 1977 as a result of having steadfastly pursued the policy fixed in 1963, Lyle Shipping Co. was equipped with a fleet of eleven modern handy-sized bulkcarriers and one ore carrier with a total deadweight tonnage of 268,759 and a total valuation of some £40 million. The average size of each vessel was 22,943 deadweight tons and the average age of the bulkcarriers was 4.8 years. This size of bulkcarrier was considerably smaller than most bulkcarriers built for the British fleet in recent years. In December 1975 no British registered bulkcarrier under five years old displaced less than 20,000 deadweight tons and two thirds of these ships were above 30,000 deadweight tons. The average displacement of all British ore/bulkcarriers at the same time was 35,705 deadweight tons and that of those carriers less than five years old was 42,705 tons.[30] By selecting to build a fleet of such small bulkcarriers, Lyle and Hogarth secured an important sector of the shipping market and managed to survive at a time when many old established companies in the United Kingdom were going out of business or being amalgamated into large combines. Although several companies in the world operate bulkcarriers of the same size as those of Lyle and Hogarth none in Britain and few in the world specialized in them to so great an extent.

From its start in 1968 Scottish Ship Management grew in size and experience. It established a world wide reputation with charterers and built up its links with the Australian market, particularly through Universal Charterers Pty Ltd of Sydney, managed by Alf Willings. From these contacts S.S.M. found new opportunities for developing its own chartering business and established a subsidiary in Hong Kong to undertake special charters. As S.S.M.'s business grew in scale it also decided, like many other British companies, to acquire its own shipbroking facilities and in 1972 it purchased from Lambert Brothers the firm of John Kilgour & Co., which had been Lyle's London broker for many years.

In addition S.S.M. evolved a strong range of management services. The difficulties encountered during the re-engining programme gave S.S.M. considerable technical expertise at an early stage in its career. Norman Bowers, with experience in the Navy and G.E.C., joined S.S.M. to supervise the re-engining programme, and on his resignation in 1975 Peter Smith, an ex Lyle master, took his place as Technical and Operations Director. The S.S.M. Board was broadened by the appointment of Jim Marshall as Finance Director in 1970. He had joined Lyle as Company Secretary in 1968, as the first qualified accountant on the staff, and transferred to S.S.M. on its establishment. Of the four original Directors, Walter Scott retired in 1974 and Herbert Walkinshaw resigned in the same year to take over as Managing Director of Lyle.

By 1977 the formation of S.S.M. had fully justified its expectations, despite the reservations of the Rochdale Committee of Enquiry into Shipping about consortia and joint management companies, expressed in its report in 1970: '. . . We do not consider that consortia, as now usually organized, are the best ultimate instruments for achieving efficiency in those areas where large scale operation is essential. We believe that they should be regarded primarily as transitional organizations designed to develop into integrated and fully independent organizations as quickly as is possible'.[31] Moreover, the coincidence of the formation of S.S.M. with the rise in freight rates that followed the 1967 Arab–Israeli War resulted in a sharp growth in the profitability of Lyle Shipping Co. From 1963, as the ore carriers began to make a steady return and the bulkcarriers entered service, profits increased from 1.11 per cent of gross tangible assets in 1962–63 to a high of 7.64 per cent in 1967–68. They fell back in 1968 to 5.29 per cent, but almost doubled in 1969 to 10.08 per cent and, with the exception of 1971, remained at over 10 per cent until 1975. This prosperity has allowed the Company to pay some of the highest dividends in its history. A dividend of 8.5 per cent was paid in 1963–64 which had grown to 18 per cent in 1970 and in 1971. (Table 9.2 and see Table 8.5 on page 132.)

In 1975, however, this affluence came to an abrupt halt. In 1974, following the Middle East October War of 1973, the oil producing countries substantially increased the price of their oil and threw the rest of the world into deep recession. S.S.M.'s relations with many of its clients were such that they agreed to contribute towards the extra cost of fuel and this in turn assisted Lyle in the short run. In the long term little could be done to protect the Company's fleet from the disastrous fall off in freight rates. The time charter index for 20/40,000 deadweight ton tramps plunged from a high of 350 in the fourth quarter of 1973 to a low of 113 in the second quarter of 1975.[32] As a result, between 1974 and 1975 profits before tax and interest fell from £2,865,000 to £785,000 and return on gross tangible assets collapsed from 13.57 to 3.02 per cent. Little improvement was made in 1976. However the modern fleet and the moves towards diversification in the 1970s (described in Chapter Ten) meant that Lyle was able to face

Table 9.2

Financial Structure of the Company, 1963–1975

Year	Gross Tangible Assets	Net Tangible Assets	Profit before tax and interest[2]	Net current assets	Profit as a percentage of gross tangible assets	Book value of fixed assets	Depreciation as a percentage of fixed assets	Percentage Dividend
1963–64	£7,691,262	£4,429,923	£173,889*	−£1,895,231	2.26	£6,561,375	6.93	8.5
1964–65	£7,570,668	£4,444,885	£277,694*	−£1,563,443	3.67	£5,988,228	7.45	12.5
1965–66	£7,288,927	£4,000,695	£405,925*	−£1,949,237	5.56	£5,929,823	7.68	13.5
1966–67	£7,494,467	£4,194,647	£377,380*	− £547,958	5.04	£4,722,505	7.8	13.5
1967–68	£8,018,399	£5,565,473	£612,207	− £350,263	7.64	£5,195,110	7.39	14
1968[1]	£10,290,325	£7,707,722	£544,944*	− £349,566	5.29	£7,324,056	4.76	17
1969	£10,211,673	£8,285,678	£1,029,756	− £185,404	10.08	£8,436,982	6.16	14
1970	£11,323,567	£8,866,676	£1,260,984	− £258,900	11.14	£9,091,476	4.8	18
1971	£15,525,954	£12,391,604	£1,137,645	− £872,523	7.33	£11,514,031	4.6	18
1972	£15,799,775	£13,807,686	£1,616,807	− £393,031	10.02	£13,212,034	3.57	15.6
1973	£19,422,221	£16,726,155	£2,726,937	£1,130,231	14.04	£14,557,441	3.12	13.6
1974	£21,117,000	£17,137,000	£2,865,000	−£2,195,000	13.57	£15,105,000	—	14.7
1975	£26,104,000	£20,485,000	£785,000	−£1,905,000	3.02	£20,559,000	—	16

[1] a ten month period   [2] includes interest payments

Source: Lyle Shipping Co. Ltd, Annual Reports, 1963–75

the economic uncertainty and depressed freight rates with much greater inherent strength than in the early 1960s.

The 1960s and 1970s provided great challenges for the British shipping industry. Faced with the long decline in the United Kingdom's share of world shipping, British owners were forced to take on foreign competition by modernising and specialising their fleets. The period witnessed an overall sizing up and rejuvenation of the vessels registered in the United Kingdom, and the adaptability of the British merchant fleet was significantly improved by the concentration of investment in container ships, large tankers, and ore/bulk/oil carriers. Lyle Shipping Co. successfully kept pace with these trends. By virtue of deliberate long-term planning in 1963, the Company met the challenges of the period by creating a bulkcarrier fleet which was ideally suited to the expanding bulk shipping market. From 1963 their efforts were also supported by government tax credits, loans and, later, investment grants. Lyle was well placed to take advantage of these facilities, as the Company had already secured sufficient term freight business to generate the income needed to meet loan repayments. Building on the experience of its ore carrier ventures, the Company ensured that it was well-equipped in the most profitable area of the shipping market.

10. 1969-1977
From Company to Group

Between 1950 and 1970, the British shipping industry was increasingly dominated by a small number of powerful groups, each seeking the economies to be
derived from large-scale operations. By 1970, ten groups controlled some two-
thirds of all shipping capacity registered in the United Kingdom, with each
group owning over 500,000 tons gross. In the 1960s, as the consolidation of
shipping groups and consortia accelerated, the largest companies diversified
their interests outside shipping in an effort to protect their profitability and
avoid the cyclical fluctuations in shipping. 'We do not make a fetish of being in
shipping,' commented Sir Nicholas Cayzer, Chairman of British and Commonwealth Shipping Co. After piloting British and Commonwealth through an
exceptionally wide diversification programme in the 1950s and 1960s, Cayzer
could compare the range of his Company's activities with those of non-shipping
conglomerates like Thomas Tilling.[1] By 1970, the principal options chosen by
the major shipowners included shipbuilding and repairing, shipbroking,
insurance, travel, air transport, road haulage, warehousing, engineering and
property development.

Many of the United Kingdom's medium and small shipping companies made
similar efforts to extend the base of their operations. In the case of Lyle Shipping
Co. this development was initially made possible by the sale of its investment
portfolio, which had been maintained at a high level during the inter-war years
but was run down in the 1950s and early 1960s as funds were required to build
new tonnage. The Company's investments fell from £3 million in 1958–59 to
£362,488 in 1966–67. Higher profits in the late 1960s coupled with the easier
acquisition of finance to build new tonnage allowed the Company to embark on
a diversification programme to relieve its dependence on the shipping cycle. The
poor performance of the stock market and the lower level of earnings on quoted
shares no longer made this traditional source of investment attractive and the
remaining investments were sold at below their cost.

Before the diversification programme began the Company had made a large
unquoted investment in Caledonian Airways (Prestwick) Ltd in 1967. This type
of diversification was characteristic of shipping companies in the 1960s; Cunard's
partnership with British Overseas Airways Corporation between 1962 and 1967
was a spectacular example, and British and Commonwealth and P. & O. had

secured large shares in Air Holdings Ltd, the parent company of British United Airways. Initially, Lyle Shipping Co. shared in the confidence in air transport. In 1967, representatives of Caledonian Airways approached the Company with an offer to negotiate a sale to the Company of a block of shares valued at £350,000 held by the Donaldson Shipping Line.[2] The Lyle Board declined to make such a heavy commitment, but, impressed by the quality of the management of Caledonian Airways, purchased newly issued shares to the value of £125,000.[3] In October 1968 a further investment of £150,000 was made in Airways Interests (Thomson) Ltd, which then controlled the airline.[4] Further substantial sums were subscribed in 1969 and 1970 to help Caledonian Airways take over British United Airways Ltd. In the subsequent re-organization, all Lyle's interest was transferred into shares of Caledonian Airways Ltd, which became the holding company of the newly formed British Caledonian Airways Ltd.

The new airline was able to operate all the scheduled services formerly flown by British United Airways and established itself as the 'Second Force' airline with regular services. It was, therefore, able to reduce its reliance on the charter market where competition later became progressively more severe. The decision proved well judged as British Caledonian retreated from the inclusive tour charter market before failure overtook Court Line in 1974 accompanied by the collapse of large package holiday operators such as Clarksons Holidays.

By the end of 1970 Lyle Shipping Co. owned 16.3 per cent of the equity of Caledonian Airways Ltd, valued at some £900,000. In the short term this investment has not proved a success. During 1971 one of Caledonian's subsidiaries (Blue Cars) made a substantial loss, reducing the overall profits of the parent company. This poor return was compounded in the following year by the rapid rises in oil prices, occasioned by the Arab–Israeli war, and the consequent fall in air traffic. No dividends were paid by Caledonian Airways after 1972, reflecting the continued depression in air freights and the protracted Government review of civil aviation, but at the present time there are signs of a turn-round in the performance of the business. A rights issue in 1973 reduced Lyle Shipping Co.'s holding to 8 per cent.

In 1968, a year after the initial stake in Caledonian Airways was acquired, Lyle Shipping Co., in association with Marshall Gibson, who had previously been a director of the Glasgow insurance brokers, William Euing & Co. Ltd, formed an insurance broking subsidiary, Lyle, Gibson & Co. Ltd. In view of the large fleet premiums placed, many British shipping companies had acquired or set up insurance broking subsidiaries over the years. The formation of Lyle, Gibson & Co. was thus a natural diversification for Lyle Shipping Co. and was, in fact, its first trading subsidiary.

Lyle, Gibson & Co. was set up with a subscribed capital of £10,000 not only to negotiate and rationalize the insurances for the Lyle fleet – the shipping

Company had previously employed five brokers – but also to establish a professional general insurance broking business. It has traded with success since its formation, extending its services to cover all aspects of insurance and negotiating business worldwide. As part of its expansion it absorbed the Glasgow insurance brokers, William Martin & Co., in 1974 and formed a subsidiary in 1977 to negotiate specialized forms of insurance. At the same time its profits grew steadily to reach £85,000 in 1976 and its staff increased to the present level of over twenty. Two other Directors were appointed in 1975 and 1976: Colin Kennedy, who had previously been employed by an international insurance broking firm in the Bahamas, and Phillip Usher, who had joined Lyle, Gibson & Co. to take charge of the life and pensions department.

During 1972, because of the mounting expense caused by the failure of the medium speed diesels, the Lyle Board considered that the acquisition of an engineering subsidiary might provide a solution to this problem. As a result, in 1972, the Company purchased for £225,000 a 90 per cent holding in the East Kilbride precision engineering company, Gordon H. Barclay (Manufacturing) Ltd. The company was renamed Lyle Barclay Ltd, and Gordon Barclay continued as Managing Director, assisted by his co-director Joe Murdoch. As the Lyle fleet's engineering problems became more complex and serious, Lyle Barclay was unable to fulfil its intended role and instead developed its connections as a supplier with the mining, motor, aircraft, computer and earth moving equipment industries. The factory at East Kilbride was built in 1972/73 and equipped with an advanced range of sophisticated numerically controlled machine tools. Lyle Barclay recorded profits of over £100,000 in 1973 and 1974 and on the strength of this performance a plan was put forward to build a precision gear cutting factory in East Kilbride. With the decline in the economy in the following year a drop in orders resulted in a substantial loss for 1975 and the first half of 1976 and the project was cancelled. Lyle Barclay returned to profitability in late 1976 when it had eighty people on its payroll.

Meanwhile the Lyle Board was seeking to adopt a more integrated approach to its policy of diversification, particularly by expanding into areas where the Company's traditional expertise could be used to advantage. After investigating and rejecting various possible alternatives – such as product carriers – for trading worldwide the directors found an outlet for their ambitions in Scottish waters. During the early 1960s oil and gas exploration began in the North Sea, and from 1964 in the United Kingdom sector. Gas was discovered in commercial quantities in the British sector the following year and the first North Sea oil in the Danish sector in 1966. Oil was not found in United Kingdom waters until 1969, when the British Gas Corporation/Amoco consortium discovered the Montrose field. In the same year the prospects for the North Sea oil industry were greatly enhanced by the discovery of the large Ekofisk oil field in the Norwegian sector. While these and other finds were consolidated exploration activity fell off until the fourth round of licensing in 1972, when 282 blocks were awarded.

A disturbing feature for the British government of the initial operations in the North Sea was the apparent lack of involvement of either Scottish or United Kingdom companies, particularly in the industries servicing the off-shore activities. In 1971 the Department of Trade and Industry commissioned the International Management and Engineering Group to conduct an independent enquiry into the problem. Their report titled *Study of Potential Benefits to British Industry from Offshore Oil and Gas Developments* commented: 'Our recommendations reflect our conviction that the key to increasing British industrial participation offshore lies in the development of a strong position in offshore engineering and contracting. British industry has to break into an area of activity in which foreign enterprise, mainly American, has established an entrenched position in off-shore works, and is daily strengthening that position by the accumulation of experience in solving the still more difficult problems of the North Sea'.[5] The report noted many examples of American and foreign services to the North Sea offshore industry which could be matched and possibly replaced by United Kingdom business.

While the British government was expressing anxiety at the failure of its domestic industry to compete in the North Sea, a number of Scottish and British businessmen were becoming aware of the possibilities of investing in the North Sea offshore oil industry. In 1969, Iain Noble and Angus Grossart had formed the merchant bank Noble Grossart Ltd in Edinburgh and soon realized the potential of the oil industry. They began to put together companies to finance offshore oil exploration and support services. As the fourth round of licensing approached, several Scottish and British companies and individuals combined to bid for the sectors that were to be allocated. Pict Petroleum Ltd was formed in 1971 by Iain Noble, with Herbert Walkinshaw as a non-executive director, and Lyle Shipping Co. invested £90,000 for a minority stake of 4.5 per cent of the equity of the concern. A further investment of £90,000 was made as a result of a rights issue in 1973 but some of Lyle's shares were later sold on to Hogarth Shipping Co., the parent company of H. Hogarth & Sons.

In 1972 Pict participated in consortia which obtained licences to drill in various sectors of the North Sea – an area covering 3,500 square miles. Although oil has been discovered in sector 15/21 and gas in sector 3/19, at the time of writing the finds are being evaluated to determine if they are commercial. In 1976–77 Pict extended its interest in the North Sea by successfully participating in a bid for part of block 3/14, next to the Alwyn Field. As an investment Pict Petroleum Ltd has so far proved a disappointment, but it enabled Lyle Shipping Co. to gain first-hand knowledge of the North Sea oil industry.

One of the areas that the report to the Department of Industry highlighted as likely to yield good returns to British enterprise was the operation of supply vessels. The report predicted that: 'The business in the North Sea is expected to double within the next years in proportion to the increased number of drilling rigs,' and advised: 'Annual charter rates for a new vessel are reckoned to be of the order of £300,000. Older and smaller vessels are chartered at much lower rates of the order of 50 per cent of this figure. A modern supply vessel costs about £1 million and the technicalities of its design and equipment as well as its operation are intricately related to the operation of drilling rigs and other manned and relatively stationary or immobile craft or platforms. Differences in specification by operators as well as questions of manoeuvreability and vessel design economics require consultation and technical interchange between rig and supply vessel operators.'[6] It was reckoned that each drilling rig required to charter between two and three supply ships to keep it supplied with cement, mud, fresh water, drilling equipment, food and other stores, yet only twenty-five out of the eighty supply ships operating in the North Sea in 1972 were registered in Britain.[7]

While the International Management and Engineering Group was conducting its investigation Lyle was acting. From its association with Pict Petroleum Ltd, the Lyle management had come to recognize that the demand for supply ships would rise as the number of rigs drilling exploration wells increased following the fourth round of allocations. It investigated the possibility of launching a Scottish-based, Scottish-owned company to provide North Sea shipping services and realized that existing supply vessels designed for the Gulf of Mexico would not suit the unique wave patterns found in the North Sea. Contact was then made with the shipbuilding firm of Cochrane & Sons Ltd of Selby, Yorkshire who were asked to quote for a series of four offshore supply vessels specifically designed for North Sea operation. Cochrane responded with a favourable quotation and the assurance of reasonable delivery.

At the time the extent of the engine problem of the Cape fleet was just becoming apparent, and the Lyle management, anxious to protect the Company against the difficulties ahead, seized this opportunity. The Board decided to proceed with the order from Cochrane and received support from Hogarth Shipping Co., who agreed to participate in the venture. Noble Grossart was employed to set up a new company to own and operate the supply ships and Seaforth Maritime Ltd was subsequently registered in April 1972 at Aberdeen. Lyle Shipping Co. and H. Hogarth & Sons subscribed 60 per cent of the issued capital of £1 million divided equally between them, with the balance spread amongst a number of other Scottish companies, particularly Sidlaw Industries Ltd. Although the new company was initially to draw on Lyle's shipping expertise, it was intended from the outset that Seaforth Maritime would have its own independent management, generating its own corporate strategy. The founder directors were Iain Noble, Herbert Walkinshaw and Max Cheales, the Managing Director of Hogarth Shipping Co. They were soon joined by James

Figure 10.1
The tug/anchor handling vessel *Seaforth Hero* passing under Clifton Suspension Bridge, Bristol, on her way down the Avon after completion at Charles Hill's yard.

Hann, as Chief Executive, and David Fleming, an oil consultant to the Bank of Scotland. Three executives were later appointed to the Board, Andrew Wilkie (Marine Director), Bill Edgar (Engineering Director) and Mike Ferrier (Finance Director). As a result of two subsequent rights issues Lyle Shipping Co. had, by 1977, invested some £1.3 million in Seaforth Maritime and owned 41.5 per cent of the equity.

On the formation of Seaforth Maritime the order for four anchor handling tug/supply vessels was confirmed with Cochrane & Sons. A visit was made to

Total Oil Co. (with whom Pict Petroleum was associated) to discuss some aspects of the detailed specifications required by oil companies and the boats *Seaforth Hero*, *Seaforth Prince* (Figure 10.1), *Seaforth Challenger* and *Seaforth Chieftain* were delivered between mid-1973 and early 1974. A contract for a further four vessels was soon placed with the same yard. These vessels, *Seaforth Champion*, *Seaforth Saga*, *Seaforth Warrior* and *Seaforth Victor* were delivered in the first half of 1975. As supply vessel technology and demand from the oil rig operators grew, four new larger ships were ordered in 1974, two from Cochrane & Sons and two from Ferguson Bros. of Port Glasgow. The two new Ferguson ships, *Seaforth Jarl* and *Seaforth Highlander*, were delivered in late 1975 and mid-1976, but the Drypool Group, of which Cochrane & Sons was a part, collapsed late in 1975 while the last two vessels, *Seaforth Conqueror* and *Seaforth Clansman*, were being built. Although Drypool was on the Labour Government's nationalisation list, the government refused to rescue the Company from receivership. Seaforth Maritime had to decide whether to abandon the two vessels and write off its investment or to continue their construction at the much higher price quoted by the Receiver.

The government offered to help Seaforth with a loan to cover the increased cost and Lyle and two other principal shareholders agreed to help with cash and guarantees. This allowed Seaforth to go ahead with the completion of the two vessels. Subsequently, however, the emergence of a worrying surplus of supply ships made these two vessels appear to be only marginally profitable. It was too late to change the design of *Seaforth Conqueror* which was delivered at the end of 1976, but the opportunity was taken with support from the newly formed Lyle Offshore Group (which took a 60 per cent interest in the vessel) to convert *Seaforth Clansman* into a sophisticated fire fighting and diving support vessel for delivery late in 1977. This new market was expanding as more production platforms came on stream; the blow-out on the Norwegian Ekofisk Bravo platform early in 1977 brought home to all concerned the need for the constant availability of 'fire engines' and maintenance facilities.[8]

From the outset Seaforth Maritime, following the example set by Scottish Ship Management, laid great stress on the training and quality of their crews. Good shiphandling and efficient working were essential for the accurate laying of moorings and for ensuring supplies to rigs in all weathers. The oil drilling companies demanded service and paid almost more attention to the master involved than the ship before placing a contract. This was recognized in the early issue of shares to masters and chief engineers, and the marine division of the Company soon gained an enviable reputation as one of the top operators in the North Sea.

Although Seaforth Maritime was conceived solely to operate tug/supply vessels in the North Sea, it soon became apparent to the Directors that, if it was to compete effectively with United Kingdom and foreign owners, some degree of integration into the offshore supply industry would be essential. The concept of 'one-stop shopping' was developed whereby the oil companies could leave the logistics of all their supplies to one company and devote the whole of their energies to drilling. The first step in this direction was taken in 1972 when Seaforth Maritime purchased an extensive office and warehousing complex on the harbour front at Aberdeen. This was equipped with silos and later improvements allowed mud, cement, oil and water to be pumped aboard supply vessels through quayside ducts rather than manually loaded, resulting in a potentially much faster turnround of supply ships. This logistic function was extended by the acquisition of J. G. Barrack & Co., an Aberdeen firm of road hauliers, which allowed Seaforth Maritime to offer complete transport service from the supplier to the rig. In addition storage and warehousing facilities were provided both at the quayside and at a large open site outside Aberdeen for drillpipe and other bulky equipment.

During 1973 Seaforth Maritime strengthened its position further by purchasing Barry Henry and Cook Ltd, one of Aberdeen's oldest and most respected engineering companies with experience of North Sea work. The range and quality of machine tools in the works was improved to meet the new requirements of the developing North Sea oil production industry, particularly the demand for components associated with pipelines and production platforms. As the balance of activity in the North Sea shifted away from exploration towards development and production Seaforth Maritime's engineering range was widened so that the Company could provide both light and heavy fabrication. In addition, the engineering division acquired the U.K. maufacturing rights for Perry diving systems and Sofec single anchor leg mooring (SALM) systems. Seaforth Maritime broke even for the first time in 1974 and 'greatly increased profits' were recorded in 1975 and again in 1976 when they totalled £560,000, by which time the Seaforth payroll had reached 875 people.[9]

From its growing experience in the North Sea oil service industry Lyle became aware of the many other opportunities arising in that area, where the Company's skills could be deployed to good effect. However, they were unwilling to over-extend Seaforth Maritime Ltd until it had consolidated its operations and overcome the financial problems caused by the Drypool collapse. Instead, in 1975, Lyle Shipping Co. expanded its management team and floated Lyle Offshore Group Ltd (LOG) with a subscribed share capital of £5 million. On this occasion Lyle, using its growing expertise in initiating and funding such projects, adopted a different approach. A prospectus was issued and Lyle's major institutional shareholders were invited to participate. Lyle Shipping Co. reserved 40 per cent of the capital and the rest of the equity was taken up mainly by Scottish investors in Aberdeen, Edinburgh and Glasgow. The Board of the new Company comprised Herbert Walkinshaw, as Chairman, Timothy Noble, Secretary of Lyle Shipping Co. since 1973, Angus Macphail of Martin Currie

Figure 10.2
The undersea engineering support vessel *Seaforth Cape*, converted from a stern factory trawler, was acquired by Lyle Offshore Group in 1976.

& Co., Edinburgh, Robert Y. Smith of Scottish United Investors Ltd, Glasgow, and Calum MacLeod of Scottish Northern Investment Trust Ltd, Aberdeen. Although independent of Lyle Shipping Co., it was arranged that LOG would be managed by Lyle.

The Lyle management had already been considering various propositions ranging from the construction of drill ships, semi-submersible rigs, diving ships, construction barges, survey vessels and support ships to marine maintenance and onshore support. Of these, considerable attention had been given to semi-submersible rigs, many of which were under construction at the time for foreign companies mainly Norwegian, but only one or two for British companies. However, it was considered that these were too costly even for a joint venture and that the possibility of securing profitable charters was too unpredictable. The decision not to pursue this alternative was proved right by the slow down in offshore oil exploration world wide in 1976. Instead Lyle, drawing on its experience of Seaforth Maritime, opted to concentrate on the maintenance market both onshore and offshore, judging that this sector would expand quickly as exploration for oil gave way to development of the oil fields and subsequently to production. Lyle Shipping Co. knew from its experience of the tough waters of the North Sea that the maintenance problems would be under-estimated. As a result LOG purchased a 260 foot long stern factory trawler in 1975 for conversion into a sophisticated diving support ship with Seaforth Perry diving equipment. Renamed *Seaforth Cape* (1,340 gross tons) she was commissioned in late 1976, placed under the management of Seaforth Maritime and chartered to Amoco for the development of the Montrose oil field. In mid-1976 a further investment in diving support ships was made when LOG took a 60 per cent interest in the *Seaforth Clansman*, in a joint venture with Seaforth Maritime (see page 166) (Figure 10.2).

In addition LOG developed onshore services to support its own offshore activities and those of Seaforth Maritime Ltd, and to fill gaps in the market. In 1975 LOG took over the premises and workforce of the bankrupt Dundee ship repair yard of Smith and Hutton, with works adjacent to the Victoria Dock. The venture was named Kestrel Marine Ltd. In two years this subsidiary guided by its Managing Director, Terence Highlands (an ex-manager in the Drypool Group), gained an impressive reputation in the North Sea for repairing and servicing supply ships of all types. In the face of strong competition, mostly from Continental yards, Kestrel captured fleet repair contracts from several American oil companies, all of which demanded very high standards and fast service. As well as its ship repair facilities this Company undertakes contracts for steel fabrication, barge stripping, ship conversions and offshore maintenance. During 1977 it took over the much larger engineering factory of the old established firm of Sturrock and Murray Ltd to increase its engineering facilities and provide steady employment in slack periods for its workforce, which had increased to 200. In the same year Kestrel, in association with the Dutch company Technology Consultants, set up Storm Petrel Maintenance Ltd to offer 'total packages' for the maintenance of oil production platforms by co-ordinating the expertise of its promoters.

During 1975 LOG acquired another subsidiary, Salamis (Marine and Industrial) Ltd, which had been established at Aberdeen in 1973 by Neil Smith to undertake shot blasting and industrial painting contracts, for example degreasing and painting entire drilling derricks, anti-skid treatment of rigs and platforms and splash zone blasting. Between 1975 and 1977 it expanded its business and increased its workforce to almost 100, moving to a new purpose built factory at Bridge of Don, Aberdeen, in 1976.

Another subsidiary established by LOG, Gael Maritime Ltd, was intended to service the production platform construction sites on the West Coast of Scotland but the downturn in demand for concrete platforms from late 1975 meant that this activity was not developed.

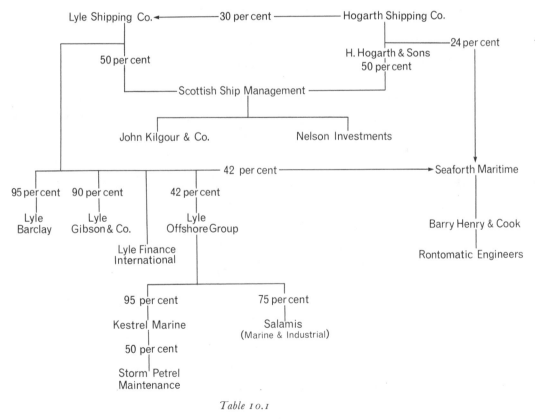

Table 10.1

Structure of Lyle Shipping Company 1977

LOG justified the faith of its subscribers by rapidly moving into profitability. Its profits rose from £9,000 in 1975 to £335,000 in 1976. Although the returns to Lyle Shipping Co. from the recently formed Seaforth Maritime Ltd and LOG were unable to offset the downturn in the freight market in 1975/76, the Lyle Directors in the years after 1972 achieved a wider and potentially profitable base for their business in a difficult market and at a difficult time. This has been achieved with the same determination that was shown during the re-equipment of their fleet with bulkcarriers.

When the Lyle family originally entered the shipping business, their ship-ownership was an adjunct of widely-based commercial interests. When it became necessary to invest heavily in a new sugar refinery in London, the family was forced to split up its different business concerns. The decision to maintain and specialise in shipping was more from sentiment than by commercial judgment, yet the decision led to the creation of a policy concerned solely with ship ownership and management. This managerial and financial expertise was matured, and in the 1960s resulted in the decision to invest in a modern bulkcarrier fleet. By the 1970s the specialist managers who then controlled the Company were sufficiently experienced and confident to broaden the base of the Company's operations again and to cover a much wider range of shipping and financial services to defend itself against the vagaries of the shipping cycle. Unlike many old-established shipping and other companies, the Lyle management elected not to abandon its original specialization or to allow this to be overshadowed by new ventures. Instead the Company exploited its long experience in shipping and ship management, and its geographical links with Scotland, building on these to diversify its interests.

I I. The Contemporary Challenge

We see no reason why the U.K. shipping industry should not remain strongly competitive with others in providing many different types of shipping service. As services become more capital intensive, crew costs are likely to become relatively less important as a proportion of total cost. The quality of management in marketing service and in exploiting technological developments to the full, will be the determining factor in the fortunes of individual enterprises . . . It is perhaps in the bulk trades – liquid and dry – that total world demand is likely to grow most rapidly. We foresee a very considerable part of the dry bulk trades being conducted on the basis of long term contracts or by shipping companies having some intimate association with individual shippers. In consequence of this changed pattern of business for a much increased bulk trade, the short term charter market will become relatively smaller.
Committee of Enquiry into Shipping – Report, Chairman Viscount Rochdale, cmnd. 4337, H.M.S.O., 1970, paragraphs 1593 and 1599.

Although the Rochdale Committee of Enquiry into Shipping reported before the world economy was plunged into deep recession by the October War of 1973, its optimistic conclusions remained a perceptive forecast of world shipping trends. The Committee's views were underlined by the confidence that the Stock Market showed in the reshaped Lyle Shipping Co., with its recently built bulkcarrier fleet, its bold management decisions, and its North Sea diversifications.

One of the additional factors to the 'wind of change' that Rochdale detected sweeping through the British shipping industry was a return to higher levels of gearing. The British shipping industry in the 1920s had been characterized by a high level of gearing which allowed Lord Kylsant to acquire control of 20 per cent of United Kingdom shipping capacity. He had extended and retained control of his group of companies, known as the Royal Mail Shipping Group, by raising an enormous loan capital. The failure of his group in 1930 had shocked the whole of the British economy and the memory of its effect on the shipping industry persisted into the 1960s. Shipowners were wary of borrowing money to finance construction, and the stock market remained suspicious of the industry, especially of companies that were highly geared. As a result during the 1950s most shipping companies were conservatively financed.

The return to a high level of borrowing in the 1960s combined with rapid inflation, resulted in a faster rate of increase of the asset value of shipping companies in comparison to their stock market valuation. This process was pronounced in the case of small firms like Lyle which had radically increased their fleet size and their gearing. The value of Lyle Shipping Co.'s assets per ordinary share advanced by 630 per cent from 129.8p to 947.2p between 1965 and 1975.

Although the share price of Lyle Shipping Co. had risen substantially, it was still low in comparison to the asset value of the fleet, and the total stock market value of the ordinary shares was very small compared with larger public companies. In these circumstances Lyle Shipping Co. became an attractive proposition for take-over bids, particularly from foreign companies who, with sterling exchange rates at a low level, saw this as a way of acquiring cheaply new tonnage and obtaining management expertise at the same time. This was made all the more possible by a widening in the ownership of the ordinary shares. After 1953, the Lyle, Macfarlane and Shearer families had gradually reduced their holdings and large institutional investors had taken their place.

During 1975 a nominee company in Panama, which had been buying a large number of shares in Sir William Reardon Smith & Sons Ltd (a shipping company with similar interests to Lyle), built up a sizeable stake in Lyle Shipping Co. over a short period. This company then sold its holdings which were purchased by Federal Commerce and Navigation Co., a Canadian concern, through its British subsidiary, Burnett Steamship Co. Federal Commerce approached Lyle, stating that it had acquired over 10 per cent of the Lyle shares and asking if the Board would be interested in starting negotiations leading to a take-over. The Lyle Board did not believe that the proposed terms would be in the interests of either shareholders or employees and declined. A year later shareholders were informed that 9 per cent of Lyle ordinary shares had been purchased gradually in the stock market by four nominee companies on behalf of a Bermudan organization. These nominee companies declined to identify the beneficial owners of their shares and, in 1976, under the terms of its articles of association, the Lyle Board took the unusual step of disenfranchizing their holdings. Eventually on 18 April 1977, Federal Commerce and the Bermudans sold their holdings to Hogarth Shipping Co. (which in the meantime had increased its traditional holding of Lyle to over 10 per cent) and the Kuwait Investment Office of the Government of Kuwait. As a result Hogarth increased its holding in Lyle Shipping Co. to just under 30 per cent.

The altered pattern of shareholdings, with greater emphasis on professional managers outside the founding families, has led to major changes in the membership of the Board. The Lyle and Macfarlane families are no longer represented. Colonel Macfarlane resigned as Chairman in 1965 after serving as a Director for over sixty years, and he died in 1968. His son, A. Keith Macfarlane, died in 1963. Lieutenant Colonel Lyle resigned as non-executive

Director in 1968 after more than twenty-two years service. James Shearer, who had resigned as Managing Director in 1958, did not offer himself for re-election to the Board at the 1964 Annual General Meeting of the Company and died later that year. Tom Shearer, now an executive director of Scottish Ship Management, is therefore the only Director representing the original families who re-founded Lyle Shipping Co. in 1903.

The initial replacements had been professional shipping managers. William Nicholson who had joined the Company in 1927 and been appointed a Director in 1946 took over as Managing Director in 1958 and played a central role in the Company's transformation. On his retirement from executive duties in 1974 he was succeeded by Herbert Walkinshaw, who had become a Director in 1960 and had been the founding spirit and first Managing Director of Scottish Ship Management.

Non-executive Directors were then appointed from outside the families. Sir Iain Stewart, who had joined the Board in 1953 when the Company went public, and who had subsequently become a well-known figure in British business life, still remains a Director. Dr. Percival Agnew, who became a Director in 1962 and Chairman in 1965, presided over a decade of tremendous changes before he retired from the Board at the end of 1974. He was succeeded as Chairman by William Nicholson, who himself retired from the Board in 1977 and was succeeded as Chairman by Herbert Walkinshaw.

In the 1970s the diversification programme led to further Board changes. Marshall Gibson became a Director in 1969 soon after the formation of Lyle Gibson & Co. Iain Noble joined the Board as a non-executive Director in 1972. In 1976 his brother Timothy, who had been Company Secretary since 1973, was appointed to the Board as an executive Director. Alastair Hogarth, the Chairman of Hogarth Shipping Co., joined the Board as a non-executive Director in 1977 when Hogarth acquired almost 30 per cent of Lyle's equity capital. He retired at the end of the year and his place on the Lyle Board was taken by John Walkinshaw.

In tracing the history of Lyle Shipping Co. up to the present time, it can be seen that the Company's past represents a microcosm of British commercial history from the stage of the entrepreneur, through diversification of his interests and then specialization, the adoption of limited liability, the employment of professional managers, the introduction of outside finance at first from individuals and then from the general public and financial institutions, and finally diversification again. On the way Lyle Shipping Co. has survived four serious economic depressions, two world wars, a voluntary liquidation, a reconstruction, and an attempted takeover; it has adapted to the enormous changes which have taken place in ship design and propulsion, in bulk trades and cargoes, and in crewing and operating ships. In this it is not unique. However, it has also survived a long period after 1880 during which it was starved of management and finance to help a sister company – which has since flourished – and it has out-lived almost all the other Clyde-based seagoing shipping companies founded in the nineteenth century. Onto this capacity for survival has been grafted the series of bold and far-sighted decisions in the last fifteen years which have created the Company's present strength and helped to counter the tarnished image of Clydeside industry.

The future of the Company, like that of its competitors throughout the world who are not protected by their governments, will be dependent on a recovery in the world economy and a consequential rise in freight rates. Although it is very probable that the world dry cargo trade will continue to increase in the next fifty years, the experience of the nineteenth century and more particularly the inter-war years makes it hazardous to predict an early return to the sustained growth characteristic of the 1950s and 1960s. It would seem more likely that in the short-term at least the world economy will remain volatile and the movement of freight rates uncertain. However, through Scottish Ship Management, Lyle has built up a highly-regarded modern bulk shipping expertise, operating ships which are both technically and economically competitive. This will allow the Company to extend the special freight-carrying relationships which have been established with individual charterers, as indicated by the Rochdale Committee in 1970. The future shipping requirements of these charterers could well lead to further substantial changes in the Company's financial structure and gearing, and the introduction of a new generation of shipping managers.

Although the principal activity of Lyle Shipping Co. is likely to continue to be bulk shipping, the Company is protected against a continued dullness in the world economy by its investment in the North Sea oil industry through Seaforth Maritime Ltd and Lyle Offshore Group Ltd, particularly in the chosen concentration of those companies on the production rather than the exploration phase of offshore oil. Moreover, the back-up services offered by both companies should allow them to build stronger and more permanent links with the offshore oil production industry. It is likely that the present commitment to North Sea oil production will continue to provide Seaforth Maritime and LOG with healthy profits through the current worldwide depression in freight rates.

In the longer term, Lyle Shipping Co. will need to adapt to further changes in the shipping industry and to continue to diversify its activities. To do this successfully is the challenge now facing the Company.

References

ABBREVIATIONS
B.P.P.   British Parliamentary Papers
G.H.T.   Greenock Harbour Trust
P.R.O.   Public Record Office
S.R.A.   Strathclyde Regional Archives
S.R.O.   Scottish Record Office

Chapter Two
1. Daniel Weir, *History of Greenock* (1829), p. 1
2. *Ibid.*, p. 3
3. Daniel Defoe, *A Tour Through The Whole Island of Great Britain* (1724–26), (Everyman's Library Edition (1962), II, p. 331)
4. Daniel Weir, *op. cit.*, p. 3
5. Greenock Statutory Register of Merchant Ships held in H.M. Customs House, Greenock, 1791
6. *Ibid.*, 1799–1800
7. Daniel Weir, *op. cit.*, p. 42
8. *Ibid.*, p. 43
9. James Cleland, *Annals of Glasgow* (1811), p. 20
10. Daniel Weir, *op. cit.*, p. 44
11. James Cleland, *op. cit.*, p. 35
12. Daniel Weir, *op. cit.*, p. 90
13. *Ibid.*, p. 91
14. *Ibid.*
15. Greenock Statutory Register of Shipping, 1791, 1799–1800
16. Daniel Weir, *op. cit.*, p. 93
17. Nothing is known about William MacDonald's wealth or occupation.
18. S.R.O., Register of Saisines for Renfrewshire, 1821–30, 3,718
19. *Ibid.*, 1821–30, 4,416
20. *Ibid.*, 1821–30, 4,272
21. *Ibid.*, 1821–30, 5,698
22. Greenock Statutory Register of Shipping, 1818, 1825, 1827.
23. *Glasgow Herald*, 7.12.1827
24. S.R.A., G.H.T., Harbour Dues Book No. 1
25. Greenock Statutory Register of Shipping, 1828
26. S.R.A., G.H.T., Harbour Dues Book No. 1
27. Daniel Weir, *op. cit.*, p. 42
28. *Ibid.*, p. 43; and L. Cope Carnford, *Aberdeen Line 1825–1925* (1925), p. 21
29. *Maritime History*, Vol. 1, No. 2, September 1971, p. 124
30. Robert Craig and Rupert Jarvis, Liverpool Registry of Merchant Shipping, *Chetham Society*, Vol. 15, 1967, p. 145
31. F.E. Hyde, *Liverpool and the Mersey* (1971), p. 41
32. Graham E. Farr (ed.), *Records of Bristol Ships 1800–1838*, Bristol Records Society, 1950, p. 12
33. Daniel Weir, *op. cit.*, p. 72

34. S.R.A., G.H.T., Harbour Dues Book No. 1

35. A.P. Lyle, *Family Notes* (1922), p. 15

36. Greenock Statutory Register of Shipping, 1829, 1832

37. A.P. Lyle, *op. cit.*, p. 15

38. S.R.O., Register of Saisines for Renfrewshire, 1931–41, 1,011

39. S.R.O., *Ibid.*, 1831–41, 1,106. The Renfrewshire Banking Co., established as the New Greenock Bank in 1785 and renamed in 1802, closed in 1842.

40. S.R.A., Ardgowan Estate Letterbooks, 10.11.1837

41. *Ibid.*, 14.7.1840

42. A.P. Lyle, *op. cit.*, p. 15

43. S.R.O., S.C.58/42/18 and 734

44. *Greenock Advertiser*, 21.9.1849

45. A.P. Lyle, *op. cit.*, p. 18

46. Greenock Statutory Register of Shipping, 1830

47. *Post Office Directories of Greenock*, Ship Lists

48. Greenock Statutory Register of Shipping, 1847

49. A.P. Lyle, *op. cit.*, p. 20

50. *Greenock Advertiser*, 9.3.1846

51. S.R.A., Ardgowan Estate Letterbooks, 13.4.1850

52. Noel Deer, *The History of Sugar* (1938), pp. 427–28

53. J. M. Hutchinson, *Notes on the Sugar Refining Industry* (1900), pp. 47–62

54. A.P. Lyle, *op. cit.*, p. 20

55. W. Hutcheson, *Greenock Directory and General Advertiser*, 1845

56. Greenock Statutory Register of Shipping, 1848–50

57. Statistics of Greenock Shipping are taken from the Greenock Ship List published annually in the Post Office's and Trade Directories of Greenock

58. *Ibid.*

59. *Ibid.*

60. Greenock Statutory Register of Shipping, 1855–72

61. A.P. Lyle, *op. cit.*, pp. 20–21

62. Leslie Jones, *Shipbuilding in Britain* (1957), pp. 10–12

63. S.R.O., SC58/42/39

64. *Post Office Directory of Greenock* (1870)

65. S.R.A., G.H.T. Coasting Arrival Book, 1866–86

66. *Clyde Bill of Entry*, 17.8.1853

67. Greenock Statutory Register of Shipping, 1857–60

68. D.N. Williams, Liverpool Merchants and the Cotton Trade, 1820–50, in J.R. Harris (ed.) *Liverpool and Merseyside*, 1967, p. 199

69. D.C. Course, *The Merchant Navy; A Social History* (1963), p. 227

70. P.R.O., BT/67/33

71. P.R.O., BT/163/33

72. P.R.O., BT/99/298

73. *Greenock Advertiser*, 29.4.1869

74. *Greenock Telegraph*, 23.12.1870

75. S.R.A., G.H.T., Harbour Dues Book No. 1, 1866–69

76. A.P. Lyle, *op. cit.*, p. 44

77. *Ibid.*, pp. 44–45

78. *Report of the Select Committee on the Sugar Industries*, B.P.P., 1880 (332), XII, p. 517, para. 79

Chapter Three
1. *Greenock Telegraph*, 15.1.1872
2. S.R.O., SC 58/42/39
3. *Ibid.*
4. *Ibid.*
5. Greenock Statutory Register of Shipping, 1864–65
6. *Greenock Telegraph*, 15.1.1872
7. S.R.O., SC 58/42/39
8. G. Rae, *The Country Banker* (1885, new edition 1976), p. 107
9. A.P. Lyle, *Family Notes* (1922), p. 54
10. *Greenock Telegraph*, 1.10.1881
11. Gerald S. Graham, 'The Ascendancy of the Sailing Ship 1855–1885', *Economic History Review*, IX, August 1956, pp. 74–88
12. *Post Office Directory of Greenock* (1880), Ship List
13. F.E. Hyde, *Shipping Enterprise and Management 1830–1939, Harrisons of Liverpool* (1967), p. 98
14. A.A. McAlister, *A Short History of H. Hogarth and Sons Ltd* (1976), passim. and L. Cope Cornford, *Aberdeen Line 1825–1925* (1925), p. 63
15. D.E.W. Gibb, *Lloyd's of London* (1951), p. 51; C. Wright and C.E. Fayle, *A History of Lloyds* (1927), p. 240
16. C. Walford, *Insurance Cyclopaedia* (1872–78)
17. *Post Office Directories of Greenock*, Ship Lists
18. In this estimate no allowance is made for depreciation, however, and with steam power becoming more competitive in this decade this loss of ship value was an increasingly important factor.
19. *Clyde Bill of Entry*
20. P.R.O., BT 99/1155
21. Greenock Telegraph, 28.3.1872
22. *Clyde Bill of Entry*
23. *Ibid.*
24. S.R.A., G.H.T., Foreign Arrival Book, No. 4
25. S.R.A., G.H.T., Day Book, No. 5
26. *Clyde Bill of Entry*
27. *Greenock Telegraph*, 7.12.1874
28. *Ibid.*, 21.8.1874
29. G.H.T., Foreign Arrival Book, No. 4
30. *Clyde Bill of Entry*
31. *Greenock Telegraph*, 6.1.1873
32. A.P. Lyle, *op. cit.*, pp. 44–45
33. *Greenock Telegraph*, 7.5.1879
34. George Martineau, *A Short History of Sugar* (1917), p. 29
35. *Ibid.*, p. 9
36. *Greenock Telegraph*, 1.7.1878
37. A.P. Lyle, *op. cit.*, p. 45
38. *Greenock Telegraph*, 22.6.1881, 6.7.1881
39. *Ibid.*, 26.9.1877
40. *Ibid.*, 6.7.1881
41. *Ibid.*, 5.8.1881
42. A.P. Lyle, *op. cit.*, pp. 45–6
43. *Greenock Telegraph*, 27.10.1881
44. Bank of Scotland, Minute Books, 10.5.1882

45. A.P. Lyle, *op. cit.*, p. 47
46. *Ibid.*, p. 48
47. *Ibid.*, p. 49
48. Lyles ceased to be listed as coopers in the Greenock trade directories
49. A.P. Lyle, *op. cit.*
50. S.R.O., SC 58/42/39
51. A.P. Lyle, *op. cit.*, p. 18
52. *Greenock Telegraph*, 3.11.1876
53. *Ibid.*
54. *Ibid.*, 19.4.1879, 20.12.1878
55. *Ibid.*, 9.8.1879
56. *Ibid.*, 15.10.1878
57. *Ibid.*, 4.10.1879
58. *Ibid.*, 1.5.1891
59. P.R.O., MT/26/33
60. A.P. Lyle, *op. cit.*, p. 18
61. *Greenock Telegraph*, 5.12.1876
62. *Ibid.*, 25.5.1877
63. *Ibid.*, 29.3.1878
64. A.P. Lyle, *op. cit.*, p. 33

Chapter Four
1. S.R.A., Association of Glasgow Underwriters and Marine Insurance Brokers, Claims
   Register, TD103/2/3, p. 271
2. Lyle Shipping Co., Board Minutes
3. Gerald S. Graham, *op. cit.*, Chapter 3 (11)
4. H.J. Dyos and D.M. Aldcroft, *British Transport. An Economic Survey from the Seventeenth
   Century to the Twentieth* (1969), pp. 285–7
5. *Ibid.*, p. 290
6. *Ibid.*
7. B.M. Deakin, *Shipping Conferences, A Study of their Origins, Development and Economic Practices*
   (1973), p. 38
8. Lyle Shipping Co., Board Minutes
9. J. McKechnie 'Marine Engineering', *Proceedings of the Institute of Mechanical Engineers*, 1901,
   p. 644
10. G. Rankin Taylor, *Thomas Dunlop and Sons, Shipowners, 1851–1951* (1951), Fleet List; J.F.
    Gibson, *J.F. Brocklebanks, 1770–1950* (1953), II, Fleet List
11. A.P. Lyle, *Family Notes* (1922), p. 61
12. *Ibid.*, p. 59
13. *Ibid.*
14. C.K. Harley, 'The Shift from Sailing Ships to Steamships, 1850–1890: A Study in Techno-
    logical Change and Its Diffusion', in D.W. McCloskey, *Essays on a Mature Economy:
    Britain after 1840* (1871), pp. 227–29
15. *Transactions of the Institution of Naval Architects*, 1895, p. xxx
16. A.P. Lyle, *op. cit.*, p. 59
17. *Ibid.*, p. 67
18. *Clyde Bill of Entry*
19. P.R.O., BT 99/1155
20. *Greenock Telegraph*, 21.8.1874

Chapter Five

1. A.P. Lyle, *Family Notes* (1922), p. 68
2. *Ibid.*
3. *Ibid.*, p. 69
4. *Ibid.*
5. S.R.O., SC53/41/18
6. A.P. Lyle, *op. cit.*, p. 69
7. *Lloyds Register*
8. *Post Office Directories of Greenock*, Ship Lists
9. 'The Story of Lyle Shipping Company Limited', *The Lithgow Journal* Spring, 1965
10. S.R.O., BT2/10543
11. *Post Office Directories of Greenock*, Ship Lists
12. S.R.O., BT2/925
13. H.J. Dyos and D.H. Aldcroft, *British Transport, An Economic Survey from the Seventeenth Century to the Twentieth* (1969), p. 28
14. Investment Ledger of William Todd Lithgow, 1878–1908. In the possession of Sir William Lithgow
15. J. Lyman, 'The Part-owners of a British Sailing Vessel, 1887–1910', *The Mariner's Mirror*, 58 (1972), pp. 463–5
16. S.R.O., BT2/5363
17. 'The Story of Lyle Shipping Co. Ltd', *The Lithgow Journal* Spring, 1965
18. P.R.O., B.T.165/531
19. H.J. Dyos and D.H. Aldcroft, *op. cit.*, p. 288
20. D.H. Aldcroft, 'The Mercantile Marine' in Aldcroft (ed.), *The Development of British Industry and Foreign Competition, 1875–1914* (1968), p. 361
21. S.G. Sturmey, *British Shipping and World Competition* (1962), p. 34
22. D.H. Aldcroft, *op. cit.*, p. 326
23. D.H. Aldcroft, 'The Depression in British Shipping 1901–1911', *Journal of Transport History*, VII, (1965), p. 19
24. In 1912 the *Cape Ortegal* made a profit of £9,811 followed by £7,228 in 1913, before depreciation on the ship was paid.
25. S.R.O., SC53/41/18
26. A.P. Lyle, *op. cit.*, p. 70
27. H. Barty-King, *The Baltic Exchange. The History of a Unique Market* (1977), p. 314
28. S.G. Sturmy, *op. cit.*, p. 50
29. A.P. Lyle, *op. cit.*, p. 119
30. P.C. Macfarlane to Mrs. Macfarlane, 27 January 1916. A letter in the possession of Air Marshal Sir Anthony Selway.
31. S.G. Sturmey, *op. cit.*, p. 49
32. A.P. Lyle, *op. cit.*, pp. 161–4
33. Michael Crowdy, *Lyle Shipping Co. Ltd, 1827–1966. The Firm and the Fleet* (1966), p. 7
34. A.P. Lyle, *op. cit.*, pp. 142–6
35. *Ibid.*, pp. 154–6
36. *Ibid.*, pp. 116, 148–54
37. See Ship List
38. A.P. Lyle, *op. cit.*, pp. 147–8
39. *Ibid.*, pp. 156–64
40. S.G. Sturmey, *op. cit.*, p. 49
41. A.P. Lyle, *op. cit.*, p. 112
42. *Ibid.*, p. 165

43. *Ibid.*, pp. 164–7
44. *Ibid.*, pp. 167–73

Chapter Six
1. H. Barty-King, *The Baltic Exchange. The History of a Unique Market* (1977), p. 349
2. H.J. Dyos and D.H. Aldcroft, *British Transport. An Economic Survey from the Seventeenth Century to the Twentieth* (1969), p. 308
3. A.P. Lyle, *Family Notes* (1922), p. 72
4. H.J. Dyos and D.H. Aldcroft, *op. cit.*, p. 345
5. Lyle Shipping Co., Board Minutes
6. *Ibid.*
7. *Ibid.*, 26.5.1922
8. *Ibid.*, 4.1.1923
9. S.R.O., GD320/5/751
10. Lyle Shipping Co. Ltd, Board Minutes, 21.7.1924
11. S.R.O. GD320/5/740. The long period between the commencement of this ship (13.2.1923) and her launch (4.8.1925) suggests her construction was delayed to allow work on non-speculative projects to go ahead smoothly.
12. S.R.O. GD320/5/785
13. Lyle Shipping Co., Board Minutes, 7.12.1926
14. *Ibid.*, 16.1.1928
15. F.E. Hyde, *op. cit.*, p. 164 (Chapter 3, 13)
16. Lyle Shipping Co., Board Minutes, 3.1.1934
17. S.R.O., GD320/5
18. Lyle Shipping Co., Board Minutes, 1.2.1934
19. The date of contract between Lithgows and Lyle Shipping Co. was 16.1.1936. The *Cape Sable* was launched less than one month later, on 12.2.1936 (S.R.O., GD320/5/1/808)
20. *Fairplay's Annual Summary of British Shipping Finance* (1935) p. 506
21. *Fairplay's Annual Summary of British Shipping Finance* (1936) p. 496
22. *Fairplay's Annual Summary of British Shipping Finance* (1937) p. 507
23. Lyle Shipping Co., Board Minutes, 1.2.1934
24. *Fairplay's Annual Summary of British Shipping Finance* (1935) p. 527
25. *Fairplay's Annual Summary of British Shipping Finance* (1937) p. 507
26. Lyle Shipping Co., Board Minutes, 4.12.1934
27. *Ibid.*, 7.1.1936
28. *Ibid.*, 27.3.1936
29. *Ibid.*, 17.4.1939, 12.7.1939
30. Lyle Shipping Co., *Lycia* Movement Book
31. Lyle Shipping Co., *Cape Wrath* Movement Book
32. S.R.O., Lithgow Collection, James Shearer junior to Mr. MacCulloch, 2.9.1938
33. Lyle Shipping Co., Ship Movement Books
34. H.J. Dyos and D.H. Aldcroft, *op. cit.*, p. 350. See also, M.E. Fletcher, 'From Coal to Oil in British Shipping', *Journal of Transport History*, 3 (1975), pp. 1–19
35. Lyle Shipping Co., Board Minutes, 21.7.1936
36. Information supplied by Mr. L.N. Cogie, a member of the staff of Lyle Shipping Co. between the wars
37. *Perthshire Advertiser*, 5.12.1946

Chapter Seven

1. D.M. Sinclair, Master of the *Cape Horn*, to Lyle Shipping Co., 15.4.1942. In the possession of John T. Rennie and Sons, Cape Town. The author is grateful to Mr. E.D. Holland for sending him a copy of this and other correspondence.
2. Lyle Shipping Co., Board Minutes, 27.6.1941
3. *Ibid.*
4. *Ibid.*, 7.10.1942
5. *Ibid.*, 15.12.1939
6. *Ibid.*, 9.1.1940
7. H. Barty-King, *The Baltic Exchange. The History of a Unique Market* (1977), pp. 374–6, 381
8. S.R.O., Lithgow Collection, James Shearer to Henry Lithgow 9.11.1945
9. *Ibid.*, 27.11.1946
10. Lyle Shipping Co., Board Minutes, 8.11.1946, 13.11.1946
11. *Ibid.*, 11.2.1947
12. *Ibid.*, 23.1.1948
13. *Ibid.*, 6.10.1947
14. *Ibid.*, 26.6.1950
15. *Ibid.*, 1.11.1951
16. *Ibid.*, 27.11.1951, 22.7.1952
17. *Ibid.*, 3.12.1951, 27.12.1951
18. *Ibid.*, 24.1.1952
19. *Ibid.*, 20.2.1952
20. *Ibid.*, 23.11.1951
21. Prospectus of Lyle Shipping Co., 9.2.1953
22. A.P. Lyle, *Family Notes* (1922), p. 69

Chapter Eight

1. *Report of Committee of Enquiry into Shipping* (1970), (Chairman, Lord Rochdale), cmnd. 4337, paras. 48–50
2. *Ibid.*, paras. 208–14.
3. *Ibid.*, Table 3.4
4. *Ibid.*, para. 512
5. Information supplied by Mr. William Nicholson
6. *Report of Committee of Enquiry into Shipping*, paras. 1261–64
7. Lyle Shipping Co., Board Minutes, 13.11.1956
8. *Report of Committee of Enquiry into Shipping*, paras. 556–64
9. Lyle Shipping Co., Board Minutes, 22.11.1951
10. *Ibid.*, 23.8.1956
11. *Ibid.*, 12.6.1956
12. *Ibid.*, 14.8.1956
13. *Ibid.*, 12.3.1958, 24.11.1958
14. *Ibid.*, 21.6.1966
15. *Ibid.*, 14.5.1958
16. *Ibid.*, 12.3.1958
17. *Ibid.*, 14.11.1958
18. *Ibid.*, 6.4.1959
19. *Ibid.*, 12.6.1959, 9.12.1959
20. G. Turner, *Business in Britain* (1969), p. 290

21. *Report of Committee of Enquiry into Shipping*, paras. 495–502
22. Lyle Shipping Co., *Annual Report* (1956)
23. *Report of Committee of Enquiry into Shipping*, paras. 1363–68
24. Lyle Shipping Co., *Annual Report*, (1958)
25. Lyle Shipping Co., Board Minutes, 12.2.1958
26. *Ibid.*, 14.11.1958, 24.11.1958
27. *Ibid.*, 6.4.1959
28. *Ibid.*, 9.3.1960
29. *Ibid.*, 11.4.1962
30. *Ibid.*, 4.9.1962

Chapter Nine
 1. *Report of Committee of Enquiry into Shipping* (Lord Rochdale, chairman), (1970), p. 2
 2. *Ibid.*, paras. 533–535
 3. Lyle Shipping Co., Board Minutes, 14.11.1962
 4. *Report of Committee of Enquiry into Shipping*, p. 138
 5. *Ibid.*, p. 164
 6. Lyle Shipping Co., Board Minutes, 12.6.1963
 7. *Ibid.*, 11.9.1963
 8. *Ibid.*, 15.10.1963
 9. *Ibid.*
10. *Ibid.*, 12.2.1964
11. *Ibid.*, 26.3.1964
12. *Ibid.*, 15.5.1964
13. *Ibid.*, 27.7.1965
14. *Ibid.*, 14.4.1967
15. *Ibid.*, 15.2.1965
16. *Ibid.*, 10.9.1965
17. *Ibid.*, 12.11.1965
18. *Ibid.*, 14.1.1966
19. *Ibid.*, 12.11.1965
20. Lyle Shipping Co., *Annual Report* (1966)
21. Lyle Shipping Co., Board Minutes, 12.11.1965
22. *Ibid.*, 11.3.1966
23. *Annual Report of Lyle Shipping Co.*, 1967
24. Lyle Shipping Co., Board Minutes, 7.6.1967
25. A.A. McAlister, *A Short History of H. Hogarth & Sons, Ltd.* (1976)
26. Lyle Shipping Co., Board Minutes, 11.9.1964
27. *Ibid.*, 16.9.1966
28. *Ibid.*, 10.11.1967
29. General Council of British Shipping, *Shipping Statistics* (1975)
30. *Ibid.*
31. *Report of Committee of Enquiry into Shipping*, para. 545
32. General Council of British Shipping, *op. cit.*

Chapter Ten
 1. G. Turner, *Business in Britain* (1969), p. 294
 2. Lyle Shipping Co., Board Minutes, 9.2.1967

3. *Ibid.*, 12.5.1967
4. *Ibid.*, 16.10.1968
5. Department of Trade and Industry, *Study of Potential Benefits to British Industry from Offshore Oil and Gas Development* by International Management and Engineering Group of Britain Ltd. (1972), pp. 7–8
6. *Ibid.*, p. 33
7. *Ibid.*
8. Seaforth Maritime Ltd Brochure (1977)
9. *Ibid.*

Appendix 1 List of Directors

	Director	Managing Director	Chairman	Vice President	President
Lyle Shipping Company Limited, 1890–1900					
Alexander P. Lyle	1890–1900				
Robert Lyle	1890–1900				
Lyle Shipping Company Limited, 1903–1920					
Alexander P. Lyle	1903–1920		1903–1920		
Peter C. Macfarlane	1903–1920				
James Shearer, senior	1903–1920				
John Birkmyre*	1903–1910				
Archibald M.P. Lyle	1907–1920				
Lyle Shipping Company Limited, from 1920					
Sir Alexander P. Lyle, Bt.*	1920–1933		1920–1925		
Sir Archibald M.P. Lyle, Bt.*	1920–1946		1925–1946		
Colonel Peter C. Macfarlane*	1920–1965		1946–1965		1965–1968
James Shearer, senior	1920–1927				
James Shearer, junior	1925–1964	1925–1958			
Major Robin A. Lyle*	1935–1944				
A. Keith Macfarlane	1946–1963				
William Nicholson	1946–1977	1958–1974	1975–1977	1977–	
Lieut. Col. A. Michael Lyle*	1946–1968				1968–
Thomas S. Shearer	1950–				
Sir Iain M. Stewart*	1953–				
Herbert A. Walkinshaw	1960–	1974–	1977–		
Dr. J. Percival Agnew*	1962–1974		1965–1974	1975–	
R. Marshall Gibson	1969–				
Iain A. Noble*	1972–				
Timothy P. Noble	1976–				
Alastair C. Hogarth*	1977–1978				
John P. Walkinshaw*	1978–				

* Non-executive

Appendix 2 List of Marine and Engineering Superintendents and Masters, 1872-1977

Marine and Engineering Superintendents

James Scobie (ship's husband)	late nineteenth century
Peter Martin	c. 1914–43
James Morton	1943–61
A.M. Duguid	1961–66
R.D. Love	from 1964

Masters

Master	Ship	Years	Master	Ship	Years
J. Grosart	Queen of the Lakes	1873–74	A.M. Smith	Cape Clear II	1897–99
Miller	Cape Comorin I	1874–76	MacKay	Cape Antibes	1903–04
G. Young	Cape Horn I	1874–78	J.A. McDonald	Cape Antibes	1904–07
	Cape Breton I	1878–87	A. Warden	Cape Breton II	1904–10
Pawley	Cape Wrath I	1874–75		Cape Ortegal I	1911–13
S. Scobie	John Kerr	1874–77	C. McLeod	Cape Corso I	1905–13
J. Page	Queen of the Lakes	1874–75	D. McKie	Cape Antibes	1907–10
	Cape Sable I	1875–80	J.A. McDonald	Cape Finisterre II	1908–13
	Cape Horn I	1881–82		Cape Ortegal I	1913–16
J. Bryson	Cape Finisterre I	1875–81	J. McNeill	Cape Antibes	1910–13
W. Scobie	Cape Race I	1874–76		Cape Finisterre II	1913–14
	John Kerr	1877–79		Cape Breton II	1915–17
A. McMillan	Cape Verde I	1875–77	T.R. Wilson	Cape Breton II	1910–14
Henderson	Cape Wrath I	1875–78		Cape Finisterre II	1914–16
J. Haswell	Cape Comorin I	1876–80	J. Lochean	Cape Antibes	1913–15
J. Henderson	Cape of Good Hope I	1877–84	R.J. Hey	Cape Corso I	1913–18
A. Scobie	Cape Verde I	1877–81		Cape Ortegal I	1919–24
	Cape Race I	1881–82		Cape Comorin II	1925–27
J.C. Prout	Cape St Vincent I	1878–89	C.H. Burch	Cape Breton II	1914–15
Fergus	Cape Wrath I	1879–81		Cape Finisterre II	1915–16
A. Douglas	Cape Comorin I	1880–82	J. Lochead	Cape Finisterre II	1916–17
Watson	Cape Horn I	1880–92	A.J.M. Henderson	Cape Ortegal I	1916–19
Robertson	Cape Finisterre I	1881–86	J.D. Milner	Cape Breton II	1917–19
Griffiths	Cape Race I	1882–89	W. Nicholson	Cape Corso I	1918
J.C. Martin	Cape Wrath I	1881–85	W. Say	Cape Breton II	1919–20
Henderson	Cape Clear I	1882–84	P.R. Wallace	Cape Breton II	1920–22
Malcolm	Cape Horn I	1882–86	W. Jarvis	Cape Comorin II	1924–25
Haswell	Cape Verde I	1882–83	C.L. Bulloch	Lycia	1926–40
Scobie	Cape Verde I	1883–89	MacMaster	Cape Ortegal I	1924–30
D. McPhail	Cape of Good Hope I	1884–85	Angus	Cape Cornwall	1927–29
Doughty	Cape Wrath I	1885–86	T.A. Jackson	Cape Verde II	1928
C. McLeod	Cape of Good Hope I	1885–94		Cape of Good Hope II	1929–35
A. Clarke	Cape Finisterre I	1886–96	F.J. Orford	Cape Verde II	1928–30
R. Rendall	Cape Wrath I	1886–92		Cape Comorin II	1929–30
S. Grierson	Cape Breton I	1887–91		Cape Ortegal I	1930
	Cape Clear II	1892–97	J.A. Jacobson	Cape Verde II	1928
A. Hart	Cape St. Vincent I	1889–91	G.H. Pike	Cape Verde II	1928
	Cape Wrath II	1892–99	W.W. Martin	Cape Comorin II	1930
J. Mitchell	Cape York I	1892–1900		Cape Cornwall	1930–31

A.T. McGlashan	Cape Cornwall	1929–30
	Cape Comorin II	1931–34
	Cape Wrath III	1934–35
	Cape of Good Hope II	1935–39
	Cape Clear III	1939–42
	Cape Hawke I	1942
	Ocean Traveller	1943–44
	Samspeed	1944
	Ocean Traveller	1945
E.S. Wilkie	Cape Verde II	1929
	Cape Ortegal I	1929–30
	Cape Horn II	1930–39
J.J. Kerr	Cape Verde II	1929–30
R. Clothier	Cape Verde II	1930
	Cape Cornwall	1931–34
	Cape Corso II	1934–36
J.A. Byars	Cape Verde II	1930–34
	Cape Nelson I	1934–41
	Cape Race II	1941
	Cape Wrath IV	1941
	Cape Sable II	1942–43
	Cape Wrath IV	1943–45
	Fort Steele	1945
	Cape Howe II	1946–47
	Cape Ortegal II	1948
D.A. MacFayden	Cape Ortegal I	1931–33
J.H. Thomson	Cape York II	1933–39
	Cape Horn II	1939–40
	Cape Wrath IV	1941–42
	Fort Wedderburne	1943
	Fort Cumberland	1944–45
	Empire Teme	1945
	Fort Wedderburne	1945
	Cape Nelson II	1948
Lamont	Cape Ortegal I	1933–34
	Cape Cornwall	1934
J. Ferguson	Cape Race II	1934–40
	Empire Mermaid	1940–41
	Cape Nelson II	1948
	Cape Corso II	1948–49
J.R. McIntyre	Cape Howe I	1936–40
	Lycia	1940
	Cape York II	1940
	Empire Buffalo	1941
	Cape Wrath IV	1941
	Cape Verde III	1941–42
	Fort Wedderburne	1942–43
	Empire Farmer	1943–45
	Cape Ortegal II	1945–48
	Cape Grenville I	1948–51
	Cape York III	1952
	Cape Grenville I	1952
	Cape Clear IV	1952–53
	Cape Rodney II	1953–54

G. Macfadyen	Cape Howe I	1934–36
	Cape Sable II	1936–39
	Cape York II	1939–40
	Lycia	1940
	Cape Rodney I	1940–41
	Cape Hawke I	1941–42
	Cape Wrath IV	1943
	Cape Sable II	1943–44
	Fort Steele	1944
J. Nicholson	Cape Corso II	1934
T.D. Scorer	Cape Ortegal I	1934–35
D.M. Sinclair	Cape Verde II	1934–35
	Lycia	1935
	Cape Wrath III	1936–37
	Cape Howe I	1937
	Cape Corso II	1938–40
Supervising master: American Steamers		
	Empire Steelhead	1940
	Cape Horn II	1941–42
	Ocean Traveller	1942–43
	Fort Lajoie	1943–44
	Fort Langley	1944
	Samtana	1944–45
	Cape Howe II	1945
J.F. McChristie	Cape Corso II	1936–38
M.J. Jones	Cape Sable II	1939
P.A. Wallace	Cape of Good Hope II	1939–40
	Cape Wrath IV	1940–41
	Cape Rodney I	1941
	Cape Clear III	1942–43
	Cape Howe II	1943–45
	Empire Nairobi	1945–46
	Cape Rodney II	1946–48
	Cape Hawke I	1949–51
	Cape Grenville I	1951–52
	Cape Grafton I	1952–54
	Cape Ortegal II	1954–56
	Cape Grenville I	1956–57
	Cape York IV	1958
J.F. Auld	Empire Buffalo	1940
A. Campbell	Cape of Good Hope II	1940–42
	Fort Lajoie	1942–43
	Fort Wedderburne	1943–44
J. Barnetson	Cape York II	1940
	Cape Race II	1940–42
	Fort Steele	1942–44
	Cape Hawke I	1945–47
	Cape Rodney II	1948–53
	Cape Grenville I	1953–56
	Cape Sable II	1956
	Cape Clear IV	1957
	Cape Grenville I	1957
W.C. Montgomerie	Lycia	1940

Name	Ship	Years	Name	Ship	Years
	Cape Corso II	1940–42		*Cape Clear III*	1943
J.J.D. Ramsay	*Empire Puma*	1940–44	C.N. Crabb	*Fort Lajoie*	1944–45
M. Ritch	*Cape Corso II*	1940	J.A. Nixon	*Fort Wedderburne*	1944–46
J. Adam	*Cape Verde III*	1941		*Cape Sable II*	1946–47
	Cape Clear III	1943–44	L.C. Hoyle	*Ocean Traveller*	1944–47
	Samspeed	1945		*Fort Lajoie*	1947
	Cape Wrath IV	1945–46		*Fort Wedderburne*	1947
J. Hill	*Empire Buffalo*	1941–42	J. Beard	*Fort Lajoie*	1945–47
K.M. Mackenzie	*Cape Nelson I*	1941	W.L. Dawson	*Cape Verde IV*	1945–48
D.M. Taylor	*Empire Steelhead*	1941–42		*Cape York III*	1949
	Cape Hawke I	1943–45	H.G. Hunter	*Cape York III*	1945–48
	Empire Teme	1945–46	C.A. Jones	*Fort Cumberland*	1945–46
	Fort Cumberland	1946–47		*Fort Anne*	1947–48
	Cape Howe II	1947–49		*Cape Nelson II*	1948–49
	Cape Ortegal II	1949–53		*Cape Howe II*	1949
	Cape Grafton I	1953–54		*Cape Grafton I*	1952
	Cape York IV	1955–58		*Cape Grenville I*	1953
	Cape Horn III	1959–62		*Cape Franklin I*	1953–54
	Cape Howe III	1962–63		*Cape Ortegal II*	1954
	Cape Sable III	1963–64		*Cape Grafton I*	1954–57
	Cape Nelson III	1965–66		*Cape Nelson II*	1958–59
	Cape Howe III	1966		*Cape Howe II*	1960–61
J.S. Binnie	*Cape Sable II*	1943		*Cape Sable III*	1962
	Fort Steel	1947–48	P. St. C. Willet	*Fort Anne*	1946
	Cape Sable II	1948		*Fort Wedderburne*	1947
	Cape Nelson II	1949–51		*Cape Corso III*	1947–51
	Cape York III	1951		*Cape Clear IV*	1952–54
G. Farmborough	*Cape Sable II*	1943	J. Mallam	*Ocean Traveller*	1947
	Empire Puma	1943		*Fort Anne*	1948
	Cape Sable II	1944–46	H.S. Todd	*Cape York III*	1947
	Fort Wedderburne	1946		*Cape Hawke I*	1947–48
	Cape Wrath IV	1946–50	W.D. Wilson	*Fort Beauharnois*	1947–48
	Cape Nelson II	1951–54		*Cape Verde IV*	1948–50
	Cape Clear IV	1954–56		*Cape Wrath IV*	1950–56
	Cape Rodney II	1957	J. Ferguson	*Cape Nelson II*	1948
	Cape Clear IV	1957–59		*Cape Corso III*	1948–49
J.T. Hair	*Fort Cumberland*	1943–44	J.R. Hall	*Cape Sable II*	1949–51
	Samtana	1944		*Cape Franklin I*	1951–52
C.G. Mallett	*Empire Day*	1943–44		*Cape Corso III*	1953–54
	Fort Steele	1945–47	W. Baird	*Cape Verde IV*	1950–52
	Cape Sable II	1947–48	Barr	*Cape Verde IV*	1952–53
	Cape Ortegal II	1948	G.E. Miles	*Table Bay*	1950–52
	Cape Franklin I	1950–51		*Lake Minnewanka*	1954
	Cape Hawke I	1951–53		*Table Bay*	1955–56
	Cape Howe II	1954–55		*Lake Pennask*	1956–57
	Cape Franklin I	1955–57		*Lake Pennask*	1962–63
	Cape York IV	1957	Hill Wilson	*Durban Bay*	1950–54
	Cape Ortegal II	1957–60		*Cape Rodney II*	1954–56
	Cape Grafton I	1960–62	N. Bellwood	*Cape Clear IV*	1952
	Cape Franklin II	1962–63	R.D. Love	*Cape Sable II*	1951–53
R. Reid	*Cape Wrath IV*	1943		*Cape Verde IV*	1954–56
	Fort Cumberland	1947–49		*Cape Ortegal II*	1956–57
	Cape Howe II	1949–52		*Cape Corso III*	1957–59
G.R. Williamson	*Empire Claymore*	1943		*Cape Nelson III*	1961–64

J.A. Ridley	Cape Grafton I	1951–52
A.B. Sutherland	Cape Corso III	1951–53
	Cape Hawke I	1953–59
	Cape Sable III	1959–62
	Cape York IV	1963–64
	Cape Sable III	1960–62
C.M. Mortimer	Cape Howe II	1952–54
A.M. Cabot	Table Bay	1953
A. Davidson	Cape Franklin I	1953–55
J. Fairgrieve	Cape Corso III	1953–57
	Cape Grenville I	1958
	Cape Sable III	1960
A.M. Fraser	Cape Sable II	1953–55
	Cape Howe II	1955–58
	Cape Grenville I	1958–59
	Cape York IV	1959–60
	Cape York IV	1962–63
	Cape Ortegal II	1964
H. Gentles	Table Bay	1953–55
J. Adam	Cape Sable II	1957–58
	Cape Rodney II	1959–61
R.O. Allen	Cape Nelson II	1954–55
	Cape Wrath IV	1957–58
	Cape Howe II	1958–60
	Cape York IV	1960–62
	Cape Sable III	1962–63
J.C. Lennie	Cape Sable II	1955–56
T. Edge	Cape Rodney II	1956
E.B. Murray	Table Bay	1956–57
J.J. Reed	Cape Verde IV	1956
	Cape Nelson II	1957
W.L. Steel	Cape Nelson II	1956–57
	Cape Ortegal II	1957
R.J. McGugan	Cape Rodney II	1957
	Lake Pennask	1957–61
	Cape Rodney II	1961–63
P. Smith	Cape Hawke I	1957
	Cape Grafton I	1958–59
	Cape Grenville I	1959–62
R.L. Barr	Cape Rodney II	1958
N. Robertson	Cape Hawke I	1959–62
	Cape Grenville I	1962
R.D. Sparling	Cape Grafton I	1959
A. Mackinley	Cape Grafton I	1959–60
D. Sinclair	Cape Ortegal II	1960–63
	Cape Rodney II	1963
R. Cameron	Lake Pennask	1961–62
	Cape Clear IV	1962–63
A. McLeod	Cape Grafton I	1962–63
	Cape Ortegal II	1964
	Cape Howe III	1967
T.R. Baker	Cape Hawke II	1962–63
	Cape Grenville I	1963–65
A. C. Hunter	Cape Ortegal II	1963–64

Masters of Lyle ships since the formation of Scottish Ship Management Ltd

G. Anderson	A. Mackinlay
W. Anderson	C.G. Mallett
T.R. Baker	A. Maxwell
I.J.I. Barclay	A.G.F. Michie
J.R.L. Cain	A.L. Milne
P. Cooney	M. Murray
F.M. Dalby	J. Paterson
K.N. Dootson	A. Peebles
G. Downie	J.R.C. Peterson
T.P. Edge	S.J. Readman
A.M. Fraser	P. Richardson
W. Greatorex	J.A. Roberts
S. Gordon	G.W. Roger
P.B. Hall	D. Sinclair
J. Hetherington	P. Smith
L.M. Hocking	C. Strachan
T.C.D. Hogg	A.B. Sutherland
A.C. Hunter	J. Tattersall
D.L. Innes	D.M. Taylor
J.E. Jennings	G. Towers
J.G. Jones	M. Turton
B.W. Lawson	I. Tyrrell
C.S. Macdonald	T.R.K. Walker
C. Maclean	N.W.G. Walsh
J. MacNab	W. Warden
A. McLeod	I.R. Wemyss
J.M. Mackay	

This list of Lyle captains is not quite complete. Some names are missing for the 1930s and the mid-1960s.

Sources: Lloyds Register of Shipping
            Records of Lyle Shipping Co. Ltd

Appendix 3 Ship List

Part One

Ships in which members of the Lyle family had an interest (1791–1832)

CHRISTIES
Sloop
30.5 tons
Built at Greenock. 1791: purchased by Robert Lyle, cooper; James Morrison and Archibald McLean, mariners. 1794: sold.

LUCY
Sloop
15 tons
1789: built Donaghadee, Ireland. 1799: purchased by Dugald MacPhaedran, Donald Mactavish, and Gideon Lyle, coopers. 1802: broken up.

CLUSTER OF PEARLS
Sloop
31 tons
1789: built at Anstruther. 1800: purchased by Robert Lyle, cooper, William Newsham, plumber, and William Campbell, mariner. 1802: sold.

FRIENDSHIP
Sloop
46 tons
1785: built Clackmannanshire. 1800: purchased by Robert Turner, smith, Malcolm Morrison, mariner, and Gideon Lyle, cooper.

COMMERCE
Brigantine
104 tons
1792: built at Weymouth. 1809: purchased by John Kerr, senior, and John Kerr, junior, merchants. 1816: acquired by Alexander Clark and Gideon Lyle, coopers.

MARIA
Sloop
27 tons
1797: built at Ramsay, Isle of Man. 1825: purchased by John Kerr II and Gideon Lyle. 1838: sold.

BELMONT
Brigantine
294 tons
1825: built at Aromueto, St. John's Province, New Brunswick, Canada. 1829: purchased by John Miller, David Sharp and Edward Paul, merchants in Greenock; and James Penell, sailmaker, Abram Lyle, cooper, and John Bog, blacksmith: sold 1829.

HELEN MACGREGOR
Barquentine
210 tons
1827: built at Miramachie, New Brunswick for Abram Lyle and William McDonald, merchants (trading as Abram Lyle & Co.); and Duncan Gibb, merchant of Liverpool. 1829: sold.

FOUNDLING
Barquentine
205 tons
1814: captured by H.M.S. *Honourable* from the French at Antigua. 1823: partially rebuilt by Robert Steele & Co., Greenock. 1828: purchased by Abram Lyle, John Kerr II, and Robert Kerr. 1832: sold.

.

Part Two

The Fleet of John Kerr & Company or the 'Diamond K' Fleet (1847–72)

D.K.1 *ESQUIMAUX* (1835–50)
Wood brig
161 tons
1832: completed at Quebec. 1835: purchased by John Kerr II and James Boyd, merchant in Glasgow. 1845: acquired by John Kerr III. 1850: missing on passage from Havana to the Clyde.

D.K.2 *AMANDA* (1847–52)
Wood brig
130 tons
1838: built at Renewze, Newfoundland. Originally owned by Kerr and McBride. 1847: purchased by John Kerr. 1852: lost.

D.K.3 *ISABELLA COOPER* (1847–48)
Wood barque
371 tons
1847: acquired by John Kerr and Archibald Robertson and James Mackenzie, commission agents, Glasgow. 1848: lost.

D.K.4 *CONSORT* (1847)
Wood barque
199 tons
1845: built at Aberdeen for George Leslie, shipowner, Aberdeen. 1847: acquired by John Kerr, Abram Lyle, master. 29.3.1847: wrecked in the Western Ocean.

D.K.5   *LADY CORNWALL* (1850–55)
Wood brig
189 tons
1830: completed at Brockwave, Gloucestershire. 1850: purchased from J.F. King, Greenock, by J. Kerr & Co. 1855: sold to Young & Co., Glasgow.

D.K.6   *ELIZABETH CAMPBELL* (1850–54)
Wood barque
316 tons
106 × 23.5 × 17.1 feet
1850: completed at Dumbarton for John Kerr & Co. 1854: purchased by J. Spiers, Glasgow.

D.K.7   *RETRIEVE* (1850–51)
Wood brig
235 tons
1840: completed at Quebec for Urie & Co., Glasgow. 1845: purchased by A. Rankin, Glasgow. 1850: purchased by John Kerr & Co. 1851: wrecked.

D.K.8   *MARGARET SMITH I* (1851–57)
Wood barque
258 tons
1851: completed by James McMillan, Greenock, for John Kerr & Co. 1857: out of register.

D.K.9   *MOUNTAINEER* (1851–54)
Wood barque
355 tons
1835: completed at Greenock for Anderson, Greenock. 1845: sold to T. Smith, Glasgow. 1851: purchased by John Kerr & Co. 1854: sold to Neill, Greenock.

D.K.10   *WILLIAM CAMPBELL* (1851–53)
Wood barque
340 tons
1851: completed by McMillan, Dumbarton, for John Kerr & Co. 1853: purchased by J. Spiers, Glasgow.

D.K.11   *BUCEPHALUS* (1852–56)
Wood barque
471 tons
1839: completed at Greenock when ship-rigged. By 1845: owned by Corbett & Co., Greenock. 1849: reduced to barque. 1852: purchased by John Kerr & Co. 1856: purchased by T. Lindsay, Leith.

D.K.12   *ISABELLA KERR I* (1852–59)
Wood barque
398 tons
1852: completed at Dumbarton for John Kerr & Co. 1859: missing off Demerara when bound Clyde to West Indies.

D.K.13 *AGNES TAYLOR* (1853–59)
Wood barque
399 tons
1853: completed by McMillan, Dumbarton, for John Kerr & Co. 1859: out of register.

D.K.14 *ISABELLA* (1853–59)
Wood brig
281 tons
1830: completed at Quebec. 1850: owned by McFee Brothers, Ardrossan. 1853: purchased by John Kerr & Co. 1859: lost on voyage from Matanzas to the Clyde.

D.K.15 *JAMAICA* (1853–55)
Wood ship
334 tons
1796: completed at Greenock. 1845: owned by Rodger & Co., Glasgow. Later reduced to barque rig. 1853: purchased by J. Kerr & Co. 1855: burnt out near Port William, Wigtownshire.

D.K.16 *JAMES CAMPBELL* (1853–55)
Wood brigantine
303 tons
1842: completed at Dumbarton. By 1845: owned by Galbreath, Glasgow. 1850: purchased by McKenzie, Glasgow. 1853: purchased by John Kerr & Co. 1855: foundered.

D.K.17 *ARCHIBALD McMILLAN* (1854–66)
Wood ship
498 tons
147.3 × 24.9 × 16.3 feet
1854: completed at Dumbarton for John Kerr & Co. 1866: wrecked at Punta Mulas, Cuba.

D.K.18 *ABYSSINIA* (1854–58)
Wood barque
399 tons
1849: completed at Sunderland for Murray & Co. 1854: purchased by John Kerr & Co. 1859: lost on a voyage to Demerara.

D.K.19 *JOHN FERGUSON* (1854–70)
Wood barque
499 tons
148 × 25 × 16.5 feet
1854: completed at Dumbarton for John Kerr & Co. 1870: wrecked in the Isle of Cloes.

D.K.20 *MARCHIONESS OF AILSA* (1854–59)
Wood barque
299 tons
1847: completed at Ayr for Sloan & Co. 1854: purchased by John Kerr & Co. 1859: lost at Troon.

D.K.21 *TRINIDAD I* (1854–66)
Wood ship
485 tons
138 × 24.7 × 17.1 feet
1854: completed at Dumbarton for John Kerr & Co. 1866: abandoned at sea.

D.K.22 *DEMERARA I* (1855–63)
Wood ship
485 tons
146.5 × 25 × 16.1 feet
1855: completed by McMillan, Dumbarton for John Kerr & Co. 1863: wrecked on the Shingles.

D.K.23 *EARL OF LONSDALE* (1855–60)
Wood ship
310 tons
1839: completed at Whitehaven. 1845: owned by Salmon, Whitehaven. 1855: purchased by John Kerr & Co. 1856: altered to barque. 1860: lost off Whitehaven.

D.K.24 *PURSUIT* (1855–57)
Wood brig
219 tons
1840: completed at Dundee. By 1845: owned by Erskine & Co., Dundee. 1850: purchased by J. Leitch, Greenock. 1852: purchased by J. Neill, Greenock. 1855: purchased by John Kerr & Co. for £1,070. 1857: out of register.

D.K.25 *VARNA* (1855–57)
Wood barque
551 tons
1855: completed at New Brunswick and purchased by John Kerr & Co. for £5,100. 1857: wrecked Tasmania.

D.K.26 *AUCHNEAGH* (1856–68)
Wood ship
629 tons
156.7 × 29.5 × 18.9 feet
2.1856: completed by McMillan, Dumbarton for John Kerr & Co. 1868: wrecked.

D.K.27 *BARBADIAN I* (1856–64)
Wood ship
569 tons
150 × 29.4 × 19 feet
1856: completed by McMillan, Dumbarton, for John Kerr & Co. 1864: burnt out.

D.K.28 *CUBAN* (1856–69)
Wood ship
477 tons
130.5 × 28.2 × 18.6 feet
1856: completed at Greenock for John Kerr & Co. 1869: lost on a voyage to Cuba.

D.K.29 *MAURITIUS I* (1856–62)
Wood ship
623 tons
160 × 30 × 19.5 feet
1856: completed by McMillan, Dumbarton for John Kerr & Co. 1862: abandoned at sea.

D.K.30 *BERBICE I* (1857–67)
Wood ship
632 tons
158.1 × 29.6 × 19.0 feet
9.1857: completed by McMillan, Dumbarton for John Kerr & Co. 1867: wrecked near home.

D.K.31 *MARGARET SMITH II* (1857–79)
Wood ship
631 tons
158.7 × 29.8 × 19.3 feet
1857: completed at Greenock for John Kerr & Co. 1872: valued at £3,170. 20.11.1879: wrecked near Mauritius.

D.K.32 *MATANZAS* (1857–61)
Wood barque
325 tons
1857: completed at Greenock for John Kerr & Co. 1861: sold to John McMillan of Dumbarton.

D.K.33 *ANTIGUA* (1858–76)
Wood ship
644 tons
158.7 × 29.6 × 19.0 feet
1858: completed by McMillan, Dumbarton for John Kerr & Co. 1872: valued at £3,215. 1876: out of register.

D.K.34 *SURINAM I* (1858–62)
Wood ship
495 tons
1858: completed at Greenock. 1862: wrecked in Gulf of St. Lawrence.

D.K.35 *BOMBAY* (1859–70)
Wood ship
890 tons
173.5 × 34.3 × 21.5 feet
1859: completed by McMillan, Dumbarton for John Kerr & Co. 1870: lost on voyage Glasgow to Bombay.

D.K.36   *GREENOCK* (1859–84)
Wood ship
640 tons
157.4 × 29.7 × 19.5 feet
12.1859: completed by McMillan, Dumbarton for John Kerr & Co. 1872: valued at
£3,515. 1873: reduced to barque. 1884: out of register.

D.K.37   *KURRACHEE* (1860–80)
Wood ship
695 tons
159 × 32.4 × 20.9 feet
8.1860: completed by McMillan, Dumbarton. 1872: valued at £4,314. 1880: out
of register.

D.K.38   *LEPHENSTRATH* (1860–80)
Wood ship
623 tons
154.9 × 29.8 × 19.3 feet
1860: completed by McMillan, Dumbarton. 1872: valued at £3,738. 1880: out of
register.

D.K.39   *CALEDONIAN* (1861–78)
Wood ship
607 tons
157 × 29.8 × 19 feet
12.1861: completed by McMillan, Dumbarton. 1872: valued at £3,762. 1873:
converted to barque. 19.7.1878: lost in Table Bay.

D.K.40   *MARGARET KERR* (1861–64)
Wood ship
650 tons
158.7 × 29.5 × 19.6 feet
4.1861: completed by McMillan, Dumbarton. 1864: wrecked on Guers Reef,
Florida.

D.K.41   *ORISSA III* (1862–69)
Wood ship
634 tons
152.5 × 31.2 × 19.5 feet
11.1862: completed by McMillan, Dumbarton. 1869: burnt out.

D.K.42   *MADRAS I* (1863–64)
Wood ship
670 tons
160 × 29.5 × 19.5 feet
1863: completed for John Kerr & Co. by McMillan, Dumbarton. 1865: lost in the
Urina Sea.

D.K.43 *MAURITIUS II* (1863–80)
Wood ship
662 tons
160 × 30 × 19.5 feet
1863: completed by McMillan, Dumbarton for John Kerr & Co. 1872: valued at £3,966. 1880: out of register.

D.K.44 *SURINAM II* (1863–64)
Wood ship
483 tons
136 × 28.5 × 18.5 feet.
1863: completed by McMillan, Dumbarton for John Kerr & Co. 1864: lost on a voyage from Trinidad.

D.K.45 *DEMERARA II* (1864–83)
Wood ship
486 tons
139.4 × 29.2 × 18.4 feet
1864: completed by McMillan, Dumbarton for John Kerr & Co. 1872: valued at £2,916. 1873: converted to a barque. 1883: sold to Foulds & Bone, Greenock. 14.7.1884: abandoned outward bound from Newport with coal.

D.K.46 *GRENADA* (1864–80)
Wood ship
684 tons
162.4 × 30.8 × 19.6 feet
1864: completed by McMillan, Dumbarton for John Kerr & Co. 1872: valued at £3,966. 1880: out of register.

D.K.47 *ISABELLA KERR II* (1864–76)
Composition ship
1,415 tons
214.8 × 38.5 × 24.2 feet
1864: completed by McMillan, Dumbarton for John Kerr & Co. 1872: valued at £11,320. 1876: out of register.

D.K.48 *QUEEN OF THE LAKES* (1864–73)
See Ship List, Part Three.

D.K.49 *BERMUDA* (1865–66)
Wood ship
677 tons
161 × 30.8 × 19.6 feet
1865: completed by McMillan, Dumbarton for John Kerr & Co. 2.1866: on maiden voyage, Greenock to Trinidad, wrecked at Westersay, near Sandera Island.

D.K.50 *MADRAS II* (1865–88)
Wood ship
668 tons
160.5 × 30.6 × 19.7 feet
3.1865: completed by McMillan, Dumbarton for John Kerr & Co. 1872: valued
at £4,335. 1883: altered to barque. 1888: purchased by D. Jones, Greenock.

D.K.51 *CEYLON* (1866–68)
Composition ship
1,073 tons
207.2 × 33.3 × 21.1 feet
1866: completed by McMillan, Dumbarton for John Kerr & Co. 1868: wrecked on
voyage, Glasgow to Bombay.

D.K.52 *BARBADIAN II* (1867–89)
Composition ship
700 tons
176.6 × 31.3 × 18.4 feet
10.1867: completed by McMillan, Dumbarton for John Kerr & Co. 1872: valued
at £6,990. 1889: purchased by G.T. Soley & Co., Liverpool.

D.K.53 *TROCHRAGUE* (1867–86)
Wood ship
677 tons
161 × 30.9 × 19.5 feet
1867: completed by McMillan, Dumbarton for John Kerr & Co. 1872: valued at
£4,639. 1886: purchased by Pande, Sundbye & Co., Christiania and renamed *Falka*.

D.K.54 *BERBICE II* (1868–88)
Composition ship
717 tons
174 × 31.5 × 18.3 feet
1868: completed by McMillan, Dumbarton for John Kerr & Co. 1872: valued
at £7,160. 6.6.1888: wrecked at the entrance to Newcastle, New South Wales.

D.K.55 *COLOMBO* (1868–79)
Iron ship
1,199 tons
230.5 × 36.3 × 22.4 feet
1868: completed by R. Duncan & Co., Port Glasgow for John Kerr & Co. 1872:
valued at £13,200. 1879: purchased by G. Petrie, Greenock.

D.K.56 *MALABAR* (1868–70)
Iron ship
1,200 tons
228.7 × 36.0 × 22.3 feet
1868: completed by Robertson, Greenock for John Kerr & Co. 20.9.1870: abandoned
on fire, Lat. 26S, Long. 31.17W.

D.K.57 *SINDE* (1868–70)
Iron ship
1,200 tons
230.5 × 36.3 × 22.4 feet
1868: completed by R. Duncan & Co. of Port Glasgow for John Kerr & Co. 1870: foundered on a voyage between Demerara and Havana.

D.K.58 *TRINIDAD II* (1868–85)
Composition ship
722 tons
171.7 × 31.6 × 18.8 feet
1868: completed by McMillan, Dumbarton for John Kerr & Co. 1872: valued at £7,220. 1885: out of register.

D.K.59 *ZANZIBAR* (1868–73)
See Ship List, Part Three, *Cape Horn I.*

D.K.60 *COCHIN* (1869–97)
Iron ship
1,200 tons
229 × 36 × 22.2 feet
1869: completed by Robertson, Greenock for John Kerr & Co. 1872: valued at £13,200. 1897: purchased by C. Hannevig, Christiania, Norway and renamed *Elfi.*

D.K.61 *JAVA* (1869–73)
See Ship List, Part Three, *Cape Comorin I.*

D.K.62 *ORISSA II* (1869–95)
Iron ship
1,199 tons
225.2 × 35.3 × 21.4 feet
10.1869: completed by J. & G. Thomson, Glasgow for John Kerr & Co. 1872: valued at £11,550. 1895: sold to O. Lohne, Mandal, Norway.

D.K.63 *COLMONELL* (1871–73)
See Ship List, Part Three, *Cape Wrath I.*

D.K.64 *CULZEAN* (1871–81)
Iron ship
1,572 tons
254 × 40 × 23.9 feet
1871: completed by J. Reid & Co., Port Glasgow for John Kerr & Co. 1872: valued at £14,786. 21.11.1881: wrecked in Sound of Jura when bound Dundee to Glasgow in tow.

D.K.65 *KILKERRAN* (1871–88)
Iron ship
1,199 tons
231 × 37 × 23.4 feet
1871: completed by J. Reid & Co., Port Glasgow. 1872: valued at £11,287. 27.9.1888: burnt out while lying at Totorabillo.

Part Three

The Fleets of Abram Lyle & Sons (1873–90) and The Lyle Shipping Company (1890–1900)

1 *QUEEN OF THE LAKES* (1873–75)
Wood ship
1,154 net tons
180.8 × 36.6 × 22.9 feet
5.1864: completed by Patterson, Quebec for James Gibb Ross, Quebec. 29.11.1864: purchased by John Kerr & Co., John Kerr holding 32 64th shares in trust for Abram Lyle. 4.1872: valued at £4,608. 26.3.1873: Abram Lyle purchased all shares. 9.12.1875: abandoned in a position 48.31N, 20.19W after her cargo had shifted while she was on a voyage from Moulmein to Greenock.

2 *CAPE COMORIN I* (1873–82)
Iron ship
1,200 net tons, 1,257 gross tons
229 × 36 × 22.2 feet
8.1869: completed by Robertson & Co., Greenock as *Java* for John Kerr & Co., John Kerr holding 32 64th shares in trust for Abram Lyle. 4.1872: valued at £13,200. 16.7.1873: Abram Lyle became sole owner of all shares. 1874: renamed *Cape Comorin*. 5.3.1880: Abram Lyle (junior), Alexander Park Lyle, Charles Lyle, William Park Lyle and Robert Lyle became joint owners of all shares. 29.9.1882: sailed from Glasgow for Buenos Aires with a crew of 27 and after passing Rathlin Island (30.9.1882) disappeared with all hands.

3 *CAPE HORN I* (1873–86)
Iron ship
1,200 net tons, 1,253 gross tons
229 × 36 × 22.3 feet
12.1868: completed by Robertson & Co., Greenock as *Zanzibar* for John Kerr & Co., John Kerr holding 32 64th shares in trust for Abram Lyle. 4.1872: valued at £13,200. 16.7.1873: Abram Lyle became sole owner of all shares. 1874: renamed *Cape Horn*. 5.3.1880: Abram Lyle (junior), A.P. Lyle, C. Lyle, W.P. Lyle and R. Lyle became joint owners of the ship. 27.2.1886: sailed from Surabaya for the U.K. and disappeared with her crew of 25.

4 *CAPE WRATH I* (1873–91)
Iron ship
1,199 net tons, 1,255 gross tons
231 × 37 × 23.4 feet
6.1871: completed by John Reid & Co., Port Glasgow, as the *Colmonell* for John Kerr & Co., with John Kerr holding 21 64th shares in trust of Abram Lyle. 4.1872: valued at £16,932. 16.7.1873: Abram Lyle became sole owner of all shares. 1874: renamed *Cape Wrath*. 5.3.1880: Abram Lyle (junior), A.P. Lyle, C. Lyle, W.P. Lyle and R. Lyle became joint owners of all shares. 30.4.1890: transferred to the ownership of The Lyle Shipping Co. Ltd. 1891: sold to C. Paulsen, Elsfleth, Germany and renamed *Lina*.

5 *JOHN KERR* (1873–79)
Iron ship
1,782 net tons, 1,864 gross tons
247.7 × 42 × 23.5 feet
12.1873: completed by John Reid & Co., Port Glasgow for Abram Lyle & Sons 2.8.1879: sailed from Middlesbrough, bound for Calcutta. 27.8.1879: Spoken in a position 12N, 25W and thereafter disappeared with her crew of 36.

6 *CAPE RACE I* (1874–89)
Iron ship
852 net tons, 907 gross tons
197.2 × 34.2 × 18.3 feet
8.1874: completed by Caird & Co., Greenock for Abram Lyle & Sons. 1889: Sold to Lawrence Tulloch, Swansea. 1902: sold to G. Chiapella, Italy, and renamed *Electa*. 1916: sold to Professor Nicolo Garaventa and moored at Genoa as a youth's correction training ship.

7 *CAPE VERDE I* (1874–89)
Iron ship
1,711 net tons, 1,786 gross tons
249 × 40.3 × 23.1 feet
9.1874: completed by Thomas Wingate & Co., Glasgow for Abram Lyle & Sons. 23.6.1889: run down and sunk while at anchor off Hobson's Bay, near Melbourne by *Iolanthe*, which was coming in too fast on a dark night. At the time of her loss *Cape Verde* was on a voyage from London to Melbourne.

8 *CAPE FINISTERRE I* (1874–89)
Iron barque
882 net tons, 935 gross tons
198.5 × 33.3 × 18.6 feet
10.1874: completed by Thomas Wingate & Co., Glasgow for Abram Lyle & Sons. 1889: sold to W.H. Ross & Co., Liverpool.

9 *CAPE SABLE I* (1874–80)
Iron ship
1,416 net tons, 1,480 gross tons
239.4 × 37.2 × 22.5 feet
12.1874: completed by Thomas Wingate & Co., Glasgow for Abram Lyle & Sons. 6.6.1880: sailed from Sunderland bound for Singapore, and after being spoken 13.6.1880 in a position 50N 5W disappeared with her crew of 28.

10 *CAPE OF GOOD HOPE I* (1876–94)
Iron ship
1,399 net tons, 1,493 gross tons
238.8 × 37.7 × 22.5 feet
7.1876: completed by J. & G. Thomson, Glasgow for Abram Lyle & Sons. Cost £22,234. 1890: passed into the ownership of The Lyle Shipping Co. Ltd. 1894: sold to J.F. Dessauer, Denmark, and renamed *Amy*.

Appendix 3.1

The iron barque *Cape Finisterre* at Canterbury, New Zealand, about 1880. The vessel astern of her is the *Canterbury*. This photograph was sent by Colin Munro, the sailmaker on the *Cape Finisterre*, to his parents. On the back he wrote: 'I enclose this card so that you will see our ship in full so that you can see how dirty we are outside, by the cleanness of the *Canterbury*'.

11 *CAPE ST. VINCENT I* (1877–91)
    Iron ship
    1,422 net tons, 1,504 gross tons
    239.1 × 37.8 × 22.2 feet
    12.1877: completed by J. & G. Thomson, Glasgow for Abram Lyle & Sons. Cost
    £21,392. 4.1890: passed into ownership of The Lyle Shipping Co .Ltd. 1891: sold to Otto
    Banck, Sweden and renamed *Lady Lina*.

12 *CAPE BRETON I* (1877–91)
    Iron ship
    1,421 net tons, 1,504 gross tons
    239.3 × 37.8 × 22.1 feet
    12.1877: completed by J. & G. Thomson, Glasgow for Abram Lyle & Sons. Cost £21,392.
    1890: passed into ownership of The Lyle Shipping Co. Ltd. 1891: sold to S. Goldberg
    & Sons, Swansea.

13 *CAPE CLEAR I* (1881–84)
Iron steamship
1,501 net tons, 2,350 gross tons
291.5 × 38.1 × 26.2 feet
Compound inverted two cylinder steam engines constructed by shipbuilders.
9.1881: completed by R. Steele & Co., Greenock for Abram Lyle & Sons. 11.1884: sold
to Union Steamship Co. of New Zealand and renamed *Tekapo* after conversion at the
yard of William Denny & Bros, Dumbarton, into a passenger vessel.

14 *CAPE YORK I* (1890–1900)
Steel four-masted barque
2,030 net tons, 2,128 gross tons
276.5 × 41.2 × 24.3 feet
8.1890: completed by Barclay Curle & Co. Ltd, Glasgow for The Lyle Shipping Co. Ltd.
1900: sold to A.D. Bordes et fils, France and renamed *Gers*.

15 *CAPE CLEAR II* (1892–9ϲ`
Steel four-masted barque
2,017 net tons, 2,129 gross tons
279.6 × 42.1 × 24.4 feet
5.1892: completed by R. Duncan & Co. Ltd, Port Glasgow for The Lyle Shipping Co.
Ltd. 1899: sold to A.D. Bordes et fils, France and renamed *Amerique*.

16 *CAPE WRATH II* (1892–99)
Steel four-masted barque
1,998 net tons, 2,140 gross tons
280.3 × 42.1 × 24.4 feet
8.1892: completed by R. Duncan & Co. Ltd, Port Glasgow for The Lyle Shipping
Co. Ltd. 1899: sold to the Dominion Ship Co. Ltd, Liverpool.

Part Four

The Fleet of Lyle Shipping Company Ltd (1903–77)

1 *CAPE ANTIBES* (1903–15)
Steamship
2,549 gross tons, 1,616 net tons
325.7 × 45.3 × 20.3 feet
Triple expansion 3 cylinder steam engines built by North Eastern Marine Engineering
Co. Ltd, Newcastle.
5.1903: completed by W. Dobson & Co., Newcastle for the Cape Antibes Steamship Co.
Ltd. Cost £32,825. 21.10.1915: mined and sunk at the entrance to the White Sea between
Cape Gorodezki and Cape Orlot while on passage from Barry to Archangel. Six members
of the crew lost their lives.

2 *CAPE BRETON II* (1904–22)
Steamship
3,872 gross tons, 2,501 net tons
360 × 49 × 17.5 feet
Triple expansion 3 cylinder steam engines built by D. Rowan & Co., Glasgow.
9.1904: completed by Russell & Co., Port Glasgow for the Cape Breton Steamship Co
Ltd. Cost £40,775. 1920: transferred to Lyle Shipping Co. Ltd. 1922: sold to the A/S
Laboremus (T. Dannevig & Co., managers), Norway, renamed *Roald Amunsden* and
converted into a whaling depot ship.

3 *CAPE CORSO I* (owned 1905–17, managed 1917–19)
Steamship
3,890 gross tons, 2,510 net tons
369.7 × 49 × 17 feet
Triple expansion 3 cylinder engines built by D. Rowan & Co., Glasgow.
9.1905: completed by Russell & Co., Port Glasgow, for the Cape Corso Steamship Co.
Ltd. Cost £41,127. 12.10.1917: torpedoed by a German submarine nine miles west of
St. Goven's lightvessel, near Milford Haven, 13 members of her crew losing their lives.
14.10.1917: Towed into Swansea where she broke her back while awaiting repair.
Abandoned to the Ministry of Shipping as a constructive total loss, she was repaired and
returned to service, Lyle Shipping Co. Ltd being appointed managers: 19.3.1919: sold
by auction to Sir William Garthwaite, Bt.

4 *CAPE FINISTERRE II* (1907–17)
Steamship
4,380 gross tons, 2,803 net tons
385 × 49.8 × 18.4 feet
Triple expansion 3 cylinder engines built by Rankin & Blackmore, Greenock.
11.1907: completed by Russell & Co., Port Glasgow, for the Cape Finisterre Steamship
Co. Ltd. Cost £50,203. 2.11.1917: torpedoed and sunk by a German submarine near
the Manacles Rocks while on passage from Falmouth to Penzance (for Brest). 35 members
of her crew were lost, only six being saved.

5 *CAPE ORTEGAL I* (1911–36)
Steamship
4,896 gross tons, 3,136 net tons
405 × 52.4 × 27.4 feet
Triple expansion 3 cylinder engines built by Rankin and Blackmore, Greenock.
2.1911: completed by Russell & Co., Port Glasgow for Lyle Shipping Co. Ltd. Cost
£43,613. 8.11.1916: heavily damaged when lying at Bakaritza, Archangel, by an
explosion aboard the Russian *Baron Driesen*, two members of her crew being killed. After
temporary repairs she sailed, via Lerwick, to the Clyde for repairs at her builders yard
which lasted from 8.12.1916 to 28.4.1917. 1936: sold to the Heston Shipping Co. Ltd
(manager: J.C. Radcliffe) for £8,250.

6 *CAPE COMORIN II* (1924–34)
Steamship
5,146 gross tons, 3,237 net tons
400 × 53.5 × 27.1 feet
Triple expansion 3 cylinder engines built by Central Marine Engine Works, West Hartlepool.
11.1912: completed by William Gray & Co. Ltd, West Hartlepool, as *Arakan* for the Rotterdamsche Lloyd (William Ruys & Zonen, managers), Netherlands. 1924: purchased by Lyle Shipping Co. Ltd for £40,000 and renamed *Cape Comorin*. 19.12.1934: arrived at Venice to be scrapped. Sold to shipbreakers for £6,975.

7 *CAPE OF GOOD HOPE II* (1925–42)
Motorship
4,963 gross tons, 3,157 net tons
405 × 52.2 × 27.5 feet
6 cylinder 4 stroke cycle single acting engines built by J.G. Kincaid & Co Ltd, Greenock.
6.1925: completed by Lithgows Ltd, Port Glasgow, for the Cape of Good Hope Motorship Co. Ltd. Cost £108,540. 11.5.1942: torpedoed and later shelled and sunk by an Italian submarine N.E. of the Virgin Islands in a position 22.48N, 58.43W, while on passage from New York to the Persian Gulf. Vessel was five days out from New York when sunk. The master's boat with 18 aboard landed at Tortola after 14 days and the chief officer's boat with 19 aboard landed at Burgentra after 17 days. No lives were lost.

8 *CAPE YORK II* (1926–40)
Motorship
5,027 gross tons, 3,117 net tons
410 × 54 × 27 feet
Twin screws each propelled by 6 cylinder 4 stroke cycle single acting oil engines built by R.W. Hawthorn Leslie & Co. Ltd, Newcastle.
3.1926: completed by Lithgows Ltd, Port Glasgow for the Cape York Motorship Co. Ltd. Cost £99,357. 1936: Re-engined by the Rotterdam Dry Dock Co. at a cost of £6,800. 26.8.1940: struck by aerial torpedo from a German aircraft off Peterhead, ten miles from Kinnaird Head, and sank the following day.

9 *CAPE CORNWALL* (1926–34)
Steamship
5,021 gross tons, 3,180 net tons
405.3 × 53 × 27.4 feet
Triple expansion 3 cylinder engines built by J.G. Kincaid & Co. Ltd, Greenock.
3.1918: completed by R. Duncan & Co. Ltd, Port Glasgow, as *Trafalgar* for Lawrence Glen, Glasgow. 1919: purchased by the Cunard Steamship Co. Ltd and renamed *Verbania*. 1926: purchased by Lyle Shipping Co. Ltd for £25,000 and renamed *Cape Cornwall*. 1934: sold to Chinese shipbreakers and broken up at Shanghai.

10 *LYCIA* (1926–40)
Motorship
2,338 gross tons, 1,249 net tons
300.5 × 44.2 × 21 feet
6 cylinder 4 stroke cycle single acting oil engines built by J.G. Kincaid & Co. Ltd, Greenock.
7.1924: completed by Dunlop, Bremner & Co. Ltd, Port Glasgow for T. and J. Brockle-bank Ltd but after a short time was returned to her builders. 9.2.1926: purchased by Lithgows and placed in the Cape York Motorship Co. Ltd. 2.1.1940: taken over by the Ministry of Shipping. 8.1940: allocated to the Miscellaneous Naval Service. 20.10.1940: compulsorily purchased by the Royal Navy. 1.1941: Lying at Scapa Flow with defective engines and shortly afterwards expended as a blockship at Scapa Flow.

11 *CAPE VERDE II* (1928–35)
Steamship
5,038 gross tons, 3,187 net tons
405.3 × 53 × 27.4 feet
Triple expansion 3 cylinder engines built by J.G. Kincaid & Co. Ltd.
28.3.1917: launched by R. Duncan & Co. Ltd, Port Glasgow as *Camperdown* for Glen & Co., Glasgow. 16.5.1918: purchased by the Canadian Pacific Railway Co. Ltd (managers: Canadian Pacific Steamships Ltd) prior to completion and renamed *Montezuma*. 14.5.1923: renamed *Bedwyn*. 19.6.1923: renamed *Balfour*. 4.2.1928: purchased by Lyle Shipping Co. Ltd for £40,000 and renamed *Cape Verde*. 6.1935: sold to Fan Shien Ho, China and renamed *Shang Ho*.

12 *CAPE HORN II* (1929–42)
Motorship
5,643 gross tons, 3,615 net tons
425 × 56 × 28.9 feet
8 cylinder 4 stroke cycle single acting oil engines built by J.G. Kincaid & Co. Ltd.
5.1929: completed by Lithgows Ltd, Port Glasgow, who owned her. Cost £124,142. Placed under Lyle management in the Cape York Motorship Co. Ltd. 14.5.1941: bombed in the Mediterranean between Suda Bay, Crete and Port Said and although six fatal casualties were suffered, reached port. 28.3.1942: blew up and sank in the South Atlantic, east of Ascencion Island following a fire and explosion which is believed to have been due to a delayed-action incendiary bomb placed in her cargo. She was at the time on a voyage to Cape Town with a cargo of ammunition. All of her crew were saved.

13 *CAPE HOWE I* (1934–40)
Steamship
4,443 gross tons, 2,728 net tons
375 × 53 × 25.6 feet
Triple expansion 3 cylinder engines built by D. Rowan & Co. Ltd, Glasgow.
7.1930: completed by Lithgows Ltd, Port Glasgow, as *Knight Almoner* at a cost of £60,016 for the Ottoman Line Ltd (managers: Pardoe-Thomas & Co. Ltd). 23.5.1930: mortgaged, joint mortgagees being James Shearer and Bertie Pardoe-Thomas. 11.3.1933: mortgage transferred to James Shearer senior and John MacCulloch (of Lithgows), joint mortgagees. 30.1.1934: purchased by Lyle Shipping Co. Ltd. 7.2.1934: renamed *Cape Howe*. 15.9.1939: taken over by the Royal Navy, converted to an anti-submarine 'Q' ship and renamed *Prunella* (pendant X.02). 21.6.1940: torpedoed and sunk south of Iceland.

14   *CAPE CORSO II* (1934–42)
Steamship
3,807 gross tons, 2,338 net tons
352.5 × 50.5 × 25 feet
Triple expansion 3 cylinder engines built by D. Rowan & Co. Ltd, Glasgow.
8.1929: completed by Lithgows Ltd, Port Glasgow, as the *Knight of St. George* for the
Newport Normandy Line Ltd (managers: Pardoe-Thomas & Co. Ltd) at a cost of £55,930.
13.8.1929: mortgaged, joint mortgagees being James Shearer and Bertie Pardoe-Thomas.
11.3.1933: mortgage transferred to James Shearer senior and John MacCulloch (of
Lithgows), joint mortgagees. 7.2.1934: sold by the mortgagees to Lyle Shipping Co. Ltd.
4.4.1934: renamed *Cape Corso*. 2.5.1942: sunk by a torpedo from a German aircraft
N.W. of North Cape in a position 73.02N, 19.46E while in a convoy to Russia. There
were only six survivors from the 56 on board.

15   *CAPE NELSON I* (1934–41)
Steamship
3,807 gross tons, 2,338 net tons
352.5 × 50.5 × 25 feet
Triple expansion 3 cylinder engines built by D. Rowan & Co. Ltd, Glasgow.
10.1929: completed by Lithgows Ltd, Port Glasgow, as *Knight of St. Michael* for the
Newport Provence Line Ltd (managers: Pardoe-Thomas & Co. Ltd) at a cost of £56,222.
14.10.1929: mortgaged, joint mortgagees being James Shearer and Bertie Pardoe-Thomas.
11.3.1933: mortgage transferred to James Shearer and John MacCulloch (of Lithgows),
joint mortgagees. 7.2.1934: sold by the mortgagees to Lyle Shipping Co. Ltd. 17.3.1934:
renamed *Cape Nelson*. 23.2.1941: torpedoed and sunk by a German submarine south of
Iceland in a position 59.30N, 21W. There were four casualties, including the master.

16   *CAPE RACE II* (1934–42)
Steamship
3,807 gross tons, 2,338 net tons
352.5 × 50.5 × 25 feet
Triple expansion 3 cylinder engines built by D. Rowan & Co. Ltd, Glasgow.
2.1930: completed by Lithgows Ltd, Port Glasgow as *Knight of St. John* for Newport
Liners Ltd (managers: Pardoe-Thomas & Co. Ltd) at a cost of £56,321. 31.1.1930:
mortgaged, joint mortgagees being James Shearer senior and Bertie Pardoe-Thomas.
11.3.1933: mortgage transferred to James Shearer and John MacCulloch (of Lithgows),
joint mortgagees. 7.2.1934: sold by the mortgagees to Lyle Shipping Co. Ltd. 19.2.1934:
renamed *Cape Race*. 10.8.1942: torpedoed and sunk by a German submarine south of
Iceland in a position 56.45N, 22.50W, although without loss of life.

17   *CAPE WRATH III* (1934–37)
Steamship
4,520 gross tons, 2,713 net tons
364.5 × 52.8 × 24.3 feet
Triple expansion three cylinder engines built by Armstrong Whitworth & Co. Ltd,
Newcastle.
6.1921: completed by Joseph L. Thompson & Sons Ltd, Sunderland as *Cycle* for Australian
Steamship Proprietary Ltd (managers: Howard Smith Ltd), Australia. 1934: purchased
by Lyle Shipping Co. Ltd for £14,000 and renamed *Cape Wrath*. 1937: purchased by Mrs.
E. Grauds, Riga, Latvia and renamed *Everelza*.

18 *CAPE SABLE II* (1936–58)
Steamship
4,398 gross tons, 2,708 net tons
375 × 53 × 25.6 feet
Triple expansion 3 cylinder engines built by D. Rowan & Co. Ltd.
1929: ordered from Lithgows as *Knight Batchelor* by the Newport Line (managers: Pardoe-Thomas & Co. Ltd) but construction halted while on the stocks. 3.1936: completed by Lithgows as the *Cape Sable* for Lyle Shipping Co. Ltd at a cost of £63,040. 19.9.1939: taken over by the Royal Navy, converted into an anti-submarine 'Q' ship and renamed *Cyprus* (pendant X.44). 1941: commissioned as an Armed Merchant Cruiser (pendant F.112). 5.1942: reverted to commercial service although remained under Ministry of War Transport requisition. 29.4.1946: returned to Lyle Shipping Co. Ltd. 1950: converted from coal to oil burning by D. & W. Henderson Ltd at a cost of £16,625. 1958: sold to the Pan Norse Steamship Co. S.A., Panama for £56,500 and renamed *Eastern Venturer*.

19 *CAPE CLEAR III* (1939–44)
Motorship
5,085 gross tons, 2,976 net tons
431.8 × 56.2 × 24.8 feet
4 cylinder 2 stroke cycle single acting oil engines by D. Rowan & Co. Ltd.
8.1939: completed by Lithgows Ltd, Port Glasgow who placed her in the Cape York Motorship Co. Ltd and under the management of Lyle Shipping Co. Ltd. Cost £144,067. 27.2.1941: damaged by a mine off the River Mersey. 21.8.1944: sank after being in collision in the Gulf of Suez with the American steamship *Henry Dearborn*, while on passage from Basra to Hampton Roads. There were no casualties.

20 *CAPE WRATH IV* (1940–58)
Steamship (dual fired)
4,512 gross tons, 2,672 net tons
411.8 × 54.2 × 23.8 feet
Triple expansion 3 cylinder engines built by Rankin & Blackmore Ltd, Greenock.
6.1940: completed by Lithgows Ltd, Port Glasgow and placed in the Cape of Good Hope Motorship Co. Ltd. Joint owned by Lithgows Ltd and Lyle Shipping Co. Ltd. Cost £106,899. 1958: sold to Gulf Steamships Ltd, Pakistan for £120,000 and renamed *Mansoor*.

21 *CAPE RODNEY I* (1940–41)
Steamship (dual fired)
4,512 gross tons, 2,672 net tons
411.8 × 54.2 × 23.8 feet
Triple expansion three cylinder engines by Rankin and Blackmore Ltd.
9.1940: completed by Lithgows Ltd, Port Glasgow and placed in the Cape of Good Hope Motorship Co. Ltd. Joint owned by Lithgows Ltd and Lyle Shipping Co. Ltd. Cost £111,831. 5.8.1941: torpedoed west of Ushant by a German submarine and sank 9.8.1941 in a position 52.44N, 11.41W while attempts were being made to salvage her.

22 *CAPE HAWKE I* (1941–63)
Motorship
5,081 gross tons, 2,933 net tons
431.8 × 56.2 × 24.8 feet
4 cylinder 2 stroke cycle single acting oil engines built by D. Rowan & Co. Ltd.
3.1941: completed by Lithgows Ltd, Port Glasgow and placed in the Cape York Motorship
Co. Ltd. Cost £163,607. Wholly owned by Lithgows Ltd until 1946 when Lyle Shipping
Co. Ltd purchased a half interest in the ship for £62,000. 1963: sold to the Kalliopi Cia.
Nav. S.A., Panama (Greek flag) for £57,000 and renamed *Kalliopi*.

23 *CAPE VERDE III* (1941–42)
Motorship
6,914 gross tons, 4,162 net tons
432.7 × 56.2 × 34.3 feet
6 cylinder 4 stroke cycle single acting oil engines built by J.G. Kincaid & Co. Ltd.
3.1941: completed by Lithgows Ltd, Port Glasgow for the Cape of Good Hope Motorship
Co. Ltd. Joint owned by Lithgows Ltd and Lyle Shipping Co. Ltd. Cost £168,313.
4.4.1941: bombed and slightly damaged forty miles north of the Smalls while on her first
voyage, from the Clyde to South Wales. 9.7.1942: torpedoed and sunk by a German
submarine, east of Grenada, British West Indies, in a position 11.32N, 60.17W. Two of
her crew were killed.

24 *CAPE HOWE II* (1943–61)
Steamship
6,999 gross tons, 4,851 net tons
432.7 × 56.2 × 33.9 feet
Triple expansion 3 cylinder engine built by D. Rowan & Co. Ltd.
2.1943: completed by Lithgows Ltd, Port Glasgow and placed in the Cape of Good Hope
Motorship Co. Ltd. Joint owned by Lyle Shipping Co. Ltd and by Lithgows Ltd. Cost
£161,671. 1961: sold to the Wing Tak S.S. Co. (Hong Kong) Ltd, Hong Kong for
£105,000 and renamed *World Pink*.

25 *CAPE ORTEGAL II* (1946–64)
Motorship
6,907 gross tons, 4,132 net tons
432.5 × 56.2 × 33.8 feet
4 cylinder 2 stroke cycle single acting oil engines built by D. Rowan & Co. Ltd.
8.1946: completed by Lithgows Ltd, Port Glasgow, and placed in the Cape of Good
Hope Motorship Co. Ltd. Joint owned by Lithgows Ltd and Lyle Shipping Co. Ltd.
Cost £239,863. 1954: damaged by fire at sea. 1964: sold to the Acres Shipping Company,
Greece for £105,000 and renamed *Megara*.

26 *CAPE RODNEY II* (1946–63)
Motorship
6,939 gross tons, 4,211 net tons
432.5 × 56.2 × 33.8 feet
4 cylinder 2 stroke cycle single acting oil engines built by D. Rowan & Co. Ltd.
11.1946: completed by Lithgows Ltd, Port Glasgow, and placed in the Cape of Good
Hope Motorship Co. Ltd. Joint owned by Lithgows Ltd and Lyle Shipping Co. Ltd.
Cost £241,179. 1963: sold to the Blue Shark Steamship Co. Ltd, Panama for £74,000 and
renamed *Blue Dolphin*.

Appendix 3.2
Cape Howe II steaming past the white cliffs of Dover sometime after the Second World War.

27 *CAPE CORSO III* (managed 1942–47, owned 1947–59)
Steamship
7,178 gross tons, 4,280 net tons
425.1 × 57 × 34.8 feet
Triple expansion 3 cylinder engines built by the Dominion Engineering Works Ltd, Montreal.
9.1942: completed by Todd-Bath Iron Shipbuilding Corporation, Portland, Maine, as *Ocean Traveller* for the Ministry of War Transport and placed under management of Lyle Shipping Co. Ltd. 1947: purchased by Lyle Shipping Co. Ltd for £115,500 less 5 per cent depreciation and renamed *Cape Corso*. 1949: taken in hand by Smiths Ltd, North Shields for conversion from coal to oil burning. 7.9.1959: sold to Teh An & Co., Hong Kong, for £57,500 and scrapped.

28 *CAPE VERDE IV* (managed 1944–47, owned 1947–57)
Steamship
7,240 gross tons, 4,415 net tons
423.3 × 57.1 × 34.8 feet
Triple expansion 3 cylinder engines built by Ellicott Machinery Corporation, Baltimore.
1944: completed by the Bethlehem Fairfield Shipyard Inc., Baltimore, Maryland as *Samtana* for the United States War Shipping Administration, bareboat chartered to the British Ministry of War Transport and placed under the management of Lyle Shipping Co. Ltd. 1947: purchased by Lyle Shipping Co. Ltd and renamed *Cape Verde*. 1957: sold to the West Africa Navigation Ltd, Liberia for £515,000 and renamed *African Night*.

29 *CAPE YORK III* (managed 1944–47, owned 1947–52)
Steamship
7,228 gross tons, 4,415 net tons
423.3 × 57.1 × 34.8 feet
Triple expansion three cylinder engines built by the Filer & Stowell Co., Milwaukee, Wisconsin.
1944: completed by the Bethlehem Fairfield Shipyard Inc., Baltimore as *Samspeed* for the United States War Shipping Administration, bareboat chartered to the British Ministry of War Transport and placed under the management of Lyle Shipping Co. Ltd. 1947: purchased by Lyle Shipping Co. Ltd and renamed *Cape York*. 1952: sold to the Nettunia Soc. Siciliana di Nav., Italy for £560,000 and renamed *Paestum*.

30 *CAPE NELSON II* (1948–59)
Steamship
7,174 gross tons, 4,314 net tons
425.1 × 57 × 34.8 feet
Triple expansion 3 cylinder engines built by the General Machinery Corporation, Hamilton, Ohio.
2.1942: completed by Todd-California Shipbuilding Corporation, Richmond, California as *Ocean Vulcan* for the Ministry of War Transport and placed under management of Idwal Williams & Co. Ltd. 1948: purchased by Lyle Shipping Co. Ltd for £182,000 and renamed *Cape Nelson*. 1949: taken in hand by Smiths Ltd, North Shields, for conversion from coal to oil burning. 1959: sold to the Marine Navigation Co. Ltd (World Wide Co. (Shipping Managers) Ltd, managers), Hong Kong for £72,500.

31 *CAPE GRENVILLE I* (1949–65)
Motorship
7,463 gross tons, 4,453 net tons
437.4 × 58.2 × 34.5 feet
6 cylinder 4 stroke cycle single acting oil engine by J.G. Kincaid & Co. Ltd.
6.1949: completed by Lithgows, Port Glasgow, and placed in the Cape York Motorship
Co. Ltd. Joint owned by Lithgows Ltd and Lyle Shipping Co. Ltd. Cost £311,684.
1965: sold to the Cosmo Maritime Corporation, Liberia for £185,000, and renamed
Cosmar.

32 *CAPE FRANKLIN I* (managed 1943–50, owned 1950–56)
Steamship
7,134 gross tons, 4,244 net tons
424.6 × 57.2 × 34.9 feet
Triple expansion 3 cylinder engine built by the Canadian Allis-Chalmers Ltd, Montreal.
5.1943: completed by the Burrard Dry Dock Co. Ltd, Vancouver, as *Fort Cumberland* for
the Canadian Government, bareboat chartered to the British Ministry of War Transport
and placed under management of Lyle Shipping Co. Ltd. 1950: sold to the Ministry of
Transport. 1950: purchased by Lyle Shipping Co. Ltd for £83,500 and renamed *Cape
Franklin*. 1956: sold to West Africa Navigation Ltd, Liberia and renamed *African Sky*.

33 *CAPE GRAFTON I* (1951–63)
Motorship
5,308 gross tons, 2,956 net tons
429.8 × 56.3 × 25.2 feet
6 cylinder 4 stroke cycle single acting oil engines built by J.G. Kincaid & Co. Ltd.
7.1943: completed by William Denny & Bros Ltd, Dumbarton as the Merchant Aircraft
Carrier *Empire MacAndrew* for the Ministry of War Transport and placed under the
management of the Hain S.S. Co. Ltd. 1947: sold to McCowen and Gross Ltd and
renamed *Derryheen*. 1951: purchased by Lyle Shipping Co. Ltd for £570,000 and renamed
Cape Grafton. 1963 sold to the Patricia Cia. Nav., S.A., Liberia, for £79,500 and renamed
Patricia.

34 *CAPE CLEAR IV* (1952–62)
Motorship
4,810 gross tons, 2,775 net tons
436 × 57.3 × 25.11 feet
3 cylinder 2 stroke cycle single acting oil engines built by William Doxford & Sons Ltd,
Sunderland.
1.1946: completed by the Burntisland Shipbuilding Co. Ltd, Burntisland as *Derryclare*
for McCowen & Gross Ltd. 1952: purchased by Lyle Shipping Co. Ltd for £600,000 and
renamed *Cape Clear*. 1962: sold to the Dynasty Shipping Co. Ltd, Hong Kong for £80,000
and renamed *Golden Sigma*.

Appendix 3.3
Cape Grafton I leaving Vancouver in the 1950s.

35 *CAPE YORK IV* (1955–65)
Motorship
8,280 gross tons, 4,608 net tons
478.6 × 60.3 × 27 feet
8 cylinder 2 stroke cycle single acting oil engines built by J.G. Kincaid & Co. Ltd.
6.1955: completed by Lithgows Ltd, Port Glasgow. 1965: sold to the Atlas Shipping
Company Ltd, Gibraltar for £380,000 and renamed *St. Joanna.*

36 *CAPE HORN III* (1957–67)
Motorship
8,484 gross tons, 4,646 net tons, 10,500 deadweight tons
478 × 60.3 × 27.5 feet
5 cylinder 2 stroke cycle single acting oil engines of Burmeister & Wain design built by
J.G. Kincaid & Co. Ltd.
6.1957: completed by Lithgows Ltd, Port Glasgow. 1967: sold to South Shipping Co.
Ltd of Gibraltar for £380,000.

37 *CAPE FRANKLIN II* (1959–74)
Ore carrier
11,815 gross tons, 6,212 net tons, 15,500 deadweight tons
524.6 × 70 × 27.3 feet
single acting oil engines built by J.G. Kincaid & Co. Ltd.
d, Port Glasgow. 7.1974: sold to Ortoria Gardella,

y Brothers Ltd. Double reduction geared to a single

nny & Brothers Ltd, Dumbarton. 1966: sold to the
anama (Liberian flag) for £530,000 and renamed

,390 deadweight tons

y Brothers Ltd. Double reduction geared to a single

y & Brothers Ltd, Dumbarton. 1966: sold to Fairfield
£525,000, and renamed *Stephanie.*

[Overlaid clipping:]

Changes of flag without change of ownership or name

	From	To
ALPHA SEA	35,450/68	Greece
ARLAND	994/68	Malta
FLOREAL	51,870/83	Panama
METEOR	3,128/69	Norway
MUNATONES	64,738/75	Sweden
VALINCO II	500/61	Cyprus
		Spain
		France

Changes of ownership or name

Y. S. ARGOSY, 4/12/88

ZAMORA, 19,752/75—m.tanker. By Flota Petrolera Ecuatoriana, Ecuador, to Mesta
Shipping Co. Ltd, Greece. Renamed DAEDALUS.
ZHU HAI, (Ceram Sea—73, Victoria I—72, Victoria—68), 15,238/64—m.bulker. By
Qingdao Ocean Shipping Co., China, to unspecified owners of St. Vincent. Renamed
SALY and broken up.
ZIM AUSTRALIA, (Zim Sydney—86, Launched as Westertal), 10,544/83—m.cont.ship.
Has been renamed WESTERTAL by Gebr. Paterson K.G., Germany.
ZIM SYDNEY, (Ville Du Mistral—86, Carman Fontana—86, C. Friendship—85, Hellenic
Friendship—84, Sea Train Bunker Hill—81), 13,098/72—m.cont.ship. By Ofer Sons
Investments (1978) Ltd, Israel, to Lavern Shipping Inc., Liberia. Renamed LAVERN
TRIESTE.

Raymund Oberhem

Appendix 3.4
Cape Franklin II going down the ways at Lithgows Ltd in 1959.

40 *CAPE NELSON III* (1961–76)
    Ore carrier
    12,351 gross tons, 6,185 net tons, 16,450 deadweight tons
    524.6 × 69.11 × 27.6 feet
    5 cylinder 2 stroke cycle single acting oil engines of Burmeister & Wain design built by
    J.G. Kincaid & Co. Ltd.
    4.1961: completed by Lithgows Ltd, Port Glasgow. 1976: sold to Compania Sydenham,
    S.A., Panama.

41 *CAPE HOWE III* (1962)
    Ore carrier
    19,032 gross tons, 11,567 net tons, 27,500 deadweight tons
    608 × 80 × 32.4 feet
    6 cylinder 2 stroke cycle single acting engines of Burmeister & Wain design built by
    J.G. Kincaid & Co. Ltd.
    11.1962: completed by Lithgows Ltd, Port Glasgow. Still in service.

Appendix 3.5
The ore carrier *Cape Howe III* entering the water from Lithgows Ltd's Port Glasgow Yard in
1962.

42 *CAPE RODNEY III* (1965–70)
Bulkcarrier
12,104 gross tons, 6,776 net tons, 17,520 deadweight tons
527.1 × 68.1 × 29.11 feet
6 cylinder 2 stroke cycle single acting oil engines built by Fairfield Rowan Ltd, Glasgow.
5.1965: completed by Lithgows Ltd, Port Glasgow. 1970: sold to Heilger's Maritime Co. Ltd of London.

43 *CAPE ST. VINCENT II* (1966–72)
Bulkcarrier
12,835 gross tons, 7,242 net tons, 20,022 deadweight tons
528 × 72.5 × 31.8 feet
6 cylinder 2 stroke cycle single acting oil engines built by John Brown & Co. (Clydebank) Ltd.
6.1966: completed by John Brown & Co. (Clydebank) Ltd for their shipowning subsidiary William Dennison Ltd and bareboat chartered to Lyle Shipping Co. Ltd for a period of fifteen years. 1972: sold to Whitwell, Cole & Co. Ltd.

44 *CAPE CLEAR V* (1967–73)
Bulkcarrier
12,624 gross tons, 6,754 net tons, 19,902 deadweight tons
530 × 71.3 × 31.9 feet
Gotaverken oil engines 760/1500 U.G–7U.
5.1967: completed by Haugesund Mekaniske Verksted, Haugesund. 1973: sold to Kalma Maritime Enterprises.

45 *CAPE WRATH VI* (1968–76)
Bulkcarrier
13,532 gross tons, 7,687 net tons, 21,870 deadweight tons
527.9 × 75.2 × 32.1 feet
Horten-Sulzer oil engines of type 6.R.D.76.
6.1968: completed by Marinens Hovedverft, Horten. 1976: sold to Mackinnon Mackenzie & Co. Ltd, Bombay. Renamed *Chandi*.

46 *CAPE SABLE IV* (1968)
Bulkcarrier
13,532 gross tons, 7,687 net tons, 21,980 deadweight tons
527.9 × 75.2 × 32.1 feet
Horten-Sulzer oil engines of type 6.R.D.76.
12.1968: completed by Marinens Hovedverft, Horten. Still in service.

47 *CAPE YORK V* (1969)
Bulkcarrier
13,543 gross tons, 7,680 net tons, 21,900 deadweight tons
527.9 × 75.2 × 32.1 feet
Horten-Sulzer oil engines of type 6.R.D.76.
5.1969: completed by Marinens Hovedverft, Horten. Still in service.

Appendix 3.6
Cape Race III on trials in 1971.

48 *CAPE HORN IV* (1971)
Bulkcarrier
14,650 gross tons, 9,895 net tons, 23,655 deadweight tons
534.4 × 75.2 × 34.1 feet
1st 2 Ruston and Hornsby 12. A.O. medium speed engines
2nd 2 Stork Werkspoor 12 T.M.410 medium speed engines
1.1971: completed by Haugesund Mekaniske Verksted, Haugesund. Still in service.

49 *CAPE RACE III* (1971)
Bulkcarrier
14,885 gross tons, 8,802 net tons, 23,310 deadweight tons
542 × 75.2 × 33.6 feet
Horten-Sulzer oil engines of type 5.R.N.D.76
1.1971: completed by Kaldnes M/V A/S Tonsberg. Hull especially strengthened for
working in ice. Still in service.

50 *CAPE HAWKE II* (1971)
Bulkcarrier
14,651 gross tons, 9,896 net tons, 23,655 deadweight tons
534.4 × 75.2 × 34.1 feet
1st 2 Ruston and Hornsby 12. A.O. medium speed engines
2nd 2 Stork Werkspoor 12 T.M.410 medium speed engines
9.1971: completed by Haugesund Mekaniske Verksted, Haugesund. Still in service.

51   *CAPE GRAFTON II* (1971)
Bulkcarrier
14,651 gross tons, 9,869 net tons, 23,710 deadweight tons
534.4 × 75.2 × 34.1 feet
1st 2 Ruston and Hornsby 12. A.O. medium speed engines
2nd 2 Stork Werkspoor 12 T.M.410 medium speed engines
12.1971: completed by Haugesund Mekaniske Verksted, Haugesund. Still in service.

52   *CAPE LEEUWIN* (1972)
Bulkcarrier
13,437 gross tons, 7,820 net tons, 21,950 deadweight tons
522.4 × 75.2 × 32.1 feet
Horten Sulzer Engines of type 5 R.N.D.76
5.1972: completed by A/S Horten Verft, Horten. Still in service.

53   *CAPE GRENVILLE II* (1973)
Bulkcarrier
14,650 gross tons, 9,896 net tons, 23,710 deadweight tons
534.4 × 75.3 × 34.1 feet
2 Stork Werkspoor 12 T.M.410 medium speed engines.
1.1973: completed by Haugesund Mekaniske Verksted, Haugesund, Still in service.

54   *CAPE ORTEGAL III* (1976)
Bulkcarrier
16,646 gross tons, 9,781 net tons, 26,930 deadweight tons
574 × 84 × 32.8 feet
B. and W. 6K7 4 E.F. type
2.1976: completed by Govan Shipbuilders Ltd. Still in service.

55   *CAPE RODNEY IV* (1976)
Bulkcarrier
16,646 gross tons, 9,781 net tons, 26,930 deadweight tons
574 × 84 × 32.8 feet
B. and W. 6K7 4 E.F. type
3.1976: completed by Govan Shipbuilders Ltd. Still in service.

56   *CAPE OTWAY* (1976)
Bulkcarrier
20,819 gross tons, 11,509 net tons, 31,992 deadweight tons
557.8 × 88.7 × 48.7 feet
Mitsui B. and W. DE 7K7 4 E.F. type
12.1976: completed by Mitsui Engineering and Shipbuilding Co. Ltd, Japan. Still in service.

Part Five

Ships managed on behalf of the Ministries of Shipping and War Transport during and after the two World Wars

1   *WAR BRACKEN* (1918–19)
Steamship
5,182 gross tons, 3,174 net tons
400.5 × 52.3 × 28.5 feet
Triple expansion 3 cylinder engines built by Caird & Co, Ltd, Greenock.
1.1918: completed by Caird & Co. Ltd, Greenock, for the Shipping Controller, and placed under the management of Lyle Shipping Co. Ltd. 1919: sold to L. Pittaluga (later Ditta Luigi Pittaluga Vapori), Italy, and renamed *Campania*.

2   *WAR PICOTEE* (1918–19)
Steamship
5,302 gross tons, 3,231 net tons
400.4 × 52.2 × 28.4 feet
Triple expansion 3 cylinder engines built by D. & W. Henderson & Co. Ltd, Glasgow.
20.8.1918: placed under the management of Lyle Shipping Co. Ltd while on the building berth of D. & W. Henderson & Co. Ltd, Glasgow. 19.12.1918: launched. 11.2.1919: handed over to Lord Inchcape to sell, and taken over by the Hain S.S. Co. Ltd, being completed in 3.1919 under the name *Tremeadow*.

3   *LIPSOS* (1919–20)
Steamship
3,979 gross tons, 2,503 net tons
365.8 × 47.1 × 24.8 feet
Triple expansion 3 cylinder engines built by G. Clark Ltd, Sunderland.
8.1902: completed by Sir James Laing & Sons Ltd, Sunderland, as *Casilda* for Bucknall Nephews, London. 1908: sold to the Societe Les Affreteurs Reunis, France and renamed *Ceres*. 1913: sold to the Deutsche Levante Linie, Germany, and renamed *Lipsos*. 8.1914: seized at Antwerp on the outbreak of war. 1919: handed over to Britain as reparations and placed by the Shipping Controller under the management of Lyle Shipping Co. Ltd. 1920: sold to the Shakespear Shipping Co. Ltd (Glover Brothers, managers), and renamed *Ovid*.

4   *OEHRINGEN* (1919–20)
Steamship
3,390 gross tons, 2,191 net tons
345.9 × 48.1 × 23 feet
Triple expansion 3 cylinder engines built by the North Eastern Marine Engineering Co. Ltd, Sunderland.
9.1907: completed by the Chantiers Navals Anversois, Hoboken, as *Oehringen* for Seetransport G.m.b.H. (R. Loesener, manager), Germany. The firm later became Rhederei Vereinigung G.m.b.H. 1919: taken over as reparations and placed by the Shipping Controller under the management of Lyle Shipping Co. Ltd. 1920: sold to the Gascony S.S. Co. Ltd (Leopold Walford & Co., managers – this firm later becoming L. Walford (London), Ltd).

5 *WARTBURG* (1919–21)
Steamship
4,295 gross tons, 2,758 net tons
387.1 × 51.8 × 16.8 feet
Triple expansion 3 cylinder engines built by Bremer Vulkan, Vegesack.
11.1905: completed by the Bremer Vulkan, Vegesack, as *Wartburg* for the Deutsche
Dampschiffahrts Ges. Hansa, Germany. 8.1914: seized at Antwerp by Belgium on the
outbreak of war. Recaptured in 10.1914 when the Germans occupied Antwerp, where
she remained until 1918. 1919: handed over to Britain as reparations and placed by the
Shipping Controller under the management of Lyle Shipping Co. Ltd. 1921: sold to the
Ornis S.S. Co. Ltd (Glover Brothers, managers) and renamed *Berkut*.

6 *MARIE REPPEL* (1920)
Steamship
4,549 gross tons, 2,370 net tons
360.4 × 50.2 × 23.2 feet
Triple expansion 3 cylinder engines built by A.G. 'Neptun', Rostock.
6.1920: completed by the A.G. 'Neptun', Rostock, for handing over to one of the allied
countries as war reparations. Initially, delivered to the British Shipping Controller and
9.7.1920 placed under the management of Lyle Shipping Co. Ltd, when she arrived at
Leith. She did not, however, do any trading between then and 8.11.1920 when she was
transferred to the Greek Government and renamed *Constantinos Vasilefs*, being registered
in the ownership of the Greek Government Service of Maritime Transport.

7 *EMPIRE PUMA* (1940–44)
Steamship
7,777 gross tons, 4,954 net tons
439.6 × 60.2 × 33.7 feet
Quadruple expansion 4 cylinder steam engines built by the William Cramp Ship and
Engine Building Company, Philadelphia.
3.1920: completed by the Pusey & Jones Corporation, Gloucester City, N.J., as *Ethan
Allen* for the United States Shipping Board. 1933: sold to the Lykes Bros.-Ripley S.S. Co.
Inc., which in 1938 was merged with the parent concern, Lykes Bros. S.S. Co. Inc.,
U.S.A. 1940: bought by the British Ministry of Shipping (later Ministry of War Transport),
placed under the management of Lyle Shipping Co. Ltd, and renamed *Empire Puma*.
4-5.5.1941: bombed while lying at Belfast, but repaired. 1944: management transferred
to Michalinos & Co. Ltd.

8 *EMPIRE MERMAID* (1940–41)
Steamship
6,381 gross tons, 3,959 net tons
401.6 × 54.9 × 32.1 feet
Triple expansion 3 cylinder steam engines built by the Hooven, Owens & Rentschler
Company, Hamilton, Ohio.
1919: completed by the Skinner & Eddy Corporation, Seattle, Wash., as *Endicott* for the
United States Shipping Board. 1933: sold to the Lykes Bros.-Ripley S.S. Co., Inc., which
in 1938 was merged with the parent concern, Lykes Bros. S.S. Co., Inc., U.S.A. 1940:
bought by the Ministry of Shipping, placed under the management of Lyle Shipping
Co. Ltd, and renamed *Empire Mermaid*. 26.3.1941: torpedoed by a German aircraft N.W.
of the Hebrides, abandoned the following day and finally sank 28.3.1941 in a position
57.33N, 12.43W. Twenty-three members of her crew were lost.

9 *EMPIRE BUFFALO* (1940–42)
Steamship
6,404 gross tons, 4,618 net tons
402.6 × 54.8 × 32.1 feet
Triple expansion 3 cylinder engines built by the Hooven, Owens & Rentschler Company, Hamilton, Ohio.
1919: completed by the Skinner & Eddy Corporation, Seattle, Wash., as *Eglantine* for the United States Shipping Board. 1933: sold to the Lykes Bros.-Ripley S.S. Co., Inc., which in 1938 was merged with the parent concern, Lykes Bros. S.S. Co. Inc., U.S.A. 1940: bought by the Ministry of Shipping, placed under the management of Lyle Shipping Co. Ltd and renamed *Empire Buffalo*. 6.5.1942: torpedoed and sunk west of the Cayman Islands (West Indies) in a position 19.14N, 82.34W. Twelve members of her crew were lost, including the Master.

10 *EMPIRE STEELHEAD* (1940–42)
Steamship
7,744 gross tons, 4,931 net tons
439.6 × 60.2 × 33.7 feet
Quadruple expansion 4 cylinder engines built by the William Cramp Ship and Engine Building Company, Philadelphia.
4.1920: completed by the Pusey & Jones Co., Gloucester City, N.J., as *Patrick Henry* for the United States Shipping Board. 1937: sold to the Lykes Bros.-Ripley S.S. Co., Inc., which in 1938 was merged with the parent concern, Lykes Bros. S.S. Co., Inc., U.S.A. 1940: bought by the Ministry of Shipping, placed under the management of Lyle Shipping Co. Ltd, and renamed *Empire Steelhead*. 1942: transferred to the Greek Government, renamed *Crete*, and managed on their behalf by Georges Nicolaou, Ltd, London.

11 *OCEAN TRAVELLER* (1942–47)
See Ship List, Part Four, *Cape Corso III*.

12 *FORT WEDDERBURNE* (1942–47)
Steamship
7,134 gross tons, 4,244 net tons
424.6 × 57.2 × 34.9 feet
Triple expansion 3 cylinder engines built by John Inglis Co. Ltd, Toronto.
10.1942: completed by the Burrard Dry Dock Co. Ltd, Vancouver, for the United States War Shipping Administration, bareboat chartered to the British Ministry of War Transport and placed under the management of Lyle Shipping Co. Ltd. 1947: returned to the United States Maritime Commission.

13 *EMPIRE DAY* (1942–44)
Motorship
7,242 gross tons, 5,021 net tons
428.8 × 56.5 × 35.5 feet
3 cylinder 2 stroke cycle single acting oil engines built by William Doxford & Sons Ltd.
7.1941: completed by William Doxford & Sons Ltd, Sunderland for the Ministry of War Transport and placed under the management of Stephens Sutton Ltd. 10.1942: purchased by Lyle Shipping Company Ltd for £185,000 for delivery at end of war and placed under Lyle management. 7.8.1944: torpedoed and sunk by a submarine off the coast of Zanzibar in a position 7.06S, 42E while on passage from Lourenco Marques to Alexandria. The chief officer, who was taken aboard the submarine, was lost when the submarine was subsequently sunk.

14 *FORT STEELE* (1942–48)
    Steamship
    7,133 gross tons, 4,244 net tons
    424.6 × 57.2 × 34.9 feet
    Triple expansion 3 cylinder engines built by the Dominion Engineering Works Ltd,
    Montreal.
    11.1942: completed by North Vancouver Ship Repairers Ltd, Vancouver, for the United
    States War Shipping Administration, bareboat chartered to the British Ministry of War
    Transport and placed under the management of Lyle Shipping Co. Ltd. 1948: returned
    to the United States Maritime Commission and laid up in the Reserve Fleet.

15 *FORT LAJOIE* (1942–47)
    Steamship
    7,134 gross tons, 4,244 net tons
    424.6 × 57.2 × 34.9 feet
    Triple expansion 3 cylinder engines built by Canada Allis-Chalmers Ltd, Montreal.
    12.1942: completed by the Burrard Dry Dock Co. Ltd, Vancouver, for the United
    States War Shipping Administration, bareboat chartered to the British Ministry of War
    Transport, and placed under the management of Lyle Shipping Co. Ltd. 1947: returned
    to the United States Maritime Commission and laid up in the Reserve Fleet.

16 *EMPIRE CLAYMORE* (1943)
    Steamship
    7,048 gross tons, 5,028 net tons
    430.9 × 56.2 × 35.2 feet
    Triple expansion 3 cylinder engine built by the North Eastern Marine Engineering Co.
    (1938) Ltd, Newcastle.
    1.1943: completed by Sir W.G. Armstrong Whitworth & Co. (Shipbuilders) Ltd, New-
    castle, for the Ministry of War Transport and placed under the management of Lyle
    Shipping Co. Ltd. 1943: transferred to the Belgian Government, renamed *Belgian Crew*,
    and managed by the Agence Maritime Internationale.

17 *FORT ANNE* (1943–45)
    Steamship
    7,134 gross tons, 4,244 net tons
    424.6 × 57.2 × 34.9 feet
    Triple expansion 3 cylinder engines built by the Dominion Engineering Works Ltd,
    Montreal.
    1.1943: completed by the Burrard Dry Dock Co. Ltd, Vancouver, for the United States
    War Shipping Administration, bareboat chartered to the British Ministry of War Trans-
    port and placed under the management of Lyle Shipping Co. Ltd. 1945: management
    transferred to the Hain S.S. Co. Ltd. 1948: returned to the United States Maritime
    Commission, and laid up in the Reserve Fleet.

18 *EMPIRE FARMER* (1943–45)
Steamship
7,049 gross tons, 4,875 net tons
430.9 × 56.2 × 35.2 feet
Triple expansion 3 cylinder engines built by the North Eastern Marine Engineering Co.
(1938) Ltd, Newcastle.
5.1943: completed by Sir W.G. Armstrong Whitworth & Co. (Shipbuilders) Ltd,
Newcastle, for the Ministry of War Transport and placed under the management of
Lyle Shipping Co. Ltd. 1945: sold to the French Government (Ministere de la Marine
Marchande), renamed *Administrateur En Chef Thomas* and managed on their behalf by the
Compagnie Generale Transatlantique.

19 *FORT CUMBERLAND* (1943–50)
See Ship List, Part Four, *Cape Franklin I.*

20 *SAMSPEED* (1944–47)
See Ship List, Part Four, *Cape York III.*

21 *SAMTANA* (1944–47)
See Ship List, Part Four, *Cape Verde IV.*

22 *EMPIRE NAIROBI* (1945–46)
Steamship
7,295 gross tons, 5,083 net tons
431.2 × 56.3 × 35.6 feet
Triple expansion 3 cylinder engines built by the North Eastern Marine Engineering Co.
(1938) Ltd, Newcastle.
4.1945: completed by Short Brothers Ltd, Sunderland, for the Ministry of War Transport
and placed under the management of Lyle Shipping Co. Ltd. 1946: sold to the Dover
Hill S.S. Co. Ltd (Counties Ship Management Co. Ltd, managers), and renamed
Dover Hill.

23 *EMPIRE TEME* (1945–46)
Steamship
3,243 gross tons, 1,859 net tons
332.5 × 46.5 × 20.5 feet
Triple expansion 3 cylinder engine built by Ottensener Maschinenfabrik G.m.b.H.,
Altona, Hamburg.
1923: completed by the Nordseewerke, Emden, as *Ilona Siemers* for T.G.H. Siemers & Co.
(later G.T.H. Siemers & Co.), Germany. 5.1945: taken as a prize, while lying damaged at
Lubeck. Handed over to Britain (Ministry of War Transport), placed under the management of Lyle Shipping Co. Ltd and renamed *Empire Teme*. 1946: allocated to Russia as
reparations and renamed *Aivazovsky.*

24 *FORT BEAUHARNOIS* (1947–48)
Steamship
7,223 gross tons, 3,871 net tons
424.6 × 57.2 × 34.89 feet
Triple expansion 3 cylinder engines built by Canadian Allis-Chalmers Ltd, Montreal.
10.1944: completed by West Coast Shipbuilders Ltd, Vancouver, as *Cornish Park* for the Canadian Government (Park S.S. Co. Ltd, managers), having been launched under the name *Fort Grand Rapids*. 1945: sold to the British Ministry of War Transport, placed under the management of Alfred Holt & Co. and renamed *Fort Beauharnois*. 1947: placed under the management of Lyle Shipping Co. Ltd. 1948: taken over by the Admiralty and converted into a Stores Ship.

Part Six

Ships managed on behalf of the Western Canada Steamship Company Limited and Lunham & Moore Limited

1 *DURBAN BAY* (1950–54)
Steamship
7,163 gross tons, 4,295 net tons
427.6 × 57.2 × 34.9 feet
Triple expansion 3 cylinder engines built by John Inglis Co. Ltd, Toronto.
5.1944: completed by North Vancouver Ship Repairers Ltd, North Vancouver, as *Dorval Park* for the Canadian Government (Park S.S. Co. Ltd, managers). 1946: sold to the Western Canada Steamships Ltd (later Western Canada S.S. Co. Ltd) and renamed *Lake Canim*. 1950: transferred from Canadian to British registry (port of registry – Glasgow), placed under the management of Lyle Shipping Co. Ltd and renamed *Durban Bay*. 1954: sold to the Sociedad de Transportes Maritimos S.A., Liberia and renamed *Sea Rover*.

2 *TABLE BAY* (1950–57)
Steamship
7,161 gross tons, 4,318 net tons
424.6 × 57.2 × 34.9 feet
Triple expansion 3 cylinder engines built by the Dominion Engineering Works, Ltd.
2.1944: completed by the Burrard Dry Dock Co. Ltd, Vancouver, as *Tipperary Park* for the Canadian Government (Park S.S. Co., Ltd, managers). 1946: sold to the Western Canada Steamships Ltd (later Western Canada S.S. Co. Ltd), and renamed *Lake Shawnigan*. 1950: transferred from Canadian to British registry (port of registry – Glasgow), placed under the management of Lyle Shipping Co. Ltd and renamed *Table Bay*. 1957: sold to the Jugoslavenska Oceanska Providba, Yugoslavia and renamed *Rumija*.

3   *LAKE MINNEWANKA* (1954)
Steamship
7,147 gross tons, 4,288 net tons
424.6 × 57.2 × 34.9 feet
Triple expansion 3 cylinder engines built by the Dominion Engineering Works Ltd.
2.1945: completed by the Burrard Dry Dock Co. Ltd, Vancouver, as *Princeton Park* for
the Canadian Government (Park S.S. Co. Ltd, managers). 1946: sold to the Western
Canada Steamships Ltd (later Western Canada S.S. Co. Ltd), and renamed *Lake
Minnewanka*. 1954: transferred from Canadian to British registry (port of registry – Glasgow)
and placed under the management of Lyle Shipping Co. Ltd. 1954: sold to the Cia. Nav.
Madraki, S.A., Liberia, and renamed *Santiago*.

4   *LAKE PENNASK* (1956–62)
Motorship
7,829 gross tons, 4,421 net tons
429 × 57.9 × 26.6 feet
4 cylinder 2 stroke cycle single acting oil engines built by William Doxford & Sons, Ltd.
6.1953: completed by William Doxford & Sons Ltd, Sunderland, as *Jersey Spray* for Morel
Ltd. 1956: sold to the Lake Pennask Shipping Co. Ltd, placed under the management
of Lyle Shipping Co. Ltd, and renamed *Lake Pennask*. 1960: owners became the Western
Canada S.S. Co. Ltd. 1962: sold to the Great Eastern Shipping Co., Ltd (A.H. Bhiwandi-
walla & Co. (Bombay) Private Ltd, managers), India, and renamed *Jag Rakshak*.

5   *ANGUSDALE/CAPE ADAN* (1954–56)
Steamship
7,331 gross tons, 4,235 net tons
424.5 × 57.2 × 34.9 feet
Triple expansion 3 cylinder engines built by the Dominion Engineering Works Ltd.
9.1945: completed by United Shipyards Ltd, Montreal, as *Fort Wayne* for the Royal
Navy for service as a Stores Issuing Ship. 1949: transferred to the Ministry of Transport.
1950: sold to Angusdale Ltd (Lunham & Moore Shipping Ltd, managers), and renamed
Angusdale. 1951: transferred to Canadian registry. 1954: transferred back to British
registry (port of registry – Glasgow) placed under the management of Lyle Shipping Co.
Ltd, and renamed *Cape Adan*. 1956 sold to the Bienvenido Steamship Co. Ltd, Liberia
and renamed *Andora*.

6   *CAPE MELAN* (1954–55)
Steamship
7,214 gross tons, 4,362 net tons
424.6 × 57.2 × 34.9 feet
Triple expansion 3 cylinder engines built by Dominion Engineering Works Ltd.
3.1944: completed by the Burrard Dry Dock Co. Ltd, Vancouver, as *Fort La Have* for
the Canadian Government, bareboat chartered to the Ministry of War Transport and
placed under the management of the Hain S.S. Co. Ltd. 1946: returned to the Canadian
Government and placed under the management of the Park S.S. Co. Ltd. 1947: sold to
Lunham & Moore (Canada) Ltd, and renamed *Angusglen*. 1948: owners became Lunham
& Moore Steamships Ltd (Lunham & Moore Shipping Ltd, managers). 1954: transferred
from Canadian to British registry (port of registry – Glasgow), placed under the manage-
ment of Lyle Shipping Co. Ltd, and renamed *Cape Melan*. 1955: sold to A.C. Hadjipateras,
Greece (Costa Rican flag), and renamed *Aghios Spyridon*.

Part Seven

Ships chartered by Lyle Shipping Company Limited, 1965–1970

1 *CAPE DALEMOS* (1965–67)
Bulkcarrier
12,240 gross tons, 6,258 net tons, 17,130 deadweight tons
533 × 63 × 32 feet
2 6 cylinder direct action engines built by Kockums M/V A/B.
1950: completed by Kockums M/V A/B of Malmo as *H. Westfal-Larsen* for Westfal-Larsen and Co. A/S of Norway. 1962: renamed *Heranger*. 1965: chartered to Lyle Shipping Co. and renamed *Cape Dalemos*. 1967: returned to her owners.

2 *CAPE MARINA* (1966–69)
Bulkcarrier
13,347 gross tons, 10,282 net tons, 24,352 deadweight tons
585 × 75 × 31 feet
2 6 cylinder single acting oil engines built by Alpha-Deisel A/S, France.
1963: completed by Chantiers de l'Atlantique, St. Nazaire, France as *Marina Grande* for Marbueno, Cia. Nav. S.A. of Liberia. 1966: time chartered to Lyle Shipping Co. 1969: returned to owners.

3 *CAPE RONA* (1965–70)
Bulkcarrier
12,186 gross tons, 7,550 net tons, 19,680 deadweight tons
555 × 70 × 30 feet
2 7 cylinder single acting oil engines built by Uddevallavarvet A/B.
1962: completed by Uddevallavarvet A/B, Uddevalla, Sweden as the *Rona Castle* for Einar Saanuin of Mandal, Norway. 1965: chartered to Lyle Shipping Co. and renamed *Cape Rona*. 1970: returned to owners.

Part Eight

Fleet of Seaforth Maritime Limited

SEAFORTH HERO (1973)
Tug/anchor handling vessel
7.1973: built by the Drypool Group and owned by Seaforth Maritime. B.H.P. rating 5,000 and bollard pull of 65 tonnes.

SEAFORTH PRINCE (1973)
Tug/anchor handling vessel
8.1973: built by Chas Hill and owned by Seaforth Maritime. B.H.P. rating 5,000 and bollard pull of 65 tonnes.

SEAFORTH CHALLENGER (1973)
Tug/anchor handling vessel
11.1973: built by the Drypool Group and owned by Seaforth Maritime. B.H.P. rating 5,000 and bollard pull of 65 tonnes.

SEAFORTH CHIEFTAIN (1974)
Tug/anchor handling vessel
2.1974: built by the Drypool Group and owned by Seaforth Maritime. B.H.P. rating 5,000 and bollard pull of 65 tonnes.

SEAFORTH CHAMPION (1975)
Tug/anchor handling vessel
1.1975: built by the Drypool Group and owned by Seaforth Maritime. B.H.P. rating 6,200 and bollard pull of 75 tonnes.

SEAFORTH WARRIOR (1975)
Tug/anchor handling vessel
3.1975: built by the Drypool Group and owned by Seaforth Maritime. B.H.P. rating 6,200 and bollard pull of 75 tonnes.

SEAFORTH VICTOR (1975)
Tug/anchor handling vessel
4.1975: built by Chas Hill and owned by Seaforth Maritime. B.H.P. rating 6,200 and bollard pull of 75 tonnes.

SEAFORTH SAGA (1975)
Tug/anchor handling vessel
5.1975: built by the Drypool Group and owned by Seaforth Maritime. B.H.P. rating 6,200 and bollard pull of 75 tonnes.

SEAFORTH JARL (1975)
Tug/anchor handling vessel
9.1975: built by Ferguson Brothers and owned by Seaforth Maritime. B.H.P. rating 7,200 and bollard pull of 103 tonnes.

SEAFORTH HIGHLANDER (1976)
Tug/anchor handling/platform support vessel
7.1976: built by Ferguson Brothers and owned by Seaforth Maritime. B.H.P. rating 7,200 and bollard pull of 103 tonnes.

SEAFORTH CONQUEROR (1976)
Tug/anchor handling/platform support vessel
12.1976: built by the Drypool Group and owned by Seaforth Maritime. B.H.P. rating 7,200 and bollard pull of 103 tonnes.

SEAFORTH CAPE (1976)
Undersea engineering support vessel
1967: built in Germany as a stern factory trawler *Tiko I.* 1976: purchased by Lyle Offshore Group and converted by Swan Hunter to an undersea engineering support vessel. Renamed *Seaforth Cape*, and managed by Seaforth Maritime.

SEAFORTH CLANSMAN (1977)
Undersea engineering support vessel (with firefighting capacity)
This vessel was delivered from Cochrane's yard in August 1977 and is 60 per cent owned by Lyle Offshore Group and 40 per cent owned by Seaforth Maritime.

Fleet of Lyle Offshore Group Limited

SEAFORTH CAPE (1976)
See under Seaforth Maritime.

SEAFORTH CLANSMAN (1977)
See under Seaforth Maritime.

Suggestions for Further Reading

H. Barty-King, *The Baltic Exchange. The History of a Unique Market* (1977).
Michael Crowdy, *Lyle Shipping Co. Ltd, 1827–1966. The Firm and the Fleet* (1966).
H.J. Dyos and D.H. Aldcroft, *British Transport. An Economic Survey from the Seventeenth Century to the Twentieth* (1969).
J.M. Hutchinson, *Notes on the Sugar Refining Industry* (1900).
Leslie Jones, *Shipbuilding in Britain* (1957).
A.P. Lyle, *Family Notes* (1922).
A.A. MacAlister and Leonard Gray, *A Short History of H. Hogarth & Sons Ltd and Fleet List* (1976).
S.G. Sturmey, *British Shipping and World Competition* (1958).

Index